Making Sense
of Cultural Studies

Making Sense of Cultural Studies

CENTRAL PROBLEMS AND CRITICAL DEBATES

Chris Barker

SAGE Publications

London • Thousand Oaks • New Delhi

SAGE Publications Ltd
6 Bonhiil Street
London EC2A 4PU

SAGE Publications Inc
2455 Teller Road
Thousand Oaks, California 91320

SAGE Publications India Pvt Ltd
32, M-Block Market
Greater Kailash – 1
New Delhi 110 048

British Library Cataloguing in Publication Data
A catalogue record for this book is available from
the British Library

ISBN 0 7619 6895 4
ISBN 0 7619 6896 2 (pbk)

Library of Congress Control Number: 2001132958

Typeset by M Rules
Printed in Great Britain by The Cromwell Press Ltd,
Trowbridge, Wiltshire

Contents

I still write. What else can I do? It is my habit and it is also my profession. For a long while I treated my pen as my sword: now I realize how helpless we are. It does not matter. I am writing, I shall write books; they are needed; they have use all the same. Culture saves nothing and nobody, nor does it justify. But it is a product of man; he projects himself through it and recognizes himself in it; this critical mirror does show him his image.

(Jean-Paul Sartre, Words (1967: 157)

My thanks to Chris Rojek, who first had the idea for this book.

1 Investigating Problems in Cultural Studies

> A man will be imprisoned in a room with a door that's locked and opens inwards; as long as it does not occur to him to pull rather than push it. (Wittgenstein, 1980: 42)

> Pragmatism could be characterized as the doctrine that all problems are at bottom problems of conduct, that all judgements are, implicitly, judgements of value, and that, as there can be ultimately no valid distinction of theoretical and practical, so there can be no final separation of questions of truth of any kind from questions of the justifiable ends of action. (C.I. Lewis, cited West, 1993: 109)

Introduction

The theoretical and institutional field of cultural studies has developed over the past thirty years or so to a stage where similar problems, issues and debates have emerged from within the literature. This book, a follow-up to my *Cultural Studies: Theory and Practice*, is intended both as a mapping exercise and as an intervention in relation to identified 'problems'. While *Cultural Studies* took a reasonably even-handed stance in describing key debates, *Making Sense* will, as its subtitle implies, be marked by a more provocative voice that, through the choice of 'problems' and the proposed 'solutions', seeks to influence the direction that cultural studies takes at the dawn of the twenty-first century. In doing so, my hope is that cultural studies can be encouraged to take a pragmatist turn.

All books are written with an image of the potential audience in the mind of the author that influences the style and content of the text. I have assumed that the readership for this book will come from the English-speaking world of Australia, the UK and the USA, and I make no pretence to be talking about the specificities of 'culture' beyond those bounds. Thus, when I talk about 'our' culture, and so forth, I mean the broad parameters of western culture. Within those bounds, I am attempting to address two overlapping readerships: new students of cultural studies who want to know about the problems, issues and debates in the field; and those professional academics who are already familiar with the domain and whose interest lies with the problems as problems. This kind of 'double-coding' involves a juggling act between providing enough background information to make the 'problems' intelligible for the new reader while not boring a more professional audience through repetition of previously stated arguments. Obviously my wish is to have been successful in this objective; where I have not been, I hope readers will bear with me.

The cultural studies family

The problem that has haunted the field since its inception has centred on the character of cultural studies itself. This topic is, I would suggest, more auspiciously pursued with the query 'how do we talk about cultural studies, and for what purposes?' than by asking 'what is cultural studies?' This therapeutic recasting of the question enables us to see that cultural studies is not an object. That is, cultural studies is not one thing that can be accurately represented, but rather is constituted by a number of ways of looking at the world which are motivated by different purposes and values.

Cultural studies is constituted by multiple voices or languages that nevertheless have sufficient resemblances to form a recognizable 'family' connected by 'kinship' ties to other families. Or, to deploy a different metaphor, cultural studies is formed by a series of currents that constitute a distinct stream of thought (albeit one that has tributaries flowing in and out of it) in the sense that, although currents may flow in this or that direction, the stream carves a characteristic pathway. Thus, cultural studies is best understood as a language-game that revolves around the theoretical terms developed and deployed by persons calling their work cultural studies. That is, to use Hall's more Foucauldian language, cultural studies can be grasped as a discursive formation, 'a cluster (or formation) of ideas, images and practices, which provide ways of talking about forms of knowledge and conduct associated with a particular topic, social activity or institutional site in society' (1997: 6).

I began by asking the question 'how do we talk about cultural studies, and for what purposes?' We might usefully follow up this inquiry by asking some further questions, namely:

- What are the constituent parts of the language-game of cultural studies?
- What are the purposes of cultural studies?
- Where are the practices of cultural studies located?

In turn, each of these questions raises a series of issues. Thus, a question regarding the 'location' of cultural studies might give rise to the issues of (a) the institutional boundaries of cultural studies and (b) the global in relation to the local. This general pattern of exploring problems through asking questions that raise further issues is one that is broadly manifested in the organization of each chapter of the book. Having said that, it does not follow that I will be exploring all possible issues that arise in relation to a given problem. Selection is a necessary aspect of writing any book.

Cultural studies as a language-game

It has always been difficult to pin down the boundaries of cultural studies as a coherent, unified, academic discipline with clear-cut substantive topics, concepts and methods. However, it is equally difficult to do so for sociology, psychology, women's studies, physics, linguistics and Buddhism. Thus Durkheim, in trying to establish sociology as a coherent discipline, instituted a stream of thought that has been influential across time and space. Nevertheless, he did not define sociology for all time since this particular language-game has mutated and splintered. In other words, the problems of definition and disciplinary boundaries are not uniquely problematic for cultural studies (as is sometimes claimed), nor do they pose problems of particular complexity.

Cultural studies has always been a multi- or post-disciplinary field of inquiry that blurs the boundaries between itself and other 'subjects'. Further, cultural studies has been something of a magpie: it has its own distinctive cast, yet it likes to borrow glittering concepts from other nests. There is nothing particularly problematic about this for it produces some original thinking. Here originality is best thought of as the rearrangement and juxtaposing of existing elements to form new patterns. That is, we generate a new way of seeing, a new perspective on or picture of the world in the same way that a kaleidoscope rearranges its existing pieces into new images. Of course, being an academic project rather than an artistic one, cultural studies uses words to write new sentences rather than colours to paint new pictures.

As Grossberg et al. have argued, there are a series of concepts that have been developed under the banner of cultural studies that have been deployed in various geographical sites. These form 'a history of real achievements that is now part of the cultural studies tradition'. To do without them would be 'to willingly accept real incapacitation' (Grossberg et al., 1992: 8). These concepts are tools for acting in the world and their meaning lies in their usage. The purposes for which these tools are commonly employed are those of writing texts and teaching students. Cultural studies, in arguing that language is constitutive of that which it names, must apply that lesson to itself. If words give meaning to material objects and social practices that are brought into view by language and made intelligible to us in terms which language delimits, then the vocabulary of cultural studies performs cultural studies. Thus, as I have argued elsewhere (Barker, 2000), culture, signifying practices, representation, cultural politics, positionality, cultural materialism, non-reductionism, social formation, articulation, power, popular culture, ideology, hegemony, texts, active audiences, subjectivity, identity, discourse and discursive formation are amongst the key theoretical concepts by which contemporary cultural studies has sought to explore and intervene in our social and cultural worlds. This is the core of the vocabulary that institutes and constitutes cultural studies.

Any academic vocabulary is located on an institutional map and deployed for particular purposes. Consequently, there remains a distinction between the study of culture and institutionally located cultural studies. Though the study of culture has taken place in a variety of academic disciplines – sociology, anthropology, English literature, etc. – and in a range of geographical and institutional spaces, this is not best thought of as cultural studies. The study of culture has no origins or single site of activity. However, cultural studies as an institutionally located activity did have a moment and place where it named itself. That was the formation and denomination of the Centre for Contemporary Cultural Studies at the University of Birmingham in the UK. Here, the quantum leap of cultural studies took it from the nameless to the named – from nothingness to institutional existence. Subsequently, cultural studies has extended its intellectual base and geographic scope. In addition to those situated in the UK, there are self-defined cultural studies practitioners in the USA, Australia, Africa, Asia, Latin America and continental Europe, with each 'formation' of cultural studies working in different ways. Thus to map cultural studies is to map its language, its locations and its purposes as it unfolded from its very own Big Bang. This is a genealogy that I do not intend to undertake. However, this argument illustrates the futility of seeking an essence or universal definition of cultural studies.

The current vocabulary of the field suggests that cultural studies is centrally concerned with culture as constituted by the meanings and representations that are generated by signifying mechanisms in the context of human practices. Further, cultural studies is concerned with the construction and consequences of those representations, and thus with matters of power, since patterns of signifying practices constitute, and are constituted by, institutions and virtual structures. For Hall, whose work has been crucial in constituting the domain of cultural studies, culture can be understood as 'the actual grounded terrain of practices, representations, languages and customs of any specific society' (1996c: 439). For Bennett, cultural studies 'is concerned with all those practices, institutions and systems of classification through which there are inculcated in a population particular values, beliefs, competencies, routines of life and habitual forms of conduct' (1998: 28). For both writers, cultural studies has sought to develop ways of thinking about culture and power that can be utilized by social agents in the pursuit of change. This, for Hall (1992a) at least, is what differentiates cultural studies from other subject areas. Hence, cultural studies is thought of as a body of theory generated by thinkers who regard the production of theoretical knowledge as a political practice. However, we should be careful not to confuse writing as a politically inspired endeavour with other kinds of civic and governmental practices, as many cultural studies practitioners are inclined to do in their enthusiasm to contribute to change and underscore their own relevance.

The purposes of cultural studies

Most writers in the field would probably agree that the purposes of cultural studies are:

- analytic,
- pedagogic,
- political.

Nevertheless, the emphasis given by a number of leading cultural studies practitioners (notably Hall above) has been to argue that it is the politics of cultural studies that endows it with distinctiveness. However, as a body of knowledge, cultural studies is no more and no less political than any other 'discipline' in terms of the establishment of world-views of power/knowledge or the institutional politics of the academy. That being so, it would be less delusional and also practically beneficial to the field if cultural studies were to become more modest in its ambitions. That is, cultural studies must come to accept that its main purpose, enacted through teaching and writing, is restricted to intellectual clarification and legitimization.

Cultural studies writers offer another variety of storytelling in the marketplace. Along with many other good stories, those of cultural studies are best thought of as inspirational guidebooks with consequences. Cultural studies, like other sets of myths and fables, acts as a symbolic guide or map of meaning and significance in the cosmos. As such, it is a potential tool for activists and policy makers rather more than a form of direct political activity. Cultural studies is no less valuable for that: storytellers have had an important role in human history, but we should avoid confusing the power and agency of the King with the play of the Fool (who tells the best stories). Indeed, the linkages between cultural studies and new social movements, which are commonly seen as the former's political agents, are tenuous given that feminism, ecology, peace campaigns, and so forth, do not need cultural studies *per se*. However, our theorizing may be of assistance and, as such, cultural studies may seek to 'clear the way' for activists through problem solving via redefinition and redescription of the world. Nevertheless, being an 'activist' is not a prerequisite for 'doing cultural studies' and 'doing cultural studies' is best thought of not as a form of 'political activism' but as a form of researching, teaching and publishing.

Of course, teaching and the production of knowledge are political in the sense that they are concerned with relations of power. However, it is not particularly helpful to merge such disparate activities as reading, writing, publishing academic books, producing campaign leaflets, picketing, door knocking at election time and teaching a class under the all-encompassing concept of the 'political'. In particular, it is a mistake to equate the demystifying or deconstructing tasks of cultural studies with the activities of new social movements,

policy makers, political parties or the institutions of government. Further, insofar as cultural studies practitioners want to engage in the cultural politics of
popular thinking, they should consider more popular forms of publishing (e.g.
journalism). Insofar as cultural studies wants to be more institutionally political,
it must assist in the formulation and implementation of policy. Both are valued
activities but should not be understood as the same pastime.

The locations of cultural studies

The prime locations of cultural studies as a set of practices are academic institutions, for example universities and publishing houses. Cultural studies' position
in the higher education systems of the West has inevitably led it to an expan-
sionist trajectory outwards from the terrain of postgraduate research and into
attracting degree students with their affiliated funding. This was a response, in
part, to the demands of students and the availability of trained staff. However,
it was perhaps more tellingly still an answer to the need for funding in a harsh
environment. Consequently, as it has become something to be taught, so cultural
studies has acquired a multitude of institutional bases, courses, textbooks and
students. In due course, this process leads to a certain 'disciplining' of cultural
studies. The courses now offered by universities for undergraduate students
constitute a broad 'definition' of the parameters of cultural studies. The textbooks that follow, including my own (Barker, 2000), reinforce this process.

Many cultural studies practitioners have felt ill at ease with the forging of
institutional disciplinary boundaries for the field. Professionalized and institutionalized cultural studies might, feared Hall, 'formalize out of existence the
critical questions of power, history and politics' (1992a: 286). However, not only
is this not an inevitable consequence of growth, but expansion in the domain of
higher education is a condition of reaching a wider audience. This readership is
made up of young people who as graduates will play an important part in the
unfolding of the twenty-first century. Indeed, such students are likely to form the
backbone of the future cadre of cultural intellectuals, policy makers, workers
and managers. As such, they are a socially and politically important audience for
cultural studies to address.

Although higher education is a branch of government, and thus teachers are
already an arm of the state, higher education remains, at least within liberal
democracies, a privileged site of critical inquiry. Few people aside from those
working in the academy have the time, resources or cultural protection to carry
out such tasks. Writers, researchers and teachers in higher education may not be
the 'organic' intellectuals whom the 'pioneers' of cultural studies hoped for.
However, they are in a position to speak with, and provide intellectual resources
for, new social movements, workers in cultural industries and policy-making
bodies. Cultural studies may find it increasingly hard to cling to its romantic and
heroic conception of itself as an 'intellectual guerrilla movement waging war on

the borders of official academia' (McGuigan, 1997: 1). Nevertheless, the establishment of cultural studies as an undergraduate subject area does not preclude research centres (now also more numerous) but rather provides new opportunities. Although the move from counter-culture to educational mainstream has not been a comfortable one for everybody, it is now necessary to see cultural studies in a new light and adapt accordingly.

In sum, I have argued that cultural studies is best described as an intellectual enterprise that is constituted by a set of overlapping language-games. The contemporary vocabulary of cultural studies suggests that it is concerned with culture, as constituted by the meanings and representations generated by human signifying practices, and the relations of power and its consequences that are inherent in such representations. The prime purposes of cultural studies, which is located in the institutions of universities, publishing houses and bookshops, are the processes of intellectual clarification and legitimation that could provide useful tools for cultural/political activists and policy makers.

Family therapy: approaching problems in cultural studies

As a general rule, I take a 'problem' in cultural studies to be constituted by a field of recurrent doubts and puzzles centred on specific sites of inquiry that give rise to repeated and as yet unresolved debates in that literature which constitutes cultural studies. Of course, as I indicated above, a problem is never 'one thing' but a clustering of questions and issues.

Therapeutic thinking

In exploring problems within cultural studies, I adopt the characteristically Wittgensteinian tactic of 'therapeutic redefinition' by which problems are dissolved through adopting a 'new way of seeing'. Or, as he puts it, to 'shew the fly the way out of the fly-bottle' (Wittgenstein, 1957: 309). For Wittgenstein, to ask a particular question with a specific grammar is to be already committed to a way of seeing. For example, to ask whether the 'mental' is a process or a state is to trap oneself in a fly-bottle since the question itself depends on a particular (and for Wittgenstein a mistaken) way of seeing.

How does the philosophical problem about mental processes and states and about behaviorism arise? The first step is one that altogether escapes notice. We talk of processes and states and leave their nature undecided. Sometime perhaps we shall know more about them – we think. But that is just what commits us to a particular way of looking at the matter. For we have a definite concept of what it means to learn to know a process better (the decisive movement in the conjuring trick had been made, and it was the very one that we thought quite innocent). And now the analogy which was to make us understand our thoughts falls to pieces. So we have to deny the yet uncomprehended process in the yet unexplored medium. And now it looks as if we had denied mental processes. And naturally we don't want to deny them. (Wittgenstein, 1957: 308)

Thinking as therapy enables problems in cultural studies to be recast in ways that, while preserving the political significance of the questions and issues involved, take some of the 'heat' out of the debates. It does this by suggesting that it is commonly the character of the question itself that constitutes part of the problem. Thus, to ask the question 'what is cultural studies?' is to assume that there is such a thing as cultural studies that we can know and name. Following Rorty's critique of representationalism (1980, 1989, 1991a, 1991b, 1998a, 1998b), I contend that we cannot know what something 'is' when 'is' suggests either a metaphysical universal truth or an accurate representation of an independent object world. Language does not accurately represent the world but is a tool for achieving our purposes (see Chapters 2 and 3). Knowledge is a matter not of getting an accurate picture of reality, but of learning how best to contend with the world. Since we have a variety of purposes, we develop a variety of languages. Thus in redescribing the question 'what is cultural studies?' as 'how do we talk about cultural studies, and for what purposes?' I made the switch from a question about representation to one concerning language use.

The idea that we cannot definitively say what an event 'is', and that we have different languages for different purposes, is not the preserve of the philosophy of language but is one shared by the 'hard' sciences (Gribbin, 1998). For example, at the core of quantum physics is a wave–particle duality by which all quantum entities can be treated as both waves and particles: as being in a particular place (particle) and in no certain place (wave). Under some circumstances it is useful to regard photons (quantities of light) as a stream of particles, while at other times they are best thought of in terms of wavelengths. Equally, in classical Newtonian physics an electron is envisaged as a particle that orbits the nuclei of an atom (protons and neutrons), while in quantum mechanics it is held to be a wave surrounding the atom's nuclei. Both descriptions 'work' according to the purposes one has in mind: physical phenomena are put 'under the description' (Davidson, 1984) of different models to achieve divergent ends.

My general approach in this book is to try to recast problems in a way that shifts the emphasis from the metaphysical representationalist question 'what is' to the more mundane and pragmatic issues of language use: that is, 'how do we talk about X?' As Wittgenstein puts it, 'Grammar tells what kind of object anything is. (Theology as grammar.)' (1957: 373). What something 'is' becomes constituted by the use of language within specific language-games. The truth of a matter is culturally and historically specific and changeable, a 'regime of truth' or a condition of being 'in the true', as Foucault (1972) would have it. In this context, problems are 'solved' by being 'dissolved', that is, by redescribing them in a different language. Indeed, any state of affairs can be explicated in a variety of ways, giving rise to variability of accounts. In particular, what may appear as a problem of binary opposites – e.g. structure and action or freedom and deter-mination – can be grasped as a case of different languages for different purposes. Thus, either/or binaries are dissolved by denying that the problem is best described in dualistic terms at all.

Solving problems in this way is not simply an abstract playing with words, for new descriptions, new languages with which to cope with world, have spe-cific consequences. Thus,

> our belief that the picture forced upon us consisted in the fact that only the one case and no other occurred to us. 'There is another solution as well' means: there is something else that I am also prepared to call a 'solution'; to which I am prepared to apply such-and-such a picture, such-and-such an analogy, and so on. (Wittgenstein, 1957: 140)

Consequently, 'what you have primarily discovered is a new way of looking at things. As if you had invented a new way of painting; or, again, a new metre, or a new kind of song' (Wittgenstein, 1957: 401).

Underlying themes

Since each chapter touches on at least three or four issues in the context of an identified 'problem', this book covers a good deal of ground, much of which will be familiar to seasoned readers of cultural studies texts. However, I also include a number of themes and intellectual resources that are less well known in a cultural studies context and that allow us to take a different perspective on familiar debates. Here I want to outline briefly some of the thinking that has shaped the themes of the book and that will be encountered again as the text unfolds.

Philosophic pragmatism

For some twenty years, cultural studies operated inside the broad parameters and problematic of western Marxism. Hence the centrality of the debates about base and superstructure, ideology, hegemony, class determinism and revolu-tionary politics. In my view we need to understand Marx as a thinker who had some interesting and useful things to say about nineteenth-century capitalism. Some of his analysis is still pertinent today – after all most of us live in capital-ist societies – but so much has changed since Marx's time that much of his work has also proved to be misleading. Certainly we cannot any longer sensibly enter-tain economic reductionism, the overwhelming priority given to class in cultural analysis or the rhetoric of revolutionary politics. Quite apart from the fact that revolution in the West is not even on the agenda, let us not forget that the con-sequences of twentieth-century social revolution have been fairly disastrous.

As cultural studies unfolded, the influence of structuralism was wedded to its Marxist foundation. One manifestation of this development was that a rupture appeared between Marxism's stress on political economy and the structuralist emphasis given to language and the autonomy of culture. Later, the break with Marxism was furthered by the widespread embracing of poststructuralism and postmodernism. However, though the work of Foucault and Derrida has much to commend it, both have a tendency to reify language into an autonomous system detached from the everyday practices of human beings. Further, neither has much to say about the gritty world of reformist public politics, preferring the rhetoric of deconstruction and insurgency. In this book I am explicitly suggesting that Rortian pragmatism is preferable to either Marxism or poststructuralism and could provide cultural studies with a more adequate framework than either of these theoretical paradigms.

Pragamatism, as espoused by Rorty (1980, 1989, 1991a, 1991b, 1998a, 1998b), is both anti-representationalist and anti-foundationalist. Anti-representationalism is understood to mean that the relationship between language and the rest of the material universe is one of causality not of adequacy of representation or expression. That is, we can usefully try to explain how human organisms come to act or speak in particular ways, but we cannot beneficially see language as representing the world in ways which more or less correspond to the material world. There are no chunks of language that line up with or correspond to chunks of reality. Above all, there is no archimedian vantage-point from which one could verify the universal 'truth' of any correspondence between the world and language. The anti-foundationalism that follows from this argument suggests that we cannot ground or justify our actions and beliefs by means of any universal truths. We can describe this or that discourse, chunk of language, as being more or less useful and as having more or less desirable consequences. However, we cannot claim it to be true in the sense of correspondence to an independent object world. We can examine the way that the word 'truth' is used, what makes a particular truth claim acceptable to us and our routine deployment of 'mundane realism'. However, we cannot give an epistemological account of truth and must steer clear of philosophical claims about transcendental and metaphysical truth.

These arguments turn our attention away from the search for universal truth and towards justification as the giving of reasons. This reason-giving is a social practice, so that to justify a belief is to give reasons in the context of a tradition and a community. Here, reasons are objective in the sense that they have an intersubjective base in the community norms for reason giving and tend towards agreement on claims that have been merited by practice. However, norms may be contradictory and understood in varying ways by the community. Further, it is possible to investigate an issue with varying degrees of conscientiousness. Thus, justification is a part of an ongoing 'conversation' of humanity, and, however we characterize 'truth', we have no reliable source for it other than our ongoing conversation with each other. Having said that, some practices of knowledge formation have yielded more capacity for predictability and control of the material world than have others. Thus, physical science has been more able to generate consensus about its forms of understanding than have the humanities precisely because of its predictive reliability.

Pragmatism shares its anti-foundationalism and anti-representationalism with the poststructuralist thinking that is currently ascendant within cultural studies. However, in contrast to poststructuralism, pragmatism combines these arguments with a commitment to social reform. Pragmatism suggests that the struggle for social change is a question of language/text *and* of material practice/policy action. Like cultural studies, in pursuit of a 'better' world, pragmatism attempts to render contingent that which appears 'natural'. However, unlike the revolutionary rhetoric of many followers of poststructuralism, pragmatism weds itself to the need for piecemeal practical political change. In this sense, pragmatism has a 'tragic' view of life for it does not share the utopian push of, say, Marxism. In contrast, it favours a trial-and-error experimentalism that seeks after new ways of doing things that we can describe as 'better' when measured against our values.

Since anti-representationalism, anti-foundationalism and pragmatism do not of necessity support any *particular* political projects, values or strategies, we may feel free to disagree with any of Rorty's programmatic suggestions. Nevertheless, his pragmatism combines a commitment to what cultural studies writers have called 'the cultural politics of difference' – that is, language-based redescriptions of the world which expand the realm of democratic cultures – together with the need for the public policy necessary to maintain it. Within liberal democratic states, a cultural politics of representation and a cultural policy orientation need not be opposed.

Rorty's politics are those of 'liberalism' in a broad sense, while in its particulars he embraces that which Europeans would understand as the social democratic left. Indeed, Gutting (1999) characterizes his Rortian-derived views as being 'pragmatic liberalism'. Here, liberalism involves a balancing act between individual freedom and the reduction of suffering through community action. The hope of liberalism is to find ways for human beings to be more free, less cruel, more leisured and richer in goods and experiences while trying to maximize their opportunities to live their lives as they see fit: that is, to pursue a private project founded on their own values and beliefs while not causing suffering to others. This involves, at least for Rorty, a strong division between the public world and the private project, for liberalism can accept a range of private values that it cannot tolerate in the public domain. Now, the division between the public and the private is contingent on cultural classifications. Indeed, since there can be no such thing as a private language, the private sphere is social and saturated with the power relations of the public world. Further, we need to avoid the implication that the 'private' is always a matter for individuals alone, for there are groups of persons who hold to beliefs that are not in tune with the liberal body politic. That said, the private–public cleavage is a useful one in maintaining our freedoms even while we may accept renegotiation of its boundaries.

Liberal democracy and cultural pluralism work imperfectly. Indeed, the liberal and democratic impulses are not always easily reconciled with each other, while liberal democratic states are themselves vehicles of oppression. Consequently, it is entirely acceptable to liberals to critique those aspects of our societies and cultures that restrict freedoms and cause suffering. This of course has been the central political project of cultural studies. However, liberals in the sense that Rorty deploys the concept do not think that the answers to our contemporary predicaments lie in a revolutionary overthrow of the institutions and practices of liberal societies. Rather, it is argued that all in all there is no viable and practical alternative to liberal democracies that poses less of a threat to our freedoms and welfare. As such, a pragmatic cultural studies can be understood as a critical wing of liberal societies drawing attention to the continuation of suffering without rejecting the fundamental viability of liberal democracy. This commitment does not mean that any particular institution of liberal democracy could not be reformed or that any specific cultural and political direction could not be improved on. Indeed, I understand the 'politics of difference' and the project of 'radical democracy' (Laclau and Mouffe, 1985) that lie at the heart of contemporary cultural studies as redefining liberal democracy in its current manifestations while remaining within its philosophical boundaries.

A commitment to liberal democracy is of course a pragmatic matter. Perhaps one day in the future we humans will come up with a way to live that we consider to be a better one. In other words, our commitment to liberal democracy has no universal foundation that is grounded in a philosophical account of human nature for example – nor does it need one. As Rorty argues, we do not require universal foundations to pursue a pragmatic improvement of the human condition on the basis of the values of our own tradition. For Rorty (1989), the contingency of language and the irony which follows from this (irony here means holding to beliefs and attitudes which one knows are contingent and could be otherwise, i.e. they have no universal foundations) leads us to ask about what kind of human being we want to be (for no transcendental truth and no transcendental God can answer this question for us). This includes questions about us as individuals – who we want to be – and questions about our relations to fellow human beings – how shall we treat others? These are pragmatic questions requiring political-value responses. They are not metaphysical or epistemological issues.

Rorty has often been bracketed with the so-called 'postmodern' philosophers, though he has tried to distance himself from this nomination. However, like postmodernism, pragmatism is against 'grand theory', being in sympathy with Lyotard's (1984) 'incredulity towards metanarratives'. Pragmatists have a radically contingent view of the world where truth ends with social practice. However, this does not mean that all theory is to be jettisoned. Rather, local theory becomes a way of redescribing the world in normative ways. That is, theory may enable us to envisage possible new and better ways of doing things. Theory does not picture the world more or less accurately; rather, it is a tool, instrument or logic for intervening in the world through the mechanisms of description, definition, prediction and control. Theory construction is a self-reflexive discursive endeavour that seeks to interpret and intercede in the world.

I take modernity and postmodernity to be periodizing concepts that refer to historical epochs. They are abstractions that broadly define the institutional parameters of social formations. As such, I cannot countenance the description of our world as postmodern but prefer Giddens, (1990, 1991) notion of 'radicalized modernity'. As a set of philosophical and epistemological concerns, modernism is associated with the enlightenment philosophy of rationality, science, universal truth and progress. In contrast, postmodern philosophy has been associated with a questioning of these categories – not depth but surface, not truth but truths, not objectivity but social commendation, not universalism or foundationalism but historically specific 'regimes of truth'. However, though reason has turned out to be partial and unbalanced rather than universal and totalizing, pragmatism is still committed to the idea that reason is a useful way of asserting human independence from arbitrary and external authorities (e.g. God and the church). Even Foucault questioned the need to be either for or against the Enlightenment. As Bauman (1991) suggests, the condition of 'postmodernity' can be understood as the modern mind reflecting upon itself from a distance and sensing the urge to change. As such, I prefer to see the self-examination of modernity by moderns as a form of 'reflexive modernism'. Nevertheless, given its common usage in cultural studies, I accept the concepts of a postmodern culture and of postmodernism as a cultural style (see Chapter 3).

Since pragmatism understands the universe as always 'in the making', so the future has ethical significance. We can, it is argued, make a difference and create new, 'better' futures. In this sense, pragmatism insists on the irreducibility of human agency even as it recognizes the causal stories of the past. Agency is to be understood here as the socially constructed capacity to act and is not to be confused with a self-originating transcendental subject. We are not constituted by an inner core that possesses attitudes, beliefs and the capacity to act; rather, we are a network of attitudes, beliefs, and so forth, that does act. Further, pragmatism shares with poststructuralist, post-Marxist cultural studies the idea that social and cultural change is a matter of 'politics without guarantees'. Without Marxism's 'laws of history', politics is centred on small-scale experimentalism, value-commitment and practical action. Here, pragmatism embraces a form of 'ethical naturalism' by which ethics do not need metaphysical foundations to be justified. That is, ethics do not require to be grounded in anything outside or beyond our beliefs and desires. However, to say that morality is rooted in our desires and ways of speaking is not to say that all moral codes have the same status. Rather, moral codes are embedded in our intersubjectivity and acculturation so that ethics are returned to questions of justification. Of course, it is a characteristic of contemporary modern cultures that we participate in a number of traditions and communities so that the justification of ethics becomes an increasingly complex matter that depends at its best on dialogue and at its worst on a descent into violence.

In sum, I am suggesting that Rorty's work is a valuable addition to the cultural studies reper-toire. However, as much can be gained by engaging Rorty in a conversation as accepting what he has to say uncritically.

For example, West (1993), a cultural critic sympathetic to pragmatism, rightly worries about Rorty's failure to analyse *power* and to deploy sociological kinds of explanation to identify the realistic and pragmatic collective routes for social change. That said, cultural studies thinkers with their concern for the province of power in social life are well placed to rectify this weakness. They are also appropriately positioned to critique the stress on individual decision making (i.e. decisionism – see Gutting, 1999) that appears in Rorty's work with a more inter-subjective and cultural account of the actions of persons.

Practices and performances

Contemporary cultural studies has been marked by its emphasis on the consti-tutive role of language as the means and medium through which we form knowledge about ourselves and the social world. Thus cultural representations are said to work 'like a language'. Indeed, it is argued that to understand culture is to explore how meaning is produced symbolically through signifying prac-tices. This understanding and its application is one of the major achievements of cultural studies. However, a reliance on structuralism and poststructuralism has led cultural studies to postulate language as a 'thing' – an autonomous system with its own rules – rather than as the marks and noises that human beings use to co-ordinate action and achieve purposes.

By contrast, Wittgenstein holds language to be an integral part of practice or conduct so that, for example, when we learn the language of pain 'we learn new pain behavior' (Wittgenstein, 1957: #244, 89). We learn language as an undivided part of learning how to do things. Consequently, new ways of seeing are also new practices or performances. While language-games are rule-bound activities, those rules are not abstract components of language (as in structuralism) but con-stitutive rules, that is, rules that are such by dint of their enactment in social practice. Thus, the rules of language constitute our pragmatic understandings of 'how to go on' in society, and to know a 'form of life' is to be able to participate in it. Thus, Wittgenstein argues that, when it comes to explaining the word 'game' to others, we are likely to show them different games and to say this is what games are. To know what games are is to be able to play games. As Giddens has argued,

I take the significance of Wittgenstein's writings for social theory to consist in the association of language with definite *social practices* . . . Language is intrinsically involved with *that which has to be done*: the constitution of language as 'meaningful' is inseparable from the constitution of forms of social life as continuing practices. (1979: 4)

There is stress on social practices, including language as a practice, in the work of Wittgenstein and Giddens that is lacking in both structuralism and poststructuralism (whatever other merits these bodies of work have) and which I commend to practitioners of cultural studies. Indeed, a reliance on structuralism and poststructuralism has sometimes led cultural studies to miss the crucial amalgam that is language and practice. This has resulted in cultural studies venturing along the road of a potentially obscure textualism where the speaking and acting subject is lost from view. I shall argue that cultural studies needs to restore the balance by adding studies of acting persons to its studies of texts and subject positions. It would be beneficial to cultural studies if more stress were laid on the utterances of persons in social contexts, thereby giving our attention to the relation between language and action. This is a matter of languages for purposes. If we want to stress 'interrelatedness', discipline and the need for structural change, the language of codes, discourse and subject positions is our tool. If we want to stress ethics, action, change and uniqueness, we can talk about the utterances of persons in social contexts.

In addition to this stress on practice, the concept of the performative also figures in the work of Wittgenstein, for whom philosophy was a performance (Genova, 1995), as well as in the subsequent speech act theory of J.L. Austin (1962). The theory of the performative unites language and practice for a performative is a statement that simultaneously puts into effect that which it describes. Thus in a marriage ceremony the words 'I pronounce you' are performative. This notion of the performative has been profitably worked by Butler (1993), for whom sex is a discursive-performative construction (though an indispensable one) that forms subjects and governs the materialization of bodies. Performativity is not a singular act or event but an iterable practice secured through being repeatedly performed. Since performativity is not a singular act but a reiteration of a set of norms, it should not be understood as a performance given by a self-conscious intentional actor. In the context of a renewed stress on language and practice, I shall argue that crucial aspects 'culture' can be understood in terms of performances.

The meaning and place of culture

The central concept of culture does not represent an entity in an independent object world but is best thought of as a mobile signifier that enables a series of different ways of talking about human activity that stress divergent uses and purposes. The multitudinous ways that culture has been talked about are not cases of right vs wrong, for none of them are erroneous in the sense of misdescribing an object. However, they do achieve different purposes and may be more or less applicable in different times and places. The concept of culture is thus political and contingent. As such, cultural studies need not feel impelled to 'define' culture in any ultimate fashion, but may utilize the concept for a variety of purposes.

The concepts of space and place are important elements of any discussion of culture. However, the idea of culture as a 'whole way of life', popularized within cultural studies by Raymond Williams, is problematic in its wedding of culture to bounded places (notably those of the modern nation-state). In the era of globalization/diaspora and the purposes associated with the politics of difference, that is, diversity and solidarity, I argue that culture is best thought of not as a bounded 'unit' but as a set of overlapping 'performative flows' with no clear limits or determinations (chaos culture). Culture can be thought of as the continual hybridization of meaningful practices or performances in a global context. Thus, culture is a matter less of locations with roots than of hybrid and creolized cultural routes in global space. Cultures are not pure, authentic and locally bounded; rather, they are syncretic and hybridized products of interactions across space.

A significant question that has been posed within cultural studies concerns the problem of the relationship between culture and the material. In relation to this issue, I argue the following:

- To point to causal links between material conditions and language/culture (or indeed the linguistic and cultural character of the material and economic) is not to deny the specificity of the other term. That phenomena have material causes does not reduce their significance to the causal agent nor take away their specificities. For example, each of us can trace biological, historical and cultural explanations for our own being, yet at no time are we anything less than unique persons capable of action.
- Since language is a tool for adapting to and controlling the environment, rather than an independent sphere that exists on its own terms to represent the material, then we are in touch with reality in all areas of culture as long as one takes this to mean 'caused by and causing' and not 'representing reality' (see Rorty, 1989). The relationship between language and the rest of the material universe is one of causality and not of adequacy of representation or expression. Human beings are animals who walk the earth, and, as such, language is never divorced from material practice, nor are we ever out of sync with reality by dint of being trapped in language.
- Cultural representations and meanings have materiality, being embedded in sounds, inscriptions, objects and images within books, magazines, television programmes, and so forth. In short, there is no cultural domain that is not material and no material world that is not, for human beings, also cultural.

That is, the material–cultural binary is a hindrance to investigation and should be put to one side.

The question of materialism leads me to another way of considering the meaning and place of culture, that is, in its evolutionary context. Dotted throughout the book are a number of references to the physical sciences and evolutionary biology/psychology in particular. I think that the potential for co-operation between evolutionary biology/psychology and cultural studies is promising. Human culture and human biology have co-evolved and are indivisible in that culture forms an environment for the human body and feeds into evolutionary change. Evolutionary biology is a useful causal story that explains human organisms in terms of relationships and consequences in which history has no *telos*. It dispenses with the idea that either the human mind or the mind of God is the ultimate source of the universe, replacing them both with the indifferent, purposeless and algorithmic processes of natural selection. This view allows us to draw a naturalistic and holistic description of human beings as animals who walk the earth adapting and changing themselves in the context of their environment. That is, we can understand culture as being both a series of adaptations to our physical circumstances and the creation of a new human environment.

Of especial interest here are the developments in evolutionary psychology that explore the cognitive mechanisms that underpin culture. Thus, evolutionary psychologists resist the demarcation between evolutionary and cultural theory, arguing that we should put our understanding of human culture in a wider context. In particular, evolutionary biology and genetic science suggest that there are limits to the plasticity of human capacities and behaviours. This argument necessarily poses a challenge to those who take the logic of social and cultural constructionism to its extreme.

One of the important features of the human condition that is explored by evolutionary psychology but under-examined by cultural studies is the place of emotions in our lives. Truth, knowledge, personal relationships, communication, ethics, behaviour and politics all have an affective dimension. That is, culture involves emotional processes that have, for the most part, been ignored by cultural studies. Cultural studies will always have an inadequate understanding of culture, politics and human behaviour in general until it incorporates questions of emotional response into its repertoire. This is both an intellectual omission and a political error, for cultural politics are driven not only by rational arguments or descriptions but also by emotional attachments and affective symbols. Indeed, in my view the latter is more significant to everyday politics than is rationality.

Some 'emotions', I would suggest, are biochemically founded universals of the human condition that are mediated and worked over by culture. Other 'emotions' work the other way around: that is, they are primarily cultural dances that set off bodily responses. Thus, emotional behaviour is the outcome of a set of conditioned bodily responses and learned cognitive appraisal mechanisms. To this situation we add a conscious 'feeling' from our working memory and words that not only label context-specific responses as 'fear', anger', 'love', and so forth, but can also themselves set off further emotional responses.

Thus, we can understand emotion as bodily biochemistry plus cognitive and cultural classificatory functions, with language as the most notable of these.

In exploring emotions, I commonly take depression and anxiety as my examples, given that the western world is experiencing something of an epidemic of 'affective disorders'.

Truth, capitalism and cultural politics

One of the central problems that confront cultural studies concerns the grounding of its theory and politics in an era where anti-foundationalism holds sway. While I argue that there are no transcendental truths, only ways of talking in culture, I also suggest that we do not need universal truths to undertake political action. Rather, politics is grounded in the values and world-views of the culture 'we' participate in. Who constitutes the 'we' is a matter of stories of power. This is a world where politics is ironic and without guarantees. I further suggest that the collapse of foundational truth has raised serious doubts about the viability and explanatory power of the concept of ideology. While cultural studies has rightly espoused an anti-representationalist and anti-essentialist view of language, a number of writers within cultural studies seem not to have entirely grasped the contradiction between an anti-essentialist position on language and the concept of ideology as falsehood. Certainly Foucault, perhaps the most cited philosopher in cultural studies, never used the concept of ideology, and for precisely this reason. While we could deploy the concept of ideology to mean the binding and justifying ideas of any group (with no reference to Truth), other words can carry this meaning just as well, so that we might be better advised to drop the concept of ideology altogether.

The concept of ideology, with its connotations of falsity, is one of the legacies of Marxism within cultural studies since it was thought to be the ideologies generated by the ruling class that held 'the people' in chains. British cultural studies of the 1970s and early 1980s was much concerned with Marxism and the attempt to explain the persistence of capitalism while maintaining that its demise could still be brought about. However, it now seems to me that capitalism is transformed and here to stay; indeed, it is capitalism itself that is the contemporary revolutionary force (as it was in Marx's day). Our world currently has no viable alternative to global capitalism. Consequently, there is little choice but to engage in a variety of reformist politics. In this context, cultural studies could play the useful role of telling stories of resistance informed by a utopian realism that must include their implications for policy development and enactment. Here 'resistance' is tactical and conjunctural rather than absolute or revolutionary. Indeed, it is becoming clear that commodities themselves can be the basis of 'resistance'.

While the pertinence of academic work to other practices of the human project does not appear to worry all scholars, it must concern cultural studies, which has long maintained that it has political applicability. Indeed, this is the basis of Hall's (1992a) distinction between 'academic' work and 'intellectual' work. Cultural studies has long justified itself with the argument that cultural criticism is an aspect of cultural politics. Provided one drops the notion of 'exposing ideology' and settles for the perspective of redescription, this is an acceptable argument. Cultural criticism can act as a tool for intervention in the social world. However, adoption of a certain deconstructive textualism along with the tone of methodological and ethical 'purity' has led some cultural studies writers into 'obscurity'. Consequently, the role cultural criticism could play in feeding more popular modes such as television, film and journalism, as well as providing beneficial tools for the formation of cultural policy, has tended to be ignored. In any case, we should avoid over-inflating the public political value of cultural studies and, in particular, try to avoid mistaking our ethical choices for radical public politics. To confuse ethics with effectiveness or cultural studies with political action is to enact category errors. Instead, the cultural left could make a contribution to the revival of social democracy and the development of democratic politics in the context of globalization: that is, the continuation of the 'long revolution' (without guarantees).

In this vein, Bennett (1992) has urged cultural studies to adopt a more pragmatic approach by working with cultural producers. He argues that the textual politics with which it has been engaged ignores the institutional dimensions of cultural power. This is so because, for Bennett (1998), culture is caught up in, and functions as a part of, cultural technologies that organize and shape social life and human conduct. Culture is a matter not just of representations and consciousness but also of institutional practices, administrative routines and spatial arrangements. While the cultural policy argument has a great deal of merit, it should not be regarded as excluding the work of theory and cultural criticism. Cultural studies needs to accept a kaleidoscope of political action that includes cultural critique, new social movements, social democracy and policy formation. In particular, it is important to continue to debate what the purposes of political action are as well as the means by which to achieve them. Indeed, there is still discussion to be had on the question of what values should guide the 'cultural left'.

It is far from clear that the most often espoused values within cultural studies – equality–justice–solidarity–difference–tolerance–diversity–respect – are mutually compatible. For example, justice may not be best served by the adoption of equality (as sameness), which itself cannot simply mean uniformity and standardization if we are to respect difference. The modernist goal of equality is beset with problems, and equality of outcome is neither possible nor desirable. Here the pragmatic inclination is to dispense with universal value approaches in favour of context- and tradition-specific resolutions of problems. When respect for difference and the reduction of suffering become our primary values (displacing an unachievable and romantic notion of equality of outcome), we may pursue justice only as a desirable, if imperfectly achievable, end. Indeed, acceptance of the imperfectibility of human beings (as measured against glorified cultural images) and our cultural world is a necessary move for a cultural studies that has been dogged by idealized fantasies of the possible. Dialogue and justice are values that may also guide us through questions of the 'Other'. We may never fully 'know' the Other, but if we approach language as a learnable practical skill and tool (not as something which mirrors the Other), then we can learn to talk amongst ourselves. Pragmatic negotiation is the only way forward.

Most western societies are broadly in post-scarcity situations: that is, no one is starving and few people are poor in an absolute sense. In this context, the problems we face in the West are increasingly psychological rather than material; specifically they are emotional and 'spiritual'. They concern our relations with others, our sense of meaninglessness, our addictions and our mental health. It is in this sense that we need to develop more emotional and spiritual intelligence as resources within our culture that are better able to deal with ancestral emotions that are triggered by contemporary cultural circumstances. The concept of the 'spiritual' is somewhat contemporary in the sense that it is separated from the religious. It does not mean the abandonment of logic and rationality or the embracing of superstition. Rather it means coming to a mature and meaningful understanding of the existential issues of our lives through the development of integrity, wisdom and transcendence. It involves acceptance of one's limitations, groundedness in the ordinary and a willingness to be surprised; what Young-Eisendrath and Miller (2000) call a 'skeptical spirituality'. Indeed, we might see it as a reflexive and ironic spirituality that plays a necessary role in the emotional lives of human beings as currently constituted. We need such a spiritual intelligence in relation to a rampant consumer culture that is producing more discontent than happiness because of the black hole of meaninglessness that remains after consumption is over. We also need it in relation to the stress, fatigue and social isolation that mark western culture.

These developments mean that cultural studies in the West faces a relative shift away from the emancipatory politics of inequality and a move towards the life-politics of meaningfulness while always being aware that the two are not entirely separable.

These are amongst the themes that constitute this book as I investigate problems in cultural studies. I begin in Chapter 2 with some of the problems that surround the central role of language in cultural analysis.

2 Language, Practice and the Material

> **Central problem:**
> **Is culture 'like a language'?**

[Wittgenstein] believed that the correct method was to fix the limit of language by oscillation between two points. In this case the outer point was the kind of objectivism which tries to offer an independent support for our linguistic practices, and the inner point is a description of the linguistic practices themselves, a description which would be completely flat if it were not given against the background of that kind of objectivism. His idea is that the outer point is an illusion, and that the inner point is the whole truth, which must, however, be apprehended through its contrast with the outer point. (Pears, 1971: 170)

Introduction

The machinery and operations of language are central concerns, and problems, for cultural studies. Indeed, the investigation of culture has often been regarded as virtually interchangeable with the exploration of meaning produced symbolically through signifying systems that work 'like a language'. In this chapter we will be concerned with an examination of the strengths and weaknesses of the metaphor of culture being 'like a language'. While the turn to studying language within cultural studies represents a major intellectual gain and research achievement, it has also involved a loss – or at least a partial sightedness. On the one hand, the enfolding of language investigations into cultural studies has gone too far in the direction of an abstracted textuality. On the other hand, cultural studies has not gone far enough in its exploration of the workings of language in the everyday lived social world of human actors. These are amongst the predicaments posed by cultural studies' engagement with language.

Language and cultural studies: dilemmas and omissions

After Saussure (1960) and Barthes (1967, 1972), cultural texts could no longer be regarded as transparent bearers of universal meanings. Rather, they were to be understood as historically contingent productions premised on inclusions, exclusions and the operations of power. The most enduring lesson learned from structuralism was the argument that all cultural texts are constructed with signs that could be read 'like a language'. Consequently, for most practitioners of cultural studies, 'culture' is understood as being constituted through signifying practices that generate and organize signs into discourses and representations.

To hold that culture works 'like a language' is to argue that all meaningful representations are assembled and generate meaning with essentially the same mechanisms as a language: that is, the selection and organization of signs into texts which are constituted through a form of grammar. Consequently, textual analysis has become the primary tool for the understanding of culture. Further, the signifying practices of language endow material objects and social practices with meanings that are brought into view and made intelligible to us in terms which language delimits. Language structures which meanings can or cannot be deployed under determinate circumstances by speaking subjects. As such, language is implicated in forms of power, with cultural politics operating at the level of signification and text.

Texts and politics

If the study of culture centres on the generation of meaningful representations, then the 'power to name' and to make particular descriptions 'stick' forms the core of cultural politics. Here, culture is understood to be a zone of contestation in which meanings and versions of the world compete for ascendancy. Consequently, issues of cultural representation are 'political' because they are intrinsically bound up with questions of power. Power, as social regulation that is productive of the self, enables some kinds of knowledge and identities to appear while excluding others.

In this context, cultural change is thought to be achievable through rethinking and redescribing the social order, together with the posing of alternative possibilities for the future. Such resignification is a social and political activity: in short, a politics of the signifier that emerges through social contradiction and conflict. For example, a good deal of 'cultural feminism' has concentrated on the textual representation of women and the subject positions of subordination that they are 'obliged' to take up. Where resistance is sought or 'found', it has been located in alternative 'texts', including magazines for young women, such as *Jackie* and *Just Seventeen* during the 1980s (McRobbie, 1991a, 1991c), the women's periodical *SHE* (Woodward, 1997) or radical modes of performative signification, including drag (Butler, 1990). Characteristic of this general approach was Kaplan's (1992) exploration of Madonna as an ambiguous text implicated in the deconstruction of gender norms. For Kaplan, Madonna plays with the codes of sex and gender to blur the boundaries of masculinity and femininity. This, she argues, is the politics of the signification: a politics of representation that centres on sex and gender as unstable 'floating signifiers'.

Gains and losses

The elevation of language to the heart of the study of culture, allied to an explicit linkage between representation and cultural power, has been the most signifi-cant and enduring achievement of cultural studies. No student of cultural studies could reasonably be unaware that culture can be read as a text. Nor should he or she be ignorant of concepts like signifiers and signifieds, significa-tion, code, discourse or the importance of power in the construction of texts in everyday life. Cultural studies has contributed to the emergence of a culturally literate set of students who have learned not only to deconstruct texts (from novels to television), but also to grasp the plasticity of gender, race, age and other forms of cultural classification. In this, it has played a significant, if unquantifiable, part in the western world's increased levels of tolerance for and solidarity with cultural difference.

However, an over-emphasis on structuralist and poststructuralist accounts of signification has led cultural studies to reify language as a 'thing' or 'system' rather than as the marks and noises that human beings use to co-ordinate action and achieve their purposes. Further, while the metaphor of culture as 'like a lan-guage' has a great deal to recommend it, there is also much to be gained, especially in policy terms, by describing culture in terms of practices, routines and spatial arrangements. Not only is language always embedded in practice, but all practices signify – there is no special layer of signifying practices as such.

The study of culture as the signifying practices of representation suggests a requirement to investigate the full range of modes by which meaning is pro-duced in a variety of contexts. However, cultural studies has been led by structuralism, poststructuralism and deconstruction to a stress on textual analy-sis. Having escaped economic reductionism, we seem to have arrived at a kind of textual determinism. Thus, textual subject positions are held to be indistin-guishable from, and constitutive of, speaking subjects. The living, embodied speaking and acting subject is lost from sight.

In my view, cultural studies needs to restore balance by adding studies of living persons to its studies of texts and subject positions. It is a matter of lan-guages for purposes. If we want to stress systemicity, interdependence, discipline and the need for structural change, the language of codes, discourse and subject positions is our tool. If we want to stress ethics, action, change and uniqueness, we need to explore the utterances of persons in social contexts. Indeed, as so-called 'ethnographic audience studies' have suggested (Ang, 1985; Morley, 1992), the identification of textual codes and subject positions does not guarantee that the prescribed meanings are 'taken up' by concrete persons in daily life. We need ethnographic studies and the exploration of utterances in social context in order to verify or deny the claims of textual analysis (even as utterances are themselves a kind of text). We need to counterpoise codes with utterances (Billig, 1997).

Finally, the turn to language has rightly emphasized the specificity of culture in order that we can explore its particular logics. Here, the language of signs has enabled us to investigate culture without resort to that economic reductionism against which cultural studies has successfully waged its war of independence. This assertion of the autonomy of culture has frequently, and valuably, been allied to the celebration of cultural power and the capacities of persons to construct their own meanings. However, it is also useful to be able to point to the actions of governments and business that shape the contours of cultural life, enabling some and disempowering others. Hence the language of political economy. Developing useful and engaging metaphors that enable us to speak more felicitously about the relationships between parts (e.g. culture–economy or sign–practice) and the whole (humans as a form of life) remains one of cultural studies' central tasks (see Chapter 4).

In sum, I remain enthusiastic about the centrality of language to the study of culture. I accept that structuralism and poststructuralism have contributed much to cultural studies. Nevertheless, they have also led to significant blind spots in the field, including:

- *the positing of language as a free-floating system rather than as a human tool;*
- *the de-coupling of signification from other practices, habits and routines, and thus to the generation of a theoretical 'gap' between signification and the material;*
- *the elevation of semiotic theory over the linguistic competencies of living persons, and thus to a concentration on codes and texts at the expense of the utterances of speaking subjects.*

Signification and cultural materialism

Sometimes it seems as if the debates surrounding the relationship between culture, signification and the material have been running within cultural studies as long as *Gone with the Wind*. This is strange given a certain obvious 'solution' to the problem: namely that signification is a material process with material consequences. That is, the binary division between the material and signification is an unnecessary one and needs to be dissolved. All material practices signify, and our understanding of the material is itself cultural (e.g. biology or the economic as cultural classification systems). Discourse and the material are indissociable (and language is itself material).

The legacy of historical materialism

In order to understand why the relationship between language and the material has been a 'problem' for cultural studies, we need to consider the origins and specificities of the debate.

The anxiety over the question of materialism is located in the triangular confrontation between cultural studies' Marxist legacy, its developing anti-reductionism and the more recent ascendancy of poststructuralism (that appears to some as a form of idealism).

For Marxism, culture is a corporeal force locked into the socially organized production of the material conditions of existence. Indeed, Marxism has been captivated and perplexed by the attempt to relate the production and reproduction of culture to the organization of the material conditions of life. It has attempted to explain this relationship through the metaphor of the base and the superstructure. The parable of the base and the superstructure tells us that the material mode of production is 'the real foundation' of legal and political superstructures, so that social, political and cultural levels are determined by it. The lesson we are directed to learn is that culture is political because 'the ideas of the ruling class are, in every age, the ruling ideas, i.e., the class which is the dominant material force in society is at the same time its dominant intellectual force' (Marx, 1961: 93). Further, the apparent freedom of the market obscures its exploitative base in the realm of production and presents a specific historically located set of social relations as natural and universal.

Cultural studies has inherited from Marxism the assumption that culture is political in the sense that it entails relationships of power. Indeed, this remains central to the project of cultural studies and one that unites its practitioners. However, an orthodox reading of Marx has proved to be too mechanical and deterministic for any useful and meaningful exploration of culture. Not only does it appear to be somewhat pointless studying culture if one's object is mere epiphenomena, but mechanistic Marxism proved hopelessly inadequate to the task of explaining the specificities of culture and subjectivity. For example, the failure of proletarian revolutions to materialize cannot itself be fully explained through a base and superstructure model. The material conditions generated by capitalism 'ought' to have given rise to revolutionary consciousness; that they did not commonly do so suggests that either Marxism had got its analysis of capitalism wrong or it was mistaken about the relationship between material conditions and cultural consciousness.

While it is possible that Marxism got it wrong on both counts, for the pioneers of cultural studies it was the linked questions of culture and subjectivity that most required attention. Even if one accepts the notion that the revolutionary potential of the proletariat was blunted by 'false consciousness' (which I do not), then the emergence of such thinking would still need to be explained, and by mechanisms other than determination by the base. This is so because in producing false consciousness, capitalism has not generated revolutionary thinking as one of the contradictions of capitalism (which Marx had predicted) but in actuality has given rise to accommodation. Consequently, the narrative of cultural studies involves a distancing of itself from Marxist reductionism in favour of a move towards the analysis of the autonomous logics of language, culture, representation and consumption: that is, the exploration of the specificities of culture.

Popular culture and the autonomy of the sign

Structuralism and the study of the sign proved to be an important influence for cultural studies in relation to exploring language and popular culture as autonomous practices. Rather than dissolving culture back into the economic (as in a base–superstructure model), structuralist analysis emphasized the irreducible character of the cultural as a set of distinct practices with their own internal organization. Subsequently, the relations between various levels of a social formation were described as being 'articulated' together in flexible ways that cannot be decided before the fact. By articulation is meant a temporary unity of discursive elements that do not have to 'go together'. An articulation is the form of the connection that *can* make a unity of two different elements under certain conditions. Articulation suggests both expressing/representing and a joining together. For example, that unity thought of as 'society' is considered to be the unique historically specific temporary stabilization of the discursively constructed relations and meanings of different levels of a social formation (Hall, 1996b).

The different instances of politics, economics and ideology are said to be articulated together to form a unity that is the result not of a single one-way base-superstructure determination, but of determinations emanating from different levels. That is, a social formation is the outcome of 'over-determination'. The spirit of this argument has subsequently been reworked by Hall and his colleagues (du Gay et al., 1997) into the metaphor of the 'circuit of culture' (see Chapter 4). Here, meanings embedded at the moments of production may or may not be taken up at the levels of representation or consumption, where new meanings are again produced. Thus, the Sony Walkman is analysed in terms of the meanings embedded at the level of design and production that are modified by the creation of new meanings as the Walkman is represented in advertising. In turn, the meanings produced through representation connect with, and help constitute, the meaningful identities of Walkman users. Overall, meanings produced at the level of production are available to be worked on at the level of consumption but do not determine them. Further, representation and consumption shape the level of production through, for example, design and marketing.

For some political economists, cultural studies had already gone too far with its declaration of the relative autonomy of language and culture, though for most in the field this represented an 'advance' in thinking. The next step for some theorists, notably Fiske (1987, 1989a, 1989b) was to separate the 'two economies' of finance and culture, with the former needing only to be 'taken into account' when studying the latter. Thus does popular culture come to be seen as a site of semiotic warfare and of popular tactics deployed to evade or resist the meanings produced and inscribed in commodities by producers. This ability to regard popular culture as an autonomous zone of activity depends on two apparently contradictory but reconcilable theoretical impulses. The first of these was the attribution to audience members of agency and the active capacity to produce meaning. Here, a whole series of 'active audience' studies (e.g. Ang, 1985; Liebes and Katz, 1991; Morley, 1980) highlighted the ability of audiences to generate meanings at odds with those identified by critics as the 'preferred meaning' of the text. In short, the meanings that audiences derived from texts were not deterministically inscribed in the text by the processes of commodity production.

The second development of significance was the observation, derived primarily from Foucault (1972), that culture is constituted by the circulation of discourses or regulated ways of speaking about a topic. Although discourses were to be investigated in their corporeal and historical specificity, including the conditions under which statements are combined to circumscribe rules of formation and regimes of truth, they were not reducible to material conditions. Indeed, the Foucauldian conception of discourse refers to a unity of language and practice that defines and produces its objects of knowledge.

The importance of discourse theory to audience studies and the notion of 'resistance' is that the multiple identities of 'readers' are formed as they cross discursive sites to be addressed in divergent ways. Consequently, discourses and modes of address developed in one site or locale can be turned to different purposes – including alternative decodings or modes of resistance – in another. These arguments place language, culture and subjectivity at a considerable distance from determination by the processes of capitalist economic production. In turn, language was elevated to a position in which it gave significance to material objects and through which audiences could assert their meaning-making capacities against the allegedly hegemonic messages of texts.

Cultural populism

So far had the tendency to understand culture as an autonomous practice gone that almost all forms of popular culture were being heralded as sites of resistance. The inevitable backlash followed, led by Jim McGuigan. For McGuigan (1992, 1996), cultural studies has taken the celebration of the productive and resistive capacities of audiences so far that it has become complicit with the ideology of consumer sovereignty. Cultural studies, argues McGuigan, over-endows audiences with the capacity to deconstruct ideology, failing to note the uneven distribution of such competencies across the divisions of class, gender, ethnicity, age, and so forth. McGuigan's central target is John Fiske (1987, 1989a, 1989b) and his conceptualization of popular culture as a site of semiotic warfare constituted by the meanings that people make for themselves rather than those identifiable within texts. McGuigan accuses Fiske of a retreat from critical thinking and an abandonment of any form of political economy, leading to the acceptance of the free market and consumer capitalism.

A more telling criticism levelled by both McGuigan and Bennett (1992, 1998) was that cultural studies had displaced its politics solely onto the level of signification. Consequently, it is said to lack a political economy of the media, housing, labour markets, educational achievement, and so forth, and thus overlooks material inequalities and relations of power. From this follows a failure to grasp the material circumstances and power relations that pertain between people, and thus cultural studies lacks the means to bring about change. Finally, an overly textual and populist cultural studies is said to be unable to engage in institutional cultural policy.

At a time when most practitioners within cultural studies had turned their attention to language, texts and audiences, McGuigan and Bennett had some valuable points to make when they chastised cultural studies for its textualism, its undifferentiated notion of resistance and its blindness in relation to institutional cultural politics and policy formation. They were right insofar as many writers within cultural studies seemed to regard political economy as an unfashionable relic of the past. However, 'unfashionable' does not necessarily mean abandoned. While cultural policy remains underdeveloped in cultural studies, the multiperspectival approach that McGuigan asks cultural studies to engage in, one that interrogates the relationships between political economy, representations, texts and audiences, is already explicitly the goal of Hall et al.'s 'circuit of culture', a model whose central elements date back to at least the early 1980s.

Accordingly, the political economy vs cultural autonomy debate represents another unnecessary binary.

We can readily accept the notion that a full analysis of any cultural practice requires the analysis of both 'economy' and 'culture', including the articulation of the relations between them. If, for practical reasons, we are concentrating on one aspect of our subject, then we can at least recognize that this is a necessarily partial view. That is, while the language of political economy and the language of texts are different languages deployed for different purposes, they are not mutually exclusive.

Language, the material and practices that signify

There are, of course, forms of the material other than the 'economic' that should interest us. In particular, a pervasive problem is the dislocation between language and material practice that has taken place within cultural studies as a consequence of the way in which it has absorbed structuralism, poststructuralism and deconstructionism.

Structuralism has been concerned with the 'systems of relations' of the underlying structure of sign systems and the grammar that makes meaning possible. Meaning production is held to be the effect of the 'deep structures' of language that are manifested in specific cultural phenomena or human speakers but which are not the outcome of the intentions of actors *per se*. That is, the distinction between the rules and conventions that organize language (*langue*) and the specific uses and utterances that individuals deploy in everyday life (*parole*) is crucial to structuralism. Subsequently, it is argued by Saussure that meaning is produced through a process of selection and combination of signs along two axes, the syntagmatic (linear – e.g. a sentence) and paradigmatic (a field of signs – e.g. synonyms), organized into a signifying system. Crucially, signs do not make sense by virtue of reference to entities in an independent object world; rather, they generate meaning by reference to each other. Thus meaning is to be understood as a social convention organized through the relations between signs.

Subsequently, poststructuralism, especially in its Derridean form, was to deconstruct the very notion of the stable structures of language. Meaning, it is argued, cannot be confined to single words, sentences or particular texts but is the outcome of relationships between texts, that is, intertextuality. Derrida accepts Saussure's argument that meaning is generated by relations of difference between signifiers rather than by reference to an independent object world. However, for Derrida, the consequence of this play of signifiers is that meaning can never be fixed. Words carry many meanings, including the echoes or traces of other meanings from other related words in other contexts. For example, if we look up the meaning of a word in a dictionary we are referred to other words in an infinite process of deferral. Meaning slides down a chain of signifiers, abolishing a stable signified. Thus, the production of meaning in the process of signification is continually deferred and supplemented.

Given this instability of meaning, Derrida proceeds to deconstruct the 'stable' binaries upon which structuralism and, indeed, western philosophy in general rely. He argues for the 'undecidablity' of binary oppositions. In particular, deconstruction involves the dismantling of hierarchical conceptual oppositions, such as speech/writing, reality/appearance, nature/culture, reason/madness, and so forth, that exclude and devalue the 'inferior' part of the binary. For Derrida, there is no original meaning circulating outside of 'representation', so that writing is in at the 'origins' of meaning. There is no primary source of signification and no self-present transparent meaning that can fix the relation between signifiers and signifieds. Thus, 'From the moment that there is meaning there is nothing but signs. We think only in signs' (Derrida, 1976: 50). It is in this sense that there is nothing outside of texts or nothing but texts (by which is *not* meant that there is no external material world).

Now, there is much that is valuable in structuralism and poststructuralism's influence within cultural studies. For example, the exploration of the conventional character of signs opened the door to an examination of representation as a 'naturalized' cultural process. Further, the notion of intertextuality has become central to cultural studies, and the concept of *'différance'* is at the heart of Hall's influential conceptualization of identity. Indeed, the 'linguistic turn' in cultural studies is core to the anti-essentialism and social constructionism that mark the field.

However, there has also been a less benign influence stemming from this structuralist and poststructuralist legacy. The relationship between signifiers and signifieds may be arbitrary in the sense of 'could have been otherwise', that is, conventional rather than universal and essential. However, it is not arbitrary in the sense that, given the history of language and culture, words do have more or less fixed meanings and usages in the world. This 'fixing', I want to suggest, is the consequence of the routine indissolubility of language and practice (and not just a matter of power, as Hall tends to argue). To neglect or fail to notice this facet of language is at best to risk formalism and a textual analysis divorced from any significant social implications. At worst, it is to join sceptics in wondering about the disjunction between words and the world or to hallucinate in hyperspace. Many practitioners of cultural studies display the first symptom and some the second.

In the beginning was the deed

In the beginning was the word? As self-conscious, self-reflexive beings whose minds appear to them as driven by language, we find this an enticing metaphor of origins. However, whether one starts with nothing and the quantum leap into the Big Bang or with the primeval chemical pool from which life emerged, it was not language that was decisive. Rather, we must look to nuclei, electrons, electromagnetic forces, atoms, molecules, the biochemistry of DNA and the indifferent processes of 'natural selection' for a story that places us humans in the universe. Certainly this is a retrospective story told by us in the language of biochemistry and evolution. In that respect biology is cultural. However, it is not credible to imagine that fully fledged speaking subjects predated our genetic ancestors. Rather, the ability to generate language represents a crucial evolutionary pathway for the human species.

In this context it is useful to heed Wittgenstein's argument that language emerges from pre-linguistic behaviour: 'The origin and the primitive form of language-game is a reaction; only from this can the more complicated forms grow.

Language – I want to say – is a refinement; in the beginning was the deed' (1980: 31). For Wittgenstein, we learn language as an integral part of learning how to *do* things. Indeed, the capacity to perform more complex tasks than other animals, that is, the achievements of humans as doers, is what has enabled our apparent evolutionary success (though it could also be said to be our downfall).

'Language', as Wittgenstein remarks, 'did not emerge from reasoning. . . . Children do not learn that there are books, that there are armchairs, etc., etc., but they learn to fetch books, sit in armchairs, etc.' (1969: 475–6). Similarly, instantaneous expressions of pain are not the outcome of thought; rather, they are spontaneous (biochemically motivated) actions. As a child develops language, so words replace actions like crying; to learn the language of pain is to learn 'new pain behavior' (Wittgenstein, 1957: #244, 89). Understood in this way, language is best described not as a coherent system or set of structural relations, but rather as an array of marks and noises used to co-ordinate action and to adapt to the environment. Language is a tool used by human organisms through which the 'pairing off the marks and noises it makes with those we make will prove a useful tactic in predicting and controlling its future behavior' (Rorty, 1989: 52).

Language as a tool

For Wittgenstein, language is not a metaphysical presence nor a coherent system but a tool used by human animals to co-ordinate their actions in the context of social relationships.

Thus, 'The meaning of a word is its use in the language' (Wittgenstein, 1957: 43). What is important is that we ask 'in what special circumstances this sentence is actually used. There does it make sense' (Wittgenstein, 1957: 117). Consequently, Wittgenstein suggests, looking for universal theoretical explanations for language is not the most profitable way to proceed. Rather, language is a context-specific tool for achieving our purposes. For Wittgenstein, a meaningful expression is one that can be given a use by living human beings as a constitutive part of our form of life. Consequently, Wittgenstein's arguments underline the pragmatic and social character of language including the significance of social relationships. Language is 'action' and meanings are temporarily stabilized by social convention for practical purposes in the context of their usage.

While the meanings of language do derive from relations of difference, they are given a degree of regulated stability through pragmatic narratives. For example, insofar as the meaning of the word 'friend' is generated through the relationship of signifiers – colleague, companion, acquaintance, associate, confidant, etc. – it is volatile and undecidable. Nevertheless, in practice its meaning is stabilized by social knowledge of the word 'friend', of what it is used for, when, under what circumstances, and so forth. That is, the meanings of words are generated and stabilized by the pragmatic narratives or language-games in which they appear. For example, in his discussion of the word 'game', Wittgenstein argues that

> you will not see something that is common to all, but similarities, relationships, and a whole series of them at that. . . . Look for example at board-games, with their multifarious relationships. Now pass to card-games; here you find many correspondences with the first group but many common features drop out, and others appear. When we pass next to ball-games, much that is common is retained, but much is lost. . . . And the result of this examination is: we see a complicated network of similarities overlapping and criss-crossing: sometimes overall similarities, sometimes similarities of detail. (1957: 31e–32e)

Thus, it is not some special or essential characteristic of a game that gives rise to meaning but a complex network of relationships and characteristics only some of which are ever present in a specific game. Games are constituted by a set of 'family resemblances' whereby members of a family share characteristics with one another without them all necessarily having any specific feature in common. In this sense the meaning of the word 'game' is relational and depends on its place in the language-game of games and of the juxtaposition of the word 'game' to not-games.

Nevertheless, despite the relational character of the word 'game', when it comes to explaining it to others we are likely to show them different games and to say that this is what games are. That is, we draw boundaries around meaning for specific purposes and forward practical explanation for particular ends rather than turn to the abstract 'meanings' generated by a reified 'language'. To know what games are is to be able to play games. The rule-bound character of language is not constituted by the theoretical regulations of grammar but is spawned by enactment in social practice. That is, the rules of language are constitutive rules which mark our pragmatic understandings of 'how to go on' in society.

The proliferation and regulation of meaning

It is worth pausing to consider Wittgenstein's arguments in relation to those of Derrida and Foucault, the two philosophers who have been most influential within contemporary cultural studies. There are certainly similarities between the writings of Derrida and Wittgenstein (see Staten, 1984). For example, both writers stress the non-representational character of language, the arbitrary relationship between signs and referents and the contextual character of truth. However, Wittgenstein more than Derrida underlines the pragmatic and social character of language.

For Derrida, meaning can never be 'fixed'; rather, words carry multiple meanings, including the echoes or traces of meanings from related words in different contexts. Here, the production of meaning in the process of signification is continually deferred and supplemented in the play of more-than-one. Hence the concept of '*différance*' – 'difference and deferral'- – by which the continual substitution and adding of meanings through the play of signifiers challenges the identity of noises and marks with fixed meaning. However, the undecidability of meaning is only a 'problem' if we think that there is something called 'language' whose job it is to originate a fixed entity called 'representational meaning'. If we think of language as constituted by the use of marks and noises that have pragmatically stabilized meanings related to the achievement of purposes, then words 'mean' what we use them to do in the context of social practice. The endless play of signification that Derrida explores is regulated and partially stabilized through pragmatic narratives and social action.

The influence of Derrida within cultural studies has too often pointed practitioners in the direction of formalism and a high textualism that rejects ethnographic or empirical work. By contrast, the influence of Wittgenstein encourages us to look at language in the context of practice and forms of life. Identifying the undecidability of concepts like justice or identity has limited value in contrast to the exploration of those ideas in context-specific practices. While meaning may formally proliferate in the rarefied world of texts, this is not so in social practice, where meaning is regulated and stabilized for pragmatic purposes. What is required is that oscillation referred to at the head of the chapter between, on the one hand, an objectivism that tries to offer an independent description of language, and which in doing so illuminates the fact that meaning cannot be fixed in the abstract, and, on the other, the linguistic practices themselves.

In this sense, Wittgenstein shares with Foucault the notion that meanings are regulated through practice. Foucault (1972) argues against structuralist theories of language that conceive of it as an autonomous rule-governed system. Instead, he is concerned with the description, analysis and effects of the regulated 'surface' of language (i.e. discourse) under determinate material and historical conditions. For Foucault, discourse constructs, defines and produces the objects of knowledge in an intelligible way while at the same time excluding other ways of reasoning as unintelligible. Here, meaning does not proliferate in an endless deferral but is regulated by power, which governs not only what can be said under determinate social and cultural conditions but also who can speak, when and where.

However, for Foucault, living persons are required to 'take up' subject positions in discourse in order to make sense of the world and appear coherent to others. A subject position is that perspective or set of regulated discursive meanings from which discourse makes sense. To speak is to take up a subject position and to be subjected to the regulatory power of that discourse. Once again we are sent in the direction of texts; this time in search of discourses that have a metaphysical presence lurking behind human subjects and pulling the strings of these puppet-like beings. By contrast, Wittgenstein directs us to languages for purposes and the utterances of living persons.

Raymond Williams (1981) once deployed the phrase 'realized signifying system' to direct our attention to the materialization of signification. An example would be the circulation of money, where a banknote signifies and constructs nationality while at the same time being used for the purposes of exchange. Yet the notion of 'realized signifying system' implies the possibility of its opposite, and it is unclear in what an 'unrealized signifying system' could consist. Wittgenstein's work teaches us that there can be no form of signification that is not practically enacted for there are no specifically separate signifying practices.

Signification does not occur in a separate domain from other practices, and all practices signify. Meaning is the product of the indistinguishability of signs and social practice.

Thus, if we continue to use the concept of 'signifying practices', then we must do so only as a heuristic device to emphasize that we are interested in the signifying aspects of practices.

Languages for purposes

The metaphor of the 'tool' captures the idea that we do things with language. That said, the concept of 'using a tool' should not be read as implying the intentionality of a pre-existent subject. Rather, 'use' is acquired through our acculturation and habituation into social practices and their associated justifications. Nevertheless, the metaphor of the 'tool' does direct us to the diverse functions words play in human life. 'We might think of words as the tools in a tool-box: there is a hammer, pliers, a screw-driver, a rule, a glue-pot, glue, nails and screws. The functions of words are as diverse as the functions of the objects' (Wittgenstein, 1957: 6).

This argument applies to our very descriptions of culture and human action. Thus, the metaphor of human life as a dance helps us to see that we are social animals who live in the world together. By contrast, the language of individual agency and responsibility encourages us to locate the source of actions in specific persons. Meanwhile, the purposes of human solidarity are tied to languages that frame human beings as the social products of cultures.

Thus, I am putting forward an understanding of communication that places an emphasis on the variety of uses to which human beings put the marks and noises we call language.

We have a variety of languages because we have a variety of purposes (see

Rorty, 1991a). Knowledge is a matter not of getting an accurate picture of reality, but of learning how to contend with the world in pursuit of those purposes.

The body 'knows': practices, habits and routines

It is one of the bedrock convictions of the humanities and social sciences that people learn the ways of a culture through imitation, discipline and the acquisition of guiding concepts that form maps of meaning. In particular, the social constructionism that pervades cultural studies lays particular emphasis on the discursive character of social and cultural life. Consequently, what it means to be a man or a woman, black or white, old or young, is a construction of language. Social categories do not have universal, essential characteristics or qualities but are constituted by the way we speak about them.

It is this anti-essentialism that leads Hall (1990, 1996a) to describe identity as a 'cut' in language: a temporary stabilization of otherwise endlessly unfolding meanings. Identity, it is argued, is best understood not as an entity but as an emotionally charged description of ourselves. Rather than a timeless essence, identity is held to be cultural 'all the way down'. What it means to be a person is plastic and changeable, being specific to particular social and cultural conjunctures. In particular, subjectivity and identity mark the composition of persons in language and culture. Without language, not only would we not be persons as we commonly understand that concept, but the very notions of personhood and identity would be unintelligible to us.

As I have argued elsewhere (Barker, 2000; Barker and Galasinski, 2001), this view of identity and language has much to commend it. However, it is based on the assumption that our maps of meaning, our culture, are learned by acquiring the propositions which guide us in the form of signs that are organized as words, sentences and discourses. By contrast, according to Wittgenstein (1969), it is through experience that we acquire a whole series of propositions in the form of practices. Much of our bedrock of convictions is part of what Giddens (1984, 1991) calls our 'practical consciousness': that is, a condition of being that is rarely made discursively explicit but which is embedded in the practical conduct of social life, namely the intertwining of language as a social institution and the taken-for-granted stocks of knowledge/practices of everyday life.

Further, the body, including the unconscious biochemical processes of the brain, 'knows' what to do just as much as do the rational aspects of the mind; it is simply not self-conscious and self-reflexive in the manner of discursive consciousness. Much of our conduct involves the body in practices that are not self-consciously worked out in advance of action but are generated as a matter of habit or routine alongside the unconscious accomplishments of brain chemistry. What we know is the outcome not of logical correctness but of 'the inherited background against which [we] distinguish between true and false' (Wittgenstein, 1969: 94). Further, the propositions which form our world-picture are like the rules of a game which are 'learned purely practically' (Wittgenstein, 1969: 95).

On certainty

What we know 'for certain', and have known for a long time, is that which forms the river bed of our form of life. We will continue to believe in these certainties until there is a shift in our thinking. 'We know the earth is round. We have definitively ascertained that it is round. We shall stick to this opinion, unless our whole way of seeing nature changes. "How do you know that?" I believe it' (Wittgenstein, 1969: 29). That the world is round is 'at the rock bottom of my convictions. And one might almost say that these foundation-walls are carried by the whole house' (Wittgenstein, 1969: 248). Nevertheless, the 'river bed of thoughts may shift' (Wittgenstein, 1969: 96), for practices and vocabularies are culturally specific and contingent. The inscriptions of vocabularies and the imprints of practices are two sides of one coin, the same 'impress of history' (Rorty, 1989).

In this sense, we can talk, on the one hand, of conduct (or action or behaviour) and, on the other, of language (or marks/noises or discourse). Of course the significance or meaning of conduct is a matter of language (itself a form of action), so that there is insight in the idea of 'discursive practice'. However, we can respond to or 'know' conduct or action without putting it into words. Everyday we undertake actions that we do not think about and some that we could not make discursive even if asked. For example, we can walk without planning each step. We can talk without knowing in advance of the noises leaving our mouth what it is we want to say. We have emotional responses (e.g. bodily responses and actions which we call fear) to a given set of circumstances that are generated outside of the cerebral cortex and thus 'before' language (see LeDoux, 1998).

The analysis of our world in terms of the indissoluble categories of conduct and language fits in well with philosophic pragmatism (see Chapter 1). Further, this emphasis on practice and pragmatism enables one to uphold an anti-representationalist view of language while avoiding the scepticism and formalism that follow when texts are distanced from social practices.

If we understand language as an evolutionary tool for adapting to and controlling the environment, we are in touch with reality in all areas of culture, providing one takes the phrase 'in touch with reality' to mean 'caused by and causing', rather than accurately or otherwise 'representing', reality.

The language of the material

The various uses of the word 'material' that I have made in this chapter (the means of subsistence, the means of production, the economic, social practice, etc.) raise the broader question of what is meant when we use this concept. Clearly, it is difficult to resolve the issue of cultural materialism and cultural autonomy without clarity of terminology. Given the relational and context-bound character of meaning in language, it comes as no great surprise to learn that there is no one agreed or universal meaning attached to the idea of the material. Rather, the concept means different things, has different usages, in a variety of contexts. Ironically, it is the science of physics, to which one might have thought one could turn for an empirically firm definition, that ultimately 'deconstructs' the solidity of the material (see Gribbin, 1998).

An account of a solid 'object' from within the procedures and vocabulary of classical physics would describe it as composed of atoms arranged in a particular way to form molecules with vast spaces between each particle of matter. Subsequently, from a human perspective, their molecular structures and atomic weights differentiate elements from each other. Further, the degree of movement between atoms and the strength of the electromagnetic bonding between them differentiates solids, liquids and gases. However, sub-atomic physics points us to the arrangements of electrons, neutrons and quarks, and so forth, within the regulation of electromagnetic energy fields. In this sense, there are no solid material objects, only forces. Indeed, the 'uncertainty principle' declares that we cannot know the exact position of a given particle since at a particular level of analysis they oscillate between points without apparently moving across the intermediate space.

Nevertheless, it is widely held by scientists that sub-atomic quantum physics does not for the most part invalidate classical atomic physics. It remains useful to describe and differentiate between iron and water in terms of atomic structure, and in everyday life we had better be able to tell the difference between the solid rock of the cliff-face and the nothingness of the space below. However, if we want to explore the origins, shape and workings of the universe, communicate across vast tracks of space, develop nuclear fuel and/or explode an atomic bomb, then at this stage in our history we need the relativity language of quantum physics. In short, the language of matter in physics is relative to our purpose.

The meaning and validity of the language of the material within cultural studies is also relative to our purpose. The distinction between the material and its opposite (and it is unclear what that could be) is a linguistic-cultural classification that depends for its sense on the context of its usage and the purposes one has in mind. In the context of cultural studies, I have pointed towards two important fields where the concept of the material has had currency:

● the distinction between economic and cultural practices;

- the differentiation between a free-floating relationally organized structure called 'language' and a set of marks and noises given 'meaning' by practices.

With regard to the former, I have suggested that the circuit of culture represents the most usable metaphor currently available to us. In relation to the latter, I have argued that it is important to reattach meaning to practice in order to curtail the heady aspirations of textualism.

From text to performances

Though the influence of semiotics within cultural studies underpinned the metaphor that culture is 'like a language', this was always meant to imply the co-existence of a variety of languages. That is, culture does not necessarily take the form of a verbal language; rather, different types of language have in common a similar mode of organization that generates meaning. This is the logic by which Barthes (1972) extended semiotic analysis from linguistic signs to other sign systems so that semiotic inquiry is brought to bear on popular culture, from magazine images to wrestling matches. This is also the line of reasoning that allows cultural studies writers to designate as texts all practices that signify.

After Barthes, we could see that texts involve the organization of signs into conventionalized and regulated sequences of meaning that turn the contingent result of an historical process into naturalized codes or myths. That is, a cultural code is a system of representation by which signs and their associated meanings are arranged by convention to stabilize significance. As Barthes argued, 'Myth has the task of giving an historical intention a natural justification, and making contingency appear as eternal' (1972: 155). Suddenly cultural studies spawned numerous examinations of cultural texts and their mythological (or ideological) codings with particular reference to the operation of cultural power.

For example, and put rather crudely, gender coding in advertising was held to associate women with domestic work and self-beautification while television news was revealed to be an encoded representation of the social milieu rather than a transparent window on the world. Thus mugging was portrayed as a black male youth crime. Here, the exploration of culture as codes seemed to herald the 'exposing of ideology' (see Chapter 3) and the potential for resistance. For example, Hebdige's (1979) semiotic study of the British punk movement concluded that it was a dislocated, self-aware and ironic mode of signification that dramatized anger and frustration in the context of British economic and social decline.

Much was gained through semiotic cultural analysis. Nevertheless, Cohen raised the problem of relating analysts' structural interpretations to the meanings held by knowing subjects when he argued that the 'nagging sense here is that these lives, selves and identities do not always coincide with what they are supposed to stand for' (1980: xviii). That is, semiotic analysis of, in this case, youth cultures failed to engage with members' accounts of subculture involvement (Widdicombe and Wooffit, 1995). However, few pieces of research within cultural studies take the time and trouble to do the fieldwork required to access participants' accounts of their actions.

The problem is that semiotics and the metaphor of the text have led too many writers to conclude that they need not do empirical work; rather, actors' understandings are implied by or 'read off' texts.

Subject positions

This problem was compounded with the entry of the poststructuralist concept of a 'subject position' into the cultural studies vocabulary. A subject position is that perspective or set of regulated discursive meanings by which discourse becomes meaningful. For Foucault, discourse offers speaking persons subject positions from which to make sense of the world while 'subjecting' speakers to the rules and discipline of those discourses. To speak is to take up a subject position and to be subjected to the regulatory power of that discourse. However, there is a difference between 'the analysis of spectatorship, conceived as a set of subject positions constructed in and through texts, and the analysis of social audiences, understood as the empirical social subjects actually engaged in watching television' (Ang, 1996: 112). Consequently, rather than regard audiences as simply reproducing textual subject positions and meanings, we need to consider what concrete people in specific locations actually do with texts: that is, the extent to which textual subject positions are in fact 'taken up' by concrete women and men.

Since the initial impact of semiotics within cultural studies that took place in the 1970s, the field has witnessed a greater interest in media reception studies (Ang, 1985; Buckingham, 1987; Hobson, 1982; Morley, 1992). It is also fair to say that cultural studies has always contained an ethnographic strand (Willis, 1977, 1978, 1990), albeit one that has consistently been in the shadow of textual analysis. Nevertheless, while the exploration of audiences and consumers has commonly involved talking to people and reporting on their attitudes, few studies within cultural studies have brought detailed language analysis to bear on the speech of informants. Semiotics taught us that texts were not to be taken at face value but were to be approached as constructions of signs that could be analysed to illustrate how meaning was generated. Ironically, the same lesson was not applied to talk as a text.

From texts to utterances

Cultural studies has been lopsided in its concentration on texts and in its general failure to analyse the utterances of living speaking subjects using the tools of linguistic analysis. However, once we take on board the significance of practice in the operations of language, then it is clear that we need to analyse the utterances of persons as social actors. The detailed analysis of language-in-use can show us how social constructions are assembled. We can see not just the overall edifice but also the design and deployment of individual bricks. Here, discursive psychology and critical discourse analysis can help us to explore the ways in which consciousness is constituted through language. This will include the processes by which people make emotional and identity claims about themselves, and what they are achieving as they do so (Billig, 1997). From a political perspective, critical discourse analysis can reveal our participation in patterns of the linguistic dance of which we are not conscious and that have consequences that we might find undesirable if we were to become aware of them.

Crucially, culture, the structures of language and individual utterances are intertwined and inseparable. Actors use linguistic constructs, or personal meanings, to make sense of what happens to them (Kelly, 1955; Viney, 1996). These constructs form a system that is forged through a series of interpretations and predictions that constitute a life-story. Here narratives are rationales for courses of action and meaning is created by people who actively impose their constructs onto life events in the context of their purposes and goals. Nevertheless, though we may feel our constructs to be highly personal, they are not simply matters of individual interpretation. Rather, they are always already a part of the wider cultural repertoire of discursive explanations, resources and maps of meaning available to members of cultures.

The requirements for telling an intelligible story about ourselves are culturally formed: that is, to possess an intelligible self requires a borrowing from a cultural repository. Those which we take to be our most personal feelings and emotions are discursive in character, drawn from the resource bank of social accounting or public discourse (Gergen, 1994). Thus do Potter and Wetherell (1987) seek to demonstrate that fundamental psychological notions such as attitudes, emotions and the inner mind could be approached through the examination of shared language. They stress the constitutive nature and action-orientation of language, arguing that we need to study the flexible ways in which language is used.

Cultural studies, while often making claims about discourse and its role in the construction of meaning, has only rarely engaged with the detailed analysis of discourse itself. Yet a characteristic of discourse analysis is, ironically, its 'textual orientation' (Fairclough, 1992). Discourse analysis is based on a close examination of texts, whether written or spoken, so that the textual metaphor need not preclude analysis of speaking subjects. Thus discourse analysis can be brought to bear on social actions accomplished by language users who communicate within specific social and cultural situations. In his review of the principles of discourse analysis, van Dijk (1997) holds the following to be the most significant:

- Discourse analysis is interested in naturally occurring text (written) and talk (verbal).
- Discourse is studied within its global and local context.
- Naturally occurring discourse is a form of social practice.
- The accomplishment of discourse is linear and sequential.
- Constitutive units of discourse may also be productive of larger units.
- Discourse analysis is interested in levels or layers of discourse and their relations.
- Language users and analysts are interested in meaning.
- Language, discourse and communication in general are rule-governed activities.

Culture as conversation

If we accept that culture is, at least in some respects, 'like a language', then, given a renewed emphasis on practice, we might adopt the dialogic metaphor of the 'conversation' to grasp the dynamic and language-oriented character of culture. This metaphor allows us to consider the formation of meaning and culture as formed in the 'joint action' of social relationships, accounting practices and conversations (Shotter, 1993). For Rorty (1991a, 1998a), the conversational metaphor underscores the importance of the social practice of reason giving in the justification of action, where our mutual questioning is the source of ethics and truth (Chapter 1). It also enables us to think through cross-cultural communication in terms of the learning of language skills, rather than holding cultural knowledge located in different places to be incommensurable. Thus, for Rorty (1980), we must set out to build the 'cosmopolitan conversation of humankind'.

Conversations are a mode of practically enacted cultural conduct involving the circulation of ideas, concepts, meanings, attitudes, beliefs, and so forth, within an intersubjectively moulded arena. Hence the conversational metaphor also directs us to the constitutive nature and action-orientation of language, which require us to consider what, in the context of social dialogue, accounts of actions, memories and attributions are designed to do (Edwards and Potter, 1992). That is, accounts of our actions and ourselves are socially produced descriptions that are marshalled for specific ends, including defence of one's credibility. The theme of conversation also highlights the variability of accounts to which any state of affairs can be put. Conversations, like cultures, involve agreement, contestation and conflict over meanings and actions. Conversations, like cultures, are shot through with power relations.

Nevertheless, I have some reservations about the analogy between culture and conversations. Though words are actions, the commonly understood connotations of 'conversation' may lead us to prioritize declarative voice over conduct, the verbal above the visual and the utterance before the body. Indeed, objects and spaces that are very much part of cultural analysis are in danger of disappearing from view. Further, what we say is only occasionally the product of self-conscious reflection and more often than not the outcome of pragmatic, ritualized or unconscious processes. That is, the undertone of the metaphor of conversation is one of intentionality when much of what we want to say about human culture includes routines, habits, compulsion and brain chemistry.

Culture as performance

Thus, according to the precise circumstances that confront us, we might also make use of the concept of performance. This aspect of culture directs our attention to the simultaneous production of the discursive, the body and a set of practices. That is, the metaphor of the performance engages with:

- the verbal and the visual;
- words and bodies;
- stasis and movement;
- objects and space;
- scripts and improvisation;
- intention and compulsion.

Like all metaphors, performance is better suited to some kinds of purpose or object than others. For example, while performance works well for public and interactional situations, it may be less well suited to more contemplative zones of culture. Thus, reading a book may fit the metaphor of performance less comfortably than does producing a film or popular music. Nevertheless, the act of reading a book is, as reader-response theory suggests, a kind of performance, as is that 'internal' conversation that we constantly have running. Still, if we are going to use the metaphor of the performance, we will probably find occasion to prefix it with a descriptor: thus, conversational performance, filmic performance, gender performance, ethnic performance, and so forth.

One problem with the idea of performance is that, like conversation, it can carry with it the connotation of intention. Consequently, Butler (1993) is right to stress that our stories are performative in that they enact and constitute that which they purport to describe. They are actions in the world that are to be evaluated according to their felicity within a procedure or social convention constituted by patterns of relationship. Indeed, for Butler, performance is required as a condition of being a certain kind of subject. I, unlike Butler, would add that it is also compelled by a definite kind of brain chemistry (see Chapter 10).

The performativity of sex

For Butler, 'sex' is cultural. It is produced as a reiteration of hegemonic norms, a citational performativity that is always derivative. The 'assumption' of sex is not a singular act or event but an iterable practice secured through citation and reiteration of the norms or conventions of the 'law': that is, through being repeatedly performed, the performative being 'that discursive practice which enacts or produces that which it names' (Butler, 1993: 13). Performance does not originate the law or its authority but invokes it through appeal to an authority that has no origin or universal foundations. Indeed, the very practice of citation produces the authority that is cited and reconstitutes the law. The maintenance of the law is a matter of reworking a set of already operative conventions and involves iterability, repetition and citationality. Thus, the statement 'It's a girl' initiates a process by which 'girling' is compelled.

> This is a 'girl', however, who is compelled to 'cite' the norm in order to qualify and remain a viable subject. Femininity is thus not the product of choice, but the forcible citation of a norm, one whose complex historicity is indissociable from relations of discipline, regulation, punishment. Indeed, there is not 'one' who takes on a gender norm. On the contrary, this citation of the gender norm is necessary in order to qualify as a 'one', to become viable as a 'one', where subject-formation is dependent on the prior operation of legitimating gender norms. (Butler, 1993: 232)

Consequently, performativity is neither a singular act nor a performance given by a self-conscious intentional actor. Rather, the performance of sex is compelled by a regulatory apparatus of heterosexuality that reiterates itself through the forcible production of 'sex'. Indeed, the very idea of an intentional sexed actor is a discursive production of performativity itself. 'Gender is *performative* in the sense that it constitutes as an effect that very subject it appears to express' (Butler, 1991: 24).

I am not trying to recommend or adopt the whole of a body of work that, I think, has its problems as well as strengths. In particular, I would want to explore sex as biochemistry as well as cultural performance (see Chapters 6 and 10). However, I am putting forward the notion of performance as central to cultural analysis and one that has advantages over the metaphors of map, discourse or conversation. The notion of performance includes bodies in space that use a variety of languages productive of meaning and carry out actions only a part of which can be understood as 'intentional' and agentive.

Conclusions

In this chapter I have put on something of a Janus face. That is, I have praised cultural studies for its turn to language at the same time that I have been critical of the lengths to which it has gone in pursuit of that interest and the omissions that this has led to. I have argued that cultural studies has too readily accepted the idea that language is a system of relations between signifiers and that the relationship between signifiers and the signified is wholly arbitrary. This has led many down the path of a disengaged textualism where culture is posited as a series of texts that 'subject' us to their picture of the world. Consequently, cultural politics is also too readily engaged with only as a textual matter rather than as an institutional or practical phenomenon.

In order to draw out my view that these problems are implicit within structuralism and poststructuralism, I deployed Wittgenstein against Derrida to contrast the former's emphasis on practice with the spiralling out of control that meaning undergoes for the latter. After Wittgenstein and Rorty, I argued that language should be treated as a tool, a series of marks and noises developed in an evolutionary context that assists us in achieving our purposes. Language has to be understood within a material context and as itself a material action. This does not imply the reduction of language and culture to the material, let alone the economic, which is merely one instance of the usage of the word 'material', though one that can be profitably pursued for specific purposes. Indeed, the phrase 'different languages for different purposes' is at the core of this chapter.

I further suggested that the emphasis on signs, codes and texts has left cultural studies unable or unwilling to deal with the context-driven speech of embodied actors. This is both analytically limited and politically damaging. In order to rectify this problem I recommended learning from discursive psychology and critical discourse analysis by deploying the tools of micro-linguistic analysis to show just how 'social construction' is achieved in the flow of everyday speech and interaction. At the same time, I expressed some reservations about the metaphor of the conversation as applied to culture and argued that we should concern ourselves with the many facets of cultural performance. Needless to say, there is no reason for us to treat culture as 'one thing', and consequently no necessity to stick to only a single metaphor. The usefulness of any given metaphor will be related to purpose.

3 Truth, Science and Ideology

Central problem:
How can we ground theory and politics?

We need to make a distinction between the claim that the world is out there and the claim that truth is out there. To say that the world is out there, that it is not our creation, is to say, with common sense, that most things in space and time are the effects of causes which do not include human mental states. To say that truth is not there is simply to say that where there are no sentences there is not truth, that sentences are elements of human languages, and that human languages are human creations. Truth cannot be out here – cannot exist independently of the human mind – because sentences cannot so exist, or be out there. The world is out here, but descriptions of the world are not. Only descriptions of the world can be true or false. The world on its own – unaided by the describing activities of human beings – cannot. (Rorty, 1989: 69)

Knowledge is limited and needs to be used within the domains where its descriptions are valid and relevant. (Kabat-Zinn, 1990: 196)

Introduction

In this chapter we are concerned with the epistemological status of cultural studies theory and the basis on which practitioners justify intervention in social and cultural affairs. That is, we shall be investigating various facets of the problem of grounding cultural theory and cultural politics. In particular, we will explore some epistemological arguments that surround the concept of ideology, which has for so long been at the core of cultural studies.

The adoption of a representationalist epistemology allows writers and researchers to make universal truth claims where truth is taken to be an accurate representation of an independent object world. It follows that once we know the truth about the workings of the social world, then we can intervene strategically in human affairs with confidence in the outcomes. Further, we can valuably cast opposing ideas not only as false but also as the self-justifying ideologies of powerful interest groups. Thus, influenced first by Marx and later by the writings of Gramsci and Althusser, cultural studies theorists have sought to 'expose' ideologies of power. The 'powerful' have been characterized initially as governing class groups and later as those of gender, race and age. In this way, cultural studies writers have hoped to arm the subordinate with the ideas by which to challenge the currently ascendant authorities.

However, the Marxist theory of ideology and its associated representationalist epistemology has largely been displaced within cultural studies by the influence of poststructuralism, postmodernism and other anti-representationalist paradigms. These widely accepted (within cultural studies) strands of thinking have undermined the notion of objective and universal truth. Instead, it is now commonplace to talk of 'regimes of truth', being 'in the true', 'multiple truth claims', 'the social construction of truth', and so forth. Despite this trend, the concept of ideology remains strongly entrenched within cultural studies as writers persist in discovering ideology lurking beneath the surface of texts. Further, these ideologies continue to be regarded as the self-serving and false claims of the powerful. Insofar as others believe them to be true, they are said to misrecognize the 'real' social and cultural conditions in which they are embedded.

In this context, cultural studies is faced with a dilemma: namely, that if one holds to an anti-representationalist position in relation to language, it is inconsistent to deploy a concept of ideology (as falsehood) that is, implicitly or explicitly, contrasted to a universal truth. In order to continue to use the concept of ideology we would need to either re-establish the legitimacy of representationalist epistemology or redefine the concept of ideology. Alternatively, cultural studies could drop the term from its vocabulary altogether. Other consequences flow from this argument, notably that without true and objective knowledge of the world we cannot guarantee the success of cultural politics nor give them universal justification. Indeed, some critics fear that cultural studies is trapped in the maelstrom of relativism wherein one set of 'truths' is as valid as any other, leaving naked power as the final arbitrator.

I shall be arguing that, at the very least, the concept of ideology must be redefined to mean the 'binding and justifying ideas' of any social group. This definition of ideology requires no concept of the truth. However, given the history of the concept of ideology, it might be better to drop the term altogether. At the same time, I do not endorse relativism, but argue instead that the philosophy of pragmatism guides us out of this self-defeating position.

Philosophy in search of the truth

Enlightenment philosophy and the theoretical discourses of modernity are widely held to have championed Reason as the source of progress in knowledge and society. That is, modern reason has been conceived as leading to certain and universal truths that would, through the demystification of religion, myth and superstition, lay the foundations for humanity's forward path. Enlightenment thinkers hailed human creativity, rationality and scientific exploration as the underpinnings of the break with tradition that modernity heralds. In search of the truth, enlightenment philosophy sought universal propositions that would apply across time, space and cultural difference.

All the social sciences, from sociology to economics and psychology, were founded on the premise that conceptual and empirical truth can be discovered. This includes cultural studies insofar as one of its early theoretical pillars was Marxism, which, with its stress on scientific thought, historical progress and the emancipatory role of the proletariat, is a form of enlightenment thought, albeit one that represents the 'underside' of modernity. This is particularly so where Marxism posits History as having its own *telos* governed by laws of human development.

Subsequently, a range of thinkers, including Adorno, Nietzsche, Foucault and Lyotard have criticized the enlightenment impulses of modernity for their will to truth, power and control: that is, for heralding not progress but domination and oppression. This critique takes two fundamental directions:

- the rejection of the claims to universal truth;
- the rejection of the logic of domination and oppression that is identified as inherent in enlightenment thinking.

In the following discussion we are primarily concerned with the first issue, namely the epistemological question of universal truth.

Breaking with the Enlightenment

Nietzsche was one of the first thinkers to reject the enlightenment philosophy of universal reason and progress. He was followed in this line of thought by post-structuralism (e.g. Foucault), postmodernism (e.g. Lyotard), neo-pragmatism (e.g. Rorty) and subsequently the mainstream of cultural studies. For Nietzsche, the idea of an objective and universal knowledge is impermissible because reason and truth are 'nothing more than the expediency of a certain race and species – their utility alone is their truth' (1967: sec. 515). Here, truth is a matter of expression in language, where sentences are the only things that can be true or false, with acculturated authority arbitrating between sentences. That is, knowledge is taken as a form of the 'will to power' and truth a 'mobile army of metaphors and metonyms'. Since there is 'no limit to the ways in which the world can be interpreted', 'truth' is a question of whose interpretations count as truth, that is, it is an issue of power.

Foucault (1972, 1973), whose work was greatly informed by that of Nietzsche, argues that discourse and history are discontinuous, being marked by historical ruptures in understanding, so that the social world is no longer perceived, described, classified and known in the same way. Different epistemes, or configurations of knowledge, shape the practices and social order of specific periods and mark out distinct historical eras. This stress on discontinuity, which is at the heart of Foucault's work, questions the modern themes of genesis, tele-ology, continuity and totality. In place of Truth, Foucault speaks instead about particular 'regimes of truth' whereby statements, combined and regulated to form and define a distinct field of knowledge/objects, are taken to be true.

Foucault's thinking diverges from the themes of enlightenment thought in a number of ways. Thus, for Foucault, the following obtain:

- truth and knowledge do not possess metaphysical, transcendental or uni-versal properties. Rather, they are specific to particular times and spaces.
- there can be no one totalizing knowledge that is able to grasp the 'objective' character of the world. Instead, we both have and require multiple view-points or truths by which to interpret a complex heterogeneous human existence. Thus, knowledge and truth are perspectival in character.
- truth is not understood as an objective or neutral way of understanding but is, as we noted above, implicated in regimes of power. That is, for Foucault, knowledge is not neutral, universal or objective but always implicated in questions of social authority.

Foucault is concerned with the description and analysis of discourse and its effects under determinate material and historical conditions. Consequently, he also breaks with the central enlightenment metaphor of 'depth' and its sense of hidden meaning. Finally, since knowledge and regimes of truth form part of the discontinuous character of discourse in history, so Foucault rejects any notion of historical *telos* or the enlightenment understanding of progress. Having said that, Foucault also refuses to mark a clear, distinctive and final break between enlightenment and post-enlightenment thought. We do not, he argues, have to be 'for' or 'against' the Enlightenment. Rather, we must accept 'this sort of revolving door of rationality that refers us to its necessity, to its indispensability, and at the same time to its intrinsic dangers' (1984b: 249).

In a not dissimilar way, the postmodern philosopher Lyotard (1984) argues that modern knowledge rests on an appeal to grand or metanarratives that lay claim to universal validity. By contrast, the postmodern, in arguing that knowl-edge is specific to language-games, embraces local, plural and heterogeneous knowledges. Thus, the postmodern condition involves a loss of faith in the foun-dational schemes that have justified the rational, scientific, technological and political projects of the modern world. This is what Lyotard describes as an 'incredulity toward metanarratives'. That is, there remain no viable metanarra-tives from which to identify universal truth. Thus, for postmodernism, no universalizing epistemology is possible. Consequently, the postmodern, for Lyotard, is not so much an historical period, but rather 'the condition of knowl-edge in the most highly developed societies' (1984: xxiii).

Philosophy and the mirror of nature

Though somewhat uncomfortable with the term 'postmodern', Richard Rorty, from within the parameters of neo-pragmatism, shares the view that knowledge cannot mirror an independent object world but is inherently ethnocentric in character. By ethnocentric, Rorty does not mean loyalty to ethnically distinct or racist knowledge; rather, he means that all truth is culture-bound and specific to times and places. Thus, 'ethnocentric', for Rorty, is akin to what cultural studies writers mean by the 'positionality' of all knowledge: that is, the who, where, when and why of speaking, judgement and comprehension located in time, space and social power. Here, truth is understood to be a social commendation rather than an accurate picture of an independent object world.

Rorty's philosophy (Rorty, 1980, 1989, 1991a, 1991b, 1998b) is anti-representationalist in relation to language and anti-foundationalist with regard to truth and knowledge (Chapter 1). Thus the relationship between language and the rest of the material universe is held to be one of causality not of adequacy of representation or expression. For Rorty, '*no* linguistic items represent *any* non-linguistic items' (1991a: 2). In addition, there is for Rorty no archimedian vantage-point from which one could verify any claimed correspondence between the world and language. From this it follows that we cannot hold our descriptions of the world to be true in the sense of correspondence to an independent object world. Nor can we found or justify actions or beliefs on the bedrock of universal truth. Rather, we can only specify this or that discourse as being more or less useful and as having more or less desirable consequences in relation to our values and purposes. That is, we must give reasons that seek to justify our statements and actions in the context of intersubjectively formed constitutive rules regarding what establishes legitimate forms of reasoning.

Against relativism

For many of its critics, anti-representationalism is a form of relativism that posits the existence of a series of epistemologically equal truth claims. This situation has led, or so it is said, to a fatal inability to make judgements between forms of knowledge. Of course, relativism *per se* is a self-contradictory and self-undermining position for its own claims are also subject to relativity. Consequently, it must be rejected. However, to argue that all knowledge is positional or culture-bound is not to embrace relativism. As Rorty suggests, relativism would imply the ability to see across different forms of knowledge and to conclude that they are of equal value. Instead, Rorty argues, we are always positioned *within* acculturated knowledge. Consequently, the true and the good refer to that which *we* believe.

It is not possible to escape values any more than we can ground them in metaphysics, so that historically and culturally specific value-based knowledge is an inevitable and inescapable condition of human existence. Subsequently, judgements are made by reference to likely or intended consequences as measured against our values rather than being founded on transcendental truth.

Needless to say, the use of 'we' and 'our' implies the drawing of boundaries to knowledge communities that are highly political in character. Hence, one of the purposes of the 'cosmopolitan conversation of humankind' (Rorty, 1980) is to enable us to redraw those perimeters in order to include all persons within the 'we' of humanity.

The place of science

We may agree that these arguments work in relation to the social and cultural world, but where does this view of knowledge leave the 'hard' sciences? Does not physics place before us indisputable and eternal truths about the universe? Although the 'official' rhetoric of science has been that of representationalism, realism and the generation of universal knowledge, only school textbooks now cling to that outdated notion. Few serious scientists currently believe that their branches of knowledge proceed through laws of certainty. Thus, for Popper (1959), science proceeds through experimentation and the principle of falsification. That is, science advances through error and is upheld by the methodology of incredulity.

Equally, Kuhn (1962) is well known for arguing that science periodically overthrows its own paradigms. That is, a period of stable 'ordinary science' is commonly preceded by the revolutionary overthrow of the existing paradigmatic wisdom. An example would be the substitution of Copernican science by a Newtonian paradigm. Subsequently, the classical physics of Newton has in part been replaced by quantum mechanics. Thus does Giddens (1991) regard modern science as premised on the methodological principle of doubt and the chronic revision of knowledge. Enlightenment science may have begun with the search for absolute laws but is now beset with uncertainty. There is no 'unified field theory' in contemporary science, nor is there going to be one, for present-day physicists talk about that which we can never know.

Science as culture

The physical sciences are cultural classification systems with their own specialized languages. Indeed, the sciences consist of sets of conceptual tools that are of more or less usefulness to us as a life-form. Thus, physics, chemistry, biology and genetics are constituted by particular vocabularies deployed for the achievement of specific purposes. The arguments of these sciences should be understood not as the revelation of objective truth or the correspondence of language to an independent object world, but as the achievements of agreed procedures. These procedures have enabled us to produce levels of *predictability* that have underpinned a degree of consensus or solidarity amongst the scientific community, leading them to call particular statements true.

Here, science is not thought to have a privileged access to a deeper truth beyond that of ordinary experience. That is, science cannot be founded on representationalism. However, as Gutting (1999) argues, the predictive successes of science do make it a privileged form of knowledge, not because it works with methods unknown to others, but rather because it extends and makes effective those empirical trial-and-error methods that we all use and does so in ways that have yielded more workable knowledge of the material world. The final test for science is not whether it can demonstrate adequacy of representation in relation to an independent object world, but whether it works for specific purposes. That is, the sciences are subject to pragmatic testing. As eminent physicist Richard Feynman once argued,

> In general we look for a new law by the following process. First we guess it. Then we compute the consequences of the guess to see what would be implied if this law that we guessed is right. Then we compare the result of the computation to nature, with experiment or experience, compare it directly with observation, to see if it works. If it disagrees with the experiment it is wrong. (cited Gribbin, 1998: 4)

Gribbin (1998) goes on to argue that even if the proposed model does agree with the experiment, this does not mean that it represents a form of universal truth. For example, molecules can be described as 'little hard balls', but that does not mean they are such entities; rather, it means that they behave, under specific circumstances, 'as if' they were little hard balls. For other purposes, or under different circumstances, atoms are described in terms of electromagnetic forces and the movement of electrons. As Gribbin goes on to suggest, 'even the best model is only a good one in its own context, . . . chisels should never be used to do the job of mallets. Whenever we describe something as being "real", what we mean is that it is the best model to use in the relevant circumstances' (1998: 7).

Truth and reality

According to this line of argument, there is no fundamental *epistemological* distinction between ethnography, physical science and a multi-layered novel; they all involve socially agreed procedures that produce texts of more or less use to us in guiding our conduct. The differences are not degrees of correspondence with reality but matters of purpose and genre. Science has proved itself to be good at prediction and control of the natural environment, while ethnographies and novels have amongst their achievements the production of empathy and the widening of the circle of human solidarity (Rorty, 1989). These arguments do not mean that material reality does not exist or that we are out of sync with that reality. Rather, language is an evolutionary tool developed through practice by human beings in order to achieve various purposes. When language is conceived as a tool for action (see Chapter 2) rather than a mirror for representing the world, then it cannot be at odds with reality. Language can only misrepresent the world if it is also able to represent it accurately. Since the former is not possible, then the latter is an irrelevancy and to ask about it is to pose a poor, because literally sense-less, question.

When we conceive of language as a tool whose signs are generated by human beings and not by the objects or relations it seeks to represent, then there must be limits to the scope of language. Wittgenstein seeks to mark out these perimeters when he speaks of the existence of a domain about which we cannot speak. He also points to 'that which we know when no one asks us about it, but no longer know when we have to give an account of it' (1957: #89, 42e). Thus, the experience of nothingness cannot be a matter of discursive knowledge or understanding but must be a state of existence. There is, of course, irony in the argument that nothingness is signed as an experience outside of representation by the sign systems of language. To speak about the limits of language is to do so in vocabularies that attempt to sign the unsayable. Beyond language is that which we cannot speak about.

In a similar vein, Zen Buddhist philosophy (J. Austin, 1999; Beck, 1997; Crook and Fontana, 1990; Kornfield, 1994, 2000; Watts, 1957, 1968) asserts the possibility of 'direct pointing at reality'. That is, Buddhism affirms the existence of a 'knowing awareness' outside of signs. This is a state of consciousness achieved through meditation in which the internal dialogue or linguistic stream of consciousness has dropped away enabling one to *be* in the world without thinking or reflecting. We might describe this as a state of awareness, yet we might also say, as Buddhist monks are inclined to do, that it is something of which we cannot speak. Beyond language is the ineffable or sublime, which, though not expressible, can be experienced. Within Buddhist thinking, the self is a sign constituted through identification with a symbol of self. Self-consciousness is, as it is for Derrida, nothing but signs. However, for Zen, we may *be* in a realm without signs through our 'original face' or knowing awareness.

In sum, neither scientific, philosophical nor cultural analysis can offer a final single resolution of questions; rather, each must engage in the substitution of one form of expression for another. There is no final vocabulary of language that is 'true' in the sense of accurately picturing an independent object world called reality. Our vocabularies are only final in the sense of being currently without tenable challenge. Thus our best bet is to go on telling stories about ourselves that aim to achieve the most valued description and arrangement of human actions and institutions.

While such stories are always formed within the conceptual terms of 'our' cultural tradition, we must nevertheless remain open to the possibility of new vocabularies that persuade us to look at the world differently and introduce a revolution in thinking. The purposes of such stories lie not in the production of a 'true' picture of the world but in the generation of meaning. This includes the creation of empathy and the widening of the circle of human solidarity. Individual identity projects and the cultural politics of collectivities require us to forge new languages, new ways of describing ourselves, that recast our place in the world. The struggle to have new languages accepted in the wider social formation is the realm of cultural politics. However, given the line of argument I have pursued, it is not now possible to conceive of that politics in terms of a struggle between false ideology and truth but only between competing values and self-conceived interests.

The mistaken character of ideology

The concept of ideology has been the subject of some debate in relation both to its scope and to its epistemological basis. Below I question the viability of the concept of ideology, thought of as misrecognition or falsity, which forms one of the legacies of Marxism within cultural studies.

The Marxist concern with the concept of ideology was rooted in the failure of proletarian revolutions to materialize and the inadequacy of historical materialism in relation to questions of subjectivity, meaning and cultural politics. For example, was the failure of proletarian revolution a consequence of working-class 'false consciousness'? There are two aspects of Marx's writing that might be grounds for pursuing this line of thought:

- Marx (1961; Marx and Engels, 1970) argues that the dominant ideas in any society are the ideas of the ruling class.
- Marx suggests that what we perceive to be the true character of social relations within capitalism are in actuality the mystifications of the market. Specifically, the appearance of market relations of equality obscures the deep structures of exploitation.

Here we have two versions of ideology that both function to legitimate the sectional interests of powerful classes. Namely:

- coherent propositions about the world that derive from and reproduce the dominance of bourgeois or capitalist ideas; and
- world-views that are the systematic outcome of the structures of capitalism that lead us to inadequate understandings of the social world.

The rise and fall of Althusser

The influence of Althusser was significant in elevating Marxist thinking about ideology to the forefront of cultural studies. For Althusser, ideology is 'a system (with its own logic and rigour) of representations (images, myths, ideas or concepts)' (1969: 231). In particular, Althusser (1971) counterpoises the concept of ideology to truth and science by describing it as the *misrecognition* of one's relationship to the real conditions of existence. There are four aspects of Althusser's work that are core to his view of ideology:

- that ideology has the general function of constituting subjects;
- that ideology as lived experience is not false;
- that ideology as misrecognition of the real conditions of existence is false;
- that ideology is involved in the reproduction of social formations and their relations of power.

For Althusser, ideology hails or interpellates concrete individuals as concrete subjects. That is, it is the work of ideology to bring subjects into being through the constitution of subject positions. Hence, subjects are said to be the 'effects' of discourse because subjectivity is constituted by the positions which discourse obliges us to take up. Here ideology is double-edged. On the one hand, it constitutes the world-views by which people live and experience the world. In that sense, ideology is not false for it forms the very categories and systems of representation by which social groups render the world intelligible. Ideology is lived experience. On the other hand, ideology is also conceived of as a more elaborate set of meanings that make sense of the world (an ideological discourse) in ways that misrecognize and misrepresent power and class relations. Here, ideology represents the imaginary relationship of individuals to their real conditions of existence. Thus, if I mistake the class relations of exploitation within capitalism for the free and equal relations of human beings to each other, then I am subject to, and formed as a subject by, the illusions and delusions of ideology.

Amongst its many problems, Althusser's work is dogged by an important epistemological puzzle. Namely that if we are all formed in ideology, how can a non-ideological view be generated that would allow us to deconstruct ideology or even recognize it as such? Althusser's answer – that the rigours of science (and of his science in particular) can expose ideology – is both elitist and untenable. Science, as I have argued above, is itself a mode of thinking and a set of procedures that produces certain kinds of understandings. It is not an elevated god-like form of knowledge that produces universal objective truth.

No universally accurate picture of the world is possible, only degrees of agreement and conflict about what counts as truth. For this reason, thinkers like Foucault and Rorty have rejected the concept of ideology altogether.

Gramsci and ideological hegemony

Gramsci offers a more flexible and less troubled understanding of ideology than does Althusser. For Gramsci, ideologies provide people with rules of practical conduct and moral behaviour equivalent 'to a religion understood in the secular sense of a unity of faith between a conception of the world and a corresponding norm of conduct' (1971: 349). Within Gramscian analysis, ideology is understood in terms of ideas, meanings and practices that, while they purport to be universal truths, are better understood as maps of cultural significance. Here, ideology is both lived experience and a body of systematic ideas whose role is to organize and bind together diverse social elements, to act as social cement, in the formation of hegemonic blocs. Though ideology may take the form of coherent sets of ideas, it more often appears as the fragmented meanings of common sense inherent in a variety of intertextually located representations.

The introduction and deployment of Gramscian concepts within cultural studies proved to be of long-lasting significance not least because of the central importance given to popular culture as a site of ideological struggle. In effect, Gramsci makes ideological struggle and conflict within civil society the central arena of cultural politics, with hegemonic analysis the mode of gauging the relevant balance of forces. According to Gramsci, 'it would be interesting to study concretely the forms of cultural organization which keep the ideological world in movement within a given country and to examine how they function in practice' (cited Bennett et al., 1981: 195–6). Thus did he provide cultural studies with its campaign slogan of the 1970s and 1980s.

As we have seen, the principal functions of ideology in Gramscian thought are twofold:

- Ideology acts as the glue that binds together diverse social groups into a 'bloc'.
- Ideology maintains and legitimates the social authority and leadership of the ascendant bloc.

The question I want to ask in the context of this chapter is this: does a Gramscian understanding contrast ideology with truth? The answer, I think, is that it does not have to but all too often it does so in the hands of cultural studies practitioners.

The binding function of lived ideology does not have to have any reference to a representational concept of truth. While actors no doubt hold their beliefs to be true, it is the common sharing of beliefs that binds, not the representational truth or falsity of ideas. However, while ideology within Gramscian thinking is held to secure diverse groups into a bloc, it is also said to connect the subordinate to the interests of the powerful. Indeed, ideology is often posed as ideas *of* the powerful: that is, ideologies that belong to the powerful and are imposed upon the subordinate against their interests. If, as Gramsci implies, the subordinate believe a set of ideas to be in their interests when critics 'know' that they are not, then there is a tendency to cast such beliefs as false and the critics' representation of what constitutes 'interests' as true. Understood in this way, the concept of ideology assumes that Marxist thinkers know (i.e. can accurately represent) what is in the 'true' interests of the subordinate and that, by contrast, ideology encompasses an inadequate and false representation of social relations.

Here, Marxism and the movement for socialism are not themselves cast as ideological. If they were, then ideology would mean 'binding and justifying ideas'. However, since this is not the case, one must conclude that a representationalist distinction between truth and falsity remains within this line of thinking. Now, by replacing the idea of truth as representationally accurate pictures of the world with the idea of justification as reason giving, we could strip this understanding of ideology of its representationalist connotations. However, this is not how the concept of ideology is commonly used within cultural studies. Rather, the representationalist connotations stick to the concept of ideology like bees around the proverbial honey pot. Any review of cultural studies literature quickly reveals the continual use of phrases like 'capitalist ideology', 'male ideology' and 'racist ideology' to suggest the operation of spellbinding devices of subordination.

It is the declaration of objective interests and the possibility of false beliefs that is the fundamental problem here. I have already outlined why I think true (representational) knowledge of objective interests is unavailable to us, and consequently I must reject this usage of the concept of ideology. Equally, the notion that the workings of the market obscure its true character must be jettisoned, and for the same reasons: namely that it is epistemologically untenable to counterpoise ideology to objective and universal truth.

The difference between ascendant and subordinate groups is one of degrees of power and differing substantive world-views, not of ideological vs non-ideological ideas. As Foucault argued, we are all implicated in power relations, and in this sense the concept of ideology could be virtually interchangeable with his notion of power/knowledge. That is, knowledge is not neutral but always implicated in questions of social power. Power and knowledge are mutually constitutive. It is important to note that for Foucault power is not simply constraining (power over) within a zero-sum model (you have it or you do not) and organized into binary power blocs through which individuals or groups are able to achieve their interests against the will of others. Rather, power is also productive and enabling (power to) as it circulates through all levels of society and all social relationships.

When the concept of ideology is read as power/knowledge, it suggests structures of signification that constitute social relations in and through power. If meaning is fluid – a question of difference and deferral – then ideology can be understood as the attempt to fix meaning for specific purposes. Ideologies are discourses that give meaning to material objects and social practices; they define and produce the acceptable and intelligible way of understanding the world while excluding other ways of reasoning as unintelligible and unjustifiable. Ideologies are thus about binding and justification rather than being concerned with truth, falsity and objective interests. They are the 'world-views' of *any* social group that both constitutes them as a group and justifies their actions.

Acceptance of the notion that the concept of ideology refers to forms of knowledge that bind and justify all groups does not mean that we are unable to distinguish between ideas in terms of their specific consequences for social groups judged against our values (i.e. what we regard as a good or bad outcome). Truth understood as the values we hold to be good (i.e. truth as social commendation) is a very different use of the word than truth as a universal actuality that is mirrored by forms of representation. The picture we now have before us is one of competing social groups operating with justifying ideas and values rather than coherent blocs of Truth and Falsity. We will certainly want to pick and choose between such ideologies and their consequences. However, we do this not because we have the Truth but because we are ourselves a part of such groups and hold to certain values and justifying ideas as an aspect of our acculturation.

In short, if we so wish, we can continue to use the concept of ideology to mean lived world-views that bind and justify, but we cannot use a concept of ideology that entails a distinction between representational truth and falsity.

However, although signs can be re-signified, this is a difficult process that cannot be guaranteed and which may remain unstable. After all, words continue to carry the traces and echoes of their intertextual uses across a variety of sites. Consequently, it is difficult for the concept of ideology to be deployed without hinting at its opposition to truth. Thus, I suggest, it would be desirable to find alternative phrases to the concept of ideology such as 'binding and justifying ideas' and 'lived world-views'.

At this stage in the argument, two further questions arise:

- Can we identify a cultural and ideological hegemonic bloc?
- What values, if any, bind together the project of cultural studies?

The concept of hegemony

For Gramsci, hegemony is conceived of in terms of an 'historical bloc' of class factions that exercises social authority and leadership over subordinate classes through a combination of force and consent. A hegemonic bloc never consists of a single socio-economic category but is formed through a series of alliances in which one group takes on a position of leadership. Ideology plays a crucial part in allowing this alliance of groups to overcome narrow self-interest in favour of 'a cultural-social unity'. Thus, by virtue of ideology, 'a multiplicity of dispersed wills, with heterogeneous aims, are welded together with a single aim' (Gramsci, 1971: 349).

Hegemony can be understood in terms of the field of play wherein the strategies and power of ascendant social groups (whether constituted by class, gender, ethnicity or nationality) are maintained and challenged. The concept of hegemony allows one to mark out the balance of forces that exist in any domain of cultural politics. In this sense, hegemony is a relational concept marking a *temporary* settlement and series of alliances between social groups that is won and not given. Further, it needs to be constantly rewon and renegotiated. Thus, culture is understood to be a terrain of conflict and struggle over meanings.

Over twenty years ago, Abercrombie et al. (1980) rejected what they called the 'dominant ideology thesis' on the grounds that there is no coherent dominant culture to be found. They further argued that class power is primarily economic and social rather than cultural. For Abercrombie et al., the brute force of economic necessity was and is quite sufficient to explain the lack of radical working-class political activity without recourse to the concept of ideology. However, the Gramscian concept of hegemony has never been interchangeable with the notion of 'dominant ideology'. Rather, the concept marks the play of power and the balance of forces involved. Consequently, I have carefully been using words like 'ascendant', 'authority', 'leadership', 'alliance' and 'bloc', rather than suggest that hegemony involves a single dominant group ideology.

The understanding of hegemony that Gramsci offers us is not one in which a single 'dominant ideology' stems from a coherent ruling class. Rather, hegemony is conceived as a situation where an 'historical bloc' of factions exercises temporary social authority and leadership within the fluid and contestable domain of lived world-views. Here, the idea of hegemony is best understood as a measure of the play of forces rather than a permanent state of affairs. Nevertheless, the concept of hegemony does have other problems associated with it.

The challenge of fragmentation

Collins (1989) rejects the notion of hegemony on the grounds that culture is heterogeneous in terms of both the variety of texts produced and of the different meanings that compete within texts. For Collins, contemporary (postmodern) culture no longer has a centre in terms of either industrial production or the generation of meaning. Here, the concept of the postmodern does not suggest an historical period but rather indicates a 'structure of feeling' and a set of cultural practices. Core to the postmodern 'structure of feeling' is a sense of the fragmentary, ambiguous and uncertain nature of living together with an awareness of the centrality of contingency. Right across the western world, it is argued, we have been witnessing the end of anything remotely resembling a 'common culture'.

Textually, postmodern culture is marked by the blurring and collapse of the traditional boundaries between culture and art, high and low culture, commerce and art, culture and commerce. Indeed, the collapse of attempts to sustain art/high culture–commercial/low culture distinctions, combined with the recognition of the interpretive work done by active audiences, has done much to undo the idea of an hegemonic culture. The notion of either an hegemonic or a common culture is also made problematic in terms of the lived cultures of social groups. In particular, the last thirty years have seen the fragmentation of lifestyle cultures through the impact of migration, the 're-emergence' of ethnicity, the rise and segmentation of youth cultures and the impact of gender politics. Above all, the cultures of class blocs have fragmented through the restructuring of global capitalism, niche marketing and the aestheticization of daily life through the creation of an array of lifestyles centred on the consumption of aesthetic objects and signs.

The majority of the populations of western societies have sufficient housing, transportation and income to be in a post-scarcity situation. Consequently, it is argued, workers' identifications, and thus identities, shift from location in the sphere of production to that of consumption. This consumption-centredness of the working class becomes the medium and instrument of its fragmentation as it is detached, through its incomes and consumption capabilities, from the underclass while becoming increasingly internally stratified through 'taste' preferences. For Crook et al. (1992), this 'postmodernization' marks the penetration of commodification into all spheres of life so that external validation collapses and choice between values and lifestyles becomes a matter of taste and style rather than 'authentic' socially formed cultural authority that could be called hegemonic.

The incoherence of hegemony

At this point, a further question arises in relation to the concept of hegemony, namely what degree of authority and leadership must a social alliance exercise before it is deemed to be hegemonic? Or, to put it the other way around, how plural and fractured must the domain of lived world-views be before the concept of hegemony is no longer warranted? Must the authority of hegemonic ideas command either a majority of persons or a preponderance of power for the concept to be valid?

Further, since the ideas of a social bloc may be hegemonic in one sphere, say the authority of parliamentary government within liberal democracies, but not in another, perhaps that of sexual mores, one must hold that hegemony is never socially over-arching but fractured into divergent domains. One might then ask whether or not the various hegemonies are connected or articulated together in any way. Could we discuss the hegemony of hegemonic ideas? That is, can we identify an over-arching hegemony that binds the divergent spheres together – in which case are we not in danger of totalizing difference into dominance?

And if we cannot, what leverage does the concept of hegemony then have if it does not unite fractured groups?

The concept of hegemony 'contains' or connotes issues of power. If the play of power is removed from the notion of hegemony, it ceases to have any validity at all. However, the notion of power that it infers through its usage in cultural studies remains that of the exercise of constraint by the powerful over the subordinate. That is, the concept of hegemony connotes an undesirable 'imposition' disguised as widespread consent. If the argument is that consent represents misrecognition of the real relations of power and interest in play, then we are back at square one with the problem of ideology as false consciousness.

Further, as both Giddens and Foucault have reminded us, power is productive and enabling as well as limiting. Consequently, one would welcome the prospect of the hegemony of anti-racist ideas. Indeed, since history suggests that disillusioned non-voting constituencies within liberal democracies are more likely to form the foundations of authoritarian rule than of the extension of democracy and justice, the undermining of liberal democratic hegemony is not, at present, to be welcomed. While the concept of hegemony could be, and occasionally is, deployed to indicate an enabling alliance, the word is so entangled with issues of 'power as subordination' that such uses invite confusion.

Some usages of the concept of hegemony are more effective than are others. For example, there is surely a difference between reference to the 'hegemony' of free enterprise and free trade philosophies amongst the powerful economic nations – where the term seems to have merit – and allusion to the 'hegemony' of particular notions of masculinity and femininity – where the concept is more of a hindrance than a help given the increasing complexity and fragmentation of gender identities.

● Do we then have different types of hegemony dependent on whether they are based on class, gender or race, and so forth?
● Is the operation of hegemony in one sphere different from its operation in another?

In this context, one wonders exactly what purpose the concept of hegemony serves that is not achieved by the vocabulary of ascendancy, authority, leadership, alliance and articulation, given that hegemony still carries connotations of dominance and is commonly (mis)used in that way even within cultural studies.

In most cases the concept of hegemony remains tied to notions of agents and their interests. Thus one reads about the hegemony of capitalist class factions in pursuit of their own well-being. The concept of 'bourgeois democracy' also falls into this kind of usage. However, liberal democracy is not a simple matter of bourgeois class interests. Liberal democracy is ascendant within western societies and is not a world-view that any longer 'belongs' to a particular class, gender or ethnic faction or alliance. There are very few coherent alternatives to liberal democracy in modern western states, and there is very little support for such views. Opposition to liberal democracy, if it can be called opposition at all, is manifest in the disengagement of the growing proportion of the electorate that does not vote (especially in the USA).

In their revision of the concept of hegemony Laclau and Mouffe (1985) put aside the final determination of class and the economic, which, for them, do not determine cultural meanings. That is, ideology has no 'class-belonging'. Rather, they stress that history has no prime agents of social change and a social formation has no one central point of antagonism. Instead, hegemonic and counter-hegemonic blocs are formed through temporary and strategic alliances of a range of discursively constructed subjects and groups of interest. Here, the 'social' is understood to be not an object but rather a field of contestation in which multiple descriptions of the self and others compete for ascendancy. For Laclau and Mouffe, it is the role of hegemonic practices to try to fix difference, to put closure around the unstable meanings of signifiers in the discursive field.

Clearly this is, from my point of view, a superior and more flexible deployment of the concept of hegemony than more traditional Marxist usage. However, one again wonders why the term 'hegemony' is required at all when it continues to carry connotations of dominance, and notions of articulation, alliance, explanatory authority and power can do the required job in a more subtle fashion. Further, the notion that it is hegemonic forces that fix the meanings of words is problematic in the light of the argument I put in Chapter 2 that routine practice necessarily secures meaning in specific contexts for the purposes in hand. In addition, even if one accepts that power is implicated in the temporary fixing of meaning, there is no necessary reason why that power must be seen as hegemonic.

The concept of hegemony as understood within cultural studies has its roots in a Gramscian paradigm that is centred on class forces. If we dispense with that paradigm, as I think we must given the changed conditions of western societies and the demise of Marxism as a source of authoritative explanation, then it becomes an increasingly tortured process to make the notion of hegemony coherent.

It is surely good enough – and indeed more flexible – to talk of 'explanatory authority', 'lived world-views' and the operations of power rather than deploy the concept of hegemony. Further, the concepts of ideology and hegemony continue at best to hint at certain knowledge, values and interests and at worst to claim them as their own. In a world without secure foundations for truth and knowledge, where *On the Origin of Species* makes more sense than the Bible or *Das Kapital*, our central concern should be with the values that we hold dear. That is, what are 'our' values (see below), and how can we forward them (see Chapter 9)? Without the emotional and epistemological props that the concepts of ideology and hegemony provide, this is increasingly 'politics without guarantees'. Indeed, this is living without guarantees.

Political values in cultural studies

Practitioners of cultural studies have, of course, their own binding and justifying world-views. These commonly flow from the core concern that unites the coalition of cultural studies writers and teachers, namely the play of power in and through culture. In this sense, cultural studies began as a modernist emancipatory project founded on the values of equality, liberty and solidarity. The purposes of such a politics in the context of material scarcity have resided in liberation from the constraints that limit life-chances. Thus, given the inequalities generated by capitalism, emancipatory politics at first directed its attention to the exploitative relations of class and the establishment of the free, open and just society that socialism was to herald.

Later, the concept of equality was to be applied in the domains of gender, sexuality and ethnicity (and to some extent age and disability) as the modern project set its sights on the freeing of social life from the fixities of tradition. Today, most cultural studies writing puts the inequalities of gender, class, race, nation, and so forth, on an equal footing and hopes that they may be linked together into a 'counter-hegemonic' coalition politics involving the articulation of 'chains of equivalence'. Here, the modernist project of emancipation begins to blend with the postmodern stress on difference.

Postmodern thinkers have argued that there can be no one totalizing knowledge that is able to grasp the 'objective' character of the world. Rather, we both have and require multiple viewpoints or truths by which to interpret a complex heterogeneous human existence. Critics of this view have feared that the abandonment of foundationalism leads to irrationalism and the inability to ground any radical politics. Yet, one may argue, to accept the legitimacy of a range of truth claims is in itself a political position for it signals support for pragmatic postmodern cultural pluralism. In this way, postmodernism has the potential to give voice to a liberatory politics of difference, tolerance and diversity.

The uncertainty, ambivalence and ambiguity of the postmodern condition, argues Bauman (1991), opens up the possibility of grasping contingency as destiny, thereby enabling us to create our own futures. This argument suggests the need for dialogue and underpins the procedural arguments for a diverse and plural public sphere of citizens where citizenship as a form of identity provides the grounds for a shared polity. To do so we must transform tolerance into solidarity:

> Survival in the world of contingency and diversity is possible only if each difference recognizes another difference as the necessary condition of the preservation of its own. Solidarity, unlike tolerance, its weaker version, means a readiness to fight; and joining the battle for the sake of the other's difference, not one's own. Tolerance is ego-centred and contemplative; solidarity is socially oriented and militant. (Bauman, 1991: 256)

Today, cultural studies is marked by a modern–postmodern mix of values that centre on a democratic tradition that holds *equality, liberty, solidarity, tolerance, difference* and *diversity*, underpinned by the notion of *justice*, to be contemporary 'goods'. These values are broadly operationalized in terms of the need for cultural pluralism and the representation of the full range of public opinions, cultural practices and social-geographical conditions. They suggest a respect for individual difference along with forms of sharing and co-operation that are genuine and not enforced. Indeed, our best chance of maintaining difference and pursuing a private identity project is to live in a culture that prides itself on being heterogeneous. Needless to say, the values of equality, liberty, solidarity, tolerance, difference and justice are not always compatible with each other, nor do they mean the same thing in divergent contexts. Further, it is far from clear how such values can be put into practice (see Chapters 6 and 9)

Life-politics and postmaterialism

The politics that flow from the adoption of the modern values of equality, liberty and solidarity remain emancipatory, being concerned with an ethics of justice, parity and participation. In contrast, given a degree of release from material deprivation, contemporary 'life-politics' is more concerned with self-actualization, choice and lifestyle. Life-politics revolves around the creation of justifiable forms of life that will promote self-actualization in a global context. They are centred on the ethics of 'how shall we live?'

> Life-politics concerns political issues which flow from processes of self-actualization in post-traditional contexts, where globalizing influences intrude deeply into the reflexive project of the self and conversely where processes of self-realization influence global strategies. (Giddens, 1992: 214)

For Giddens, the more we 'make ourselves', the more the questions of 'what is a person?' and 'who do I want to be?' are raised in the context of global circumstances that no one can escape. For example, the recognition of the finite character of global resources and the limits of science and technology may lead to a de-emphasis on economic accumulation and the need to adopt new lifestyles. This reflexivity, involving the re-moralizing of social life, lies behind many contemporary New Social Movements (see Chapter 9).

In the context of western culture's relative affluence, political conflict is becoming less centred on questions of economic inequality and the injustices that flow from this and more concerned with questions of identity, self-actualization and postmaterialist values. In the context of a culture that has continually stressed that growth is about 'more of everything', a shift from quantity to quality is politically significant. For example, questions of emotional and spiritual 'intelligence' have emerged as important concerns in contemporary culture (see Chapter 10).

These issues are manifested in concerns about health, relationships and happiness in the face of, for example, the rise of depression to epidemic proportions. (See Chapter 6 for a discussion of depression as it relates to men.) Though depression has a genetic and biochemical basis, changes at this level of the body take place at too slow a rate to explain the post-Second World War rise in depression. Rather, this is better accounted for in terms of diet, industrial pollution (i.e. chemical poisoning), the stress associated with the accelerated demands of work, the collapse of community and social networks, the unachievable personnel targets set by consumer culture and rising cultural expectations of undiluted happiness through material gain. That is, the rise in depression is a direct consequence of our way of life – our culture.

Further, it can be convincingly argued that violence, sex addiction, gambling, alcohol and drug abuse are forms of self-medication and attempted defence against covert depression stemming from shame and 'toxic' family relationships. Low self-esteem (itself an outcome of family life), along with the self-perceived failure to meet cultural expectations, often lies at the root of depression and drug abuse so that much behaviour that appears to the 'outsider' as needless self-destruction is underpinned by personal pain, anxiety and depression. In short, these are important *cultural* questions wherein 'liberation' does not so much entail emancipatory actions directed against a simple oppressor but rather involves changes in lifestyle and emotional meanings.

In the context of western culture, emancipation can no longer be the only politics in play. Rather, we must take on the qualitative and postmaterialist values of emotional and spiritual contentment or happiness in the context of globally sustainable and justifiable forms of life that promote self-actualization. Cultural studies must increasingly engage with life-politics that are, at their core, cultural questions. In any case, such a politics has much to do with justifying cultural values and lifestyles and little or nothing to do with ideology as untruth.

Conclusions

Cultural studies during the 1970s and 1980s was marked by its vocabulary of ideology and hegemony. Indeed, cultural studies was dubbed 'ideological studies' (Turner, 1990), with theory regarded as an 'exposing' of ideology. Later, in its turn to language, cultural studies rightly espoused anti-representationalism and anti-essentialism. However, there remains a contradiction between these two arguments, namely that an anti-representationalist position on language cannot deploy a concept of ideology (as falsehood) posited in contrast to an objective universal truth.

I argued that there are no grounds for claiming knowledge as universal transcendental truth. Rather, there are only varieties of describing and speaking about the world from within our own milieu. Truth is culture-bound, contingent and specific to the historical and cultural conditions of its production. Truth is the word we use when we want to praise a world-view and its associated values. Thus the concept of ideology as falsity has lost its power as an explanatory concept and cultural studies must drop the idea that it has found the truth which ideology had masked. Indeed, the concept of ideology functions increasingly less as a useful tool of analysis and more as an emotional support and guarantor of cultural critics' world-views.

We could deploy the concept of ideology to mean 'binding and justifying ideas' or 'power/knowledge', but words are not easily re-signified; they tend to carry historical connotations (in this case of truth vs falsity). The concept of hegemony remains useful as an indicator that descriptions of the world justify and maintain powerful groups, but we should understand that there are centres of power, not a centre of power. Overall, simple phrases such as 'lived world-views', 'binding and justifying ideas' and 'explanatory authority' might usefully replace ideology and hegemony in the vocabulary of cultural studies.

In any case, we do not need the concepts of universal truth and falsity to pursue political action. Rather, we should be concerned with the grounds by which truth claims are *justified*, the rules that allow justification to be warranted, and the potential *consequences* of given world-views. This leads us to the ethical and value-based character of politics whose acts are grounded in values and descriptions 'we' share. On the one hand, this is an ironic politics without guarantees. On the other hand, it is a matter of the stories of power that underpin and justify values, actions and the boundaries of the 'we'.

Finally, cultural studies should understand theory not as a grand narrative but as a local tool, a redescription of specific aspects of our world that seeks to maintain solidarity and widen the circle of the 'we'. This 'we' is constituted by those who share a democratic pluralist tradition that values difference, solidarity, diversity, liberty and the reduction of suffering. The latter includes the postmateralist values of emotional and spiritual contentment pursued through the life-politics of ecology, relationships and lifestyle.

4 Culture as a Way of Life

Central problem:
Is culture best described as a whole way of life?

We use the word culture in these two senses: to mean a whole way of life – the common meanings; to mean the arts and learning – the special processes of discovery and creative effort. Some writers reserve the word for one or other of these senses; I insist on both, and on the significance of their conjunction. The questions I ask about our culture are questions about our general and common purposes, yet also questions about deep and personal meanings. Culture is ordinary, in every society and in every mind. (Williams, 1989: 4)

[Local cultures are] constellations of temporary coherence . . . set within a social space which is the product of relations and interconnections from the very local to the intercontinental. (Massey, 1998: 125)

Introduction

In this chapter I am concerned to mark a shift in the use and purposes of the concept of culture through an interrogation of the founding language of cultural studies, in which culture was characterized as a 'whole way of life'. I conclude that this phrase glosses over too many problems to be accepted without criticism. In particular, culture as a 'whole way of life' ties culture to place and even more problematically to nationalism and the domain of the nation-state. In the era of globalization, I argue, culture is more profitably thought of in terms of 'fields', 'flows' and 'knots' involving the continual hybridization of meaningful practices or performances in global space. And yet, the holism implied by the phrase a 'whole way of life' is worth preserving. As with the metaphor of the photon in quantum physics, the duality of culture lies in its being 'in-place' and of 'no-place' at the same time. Whether one treats culture as a particle (in-place) or a wave (no-place) depends on what one hopes to achieve. That is, the boundaries of a local culture or of a whole way of life are not intrinsic to culture but are the somewhat arbitrary tools of cultural classification and analysis.

Insofar as cultural studies has a distinguishing take on the concept of culture, it is a 'political' one that stresses the intersection of power and meaning with a view to promoting social change and improving the human condition as 'we' would define it. 'Culture' is both a name for the domain in which contestation over value, meaning and practices takes place and a tool by which to intervene in social life. Thus, the very debate over the meaning of the word 'culture' is itself a form of cultural politics. To talk about culture as flow, as hybrid, as global, as constellations of temporary coherence, and so forth, is to celebrate difference and diversity. It is to exhort and promote global cultural dialogue and the 'cosmopolitan conversation of humankind' (Rorty, 1980). However, there is also the danger here of losing sight of any manageable unit of analysis. By contrast, to locate culture 'in-place' is to mark out such a unit of analysis but to run the risk, given the national 'origins' and connotations of the phrase 'a whole way of life', of legitimizing the matrix of cultural absolutism, nationalism and fundamentalism. We need a unit of analysis that operates below the level of the nation but which can migrate on a global scale. I look to the notion of 'performance' to fulfil this function.

Raymond Williams: culture as a whole way of life

The publication of Raymond Williams' *Keywords* (1983) was a seminal moment in the field of cultural inquiry, not least because it marked the significance of an historical mapping of, and investigation into, the changing meanings of words. Consequently, the important question we face is not so much how to define culture for all time, but rather to consider how the concept has been deployed, and for what purposes, under varying circumstances.

As such, the concept of culture is a tool for exploring human conduct from a variety of perspectives. Indeed, no story centred on the meaning of culture is 'just' a description; it is also an evaluation and implicit justification of concerns contemporary to that account.

Williams (1981, 1983) suggests that the word 'culture' began as a noun of process connected to growing crops, that is, cultivation. We may note that cultivation is located in specific settled places, a connotation that clings to Williams' work. Having germinated from the soil, the concept of culture grew to encompass human beings, so that to be a cultivated person was to be a cultured person. However, during the nineteenth century it was apparent to the cultured that not all persons were equally civilized. At worst, the capability to be cultured was held to be a product of natural selection; at best, it was a condition to be aspired to and acquired by, in practice, the educated classes. Hence Matthew Arnold's view that acquiring culture – 'the best that has been thought and said in the world' (1960: 6) – was the means toward moral perfection and social good. Culture as human 'civilization' is counterposed to the 'anarchy' of the 'raw and uncultivated masses'. Later, F.R. Leavis (see Leavis and Thompson, 1933) was to hold that high or literary culture, captured in the artistic and scholarly tradition, nurtured the ability to discriminate between the best and the worst of culture: that is, the canon of good works and the 'addictions' and 'distractions' of mass culture, as he saw it.

Culture is ordinary

By contrast, Williams utilized the spirit of a nineteenth-century anthropological understanding of culture associated with Malinowski and Radcliffe-Brown to designate culture as 'a whole and distinctive way of life'. For Williams, it was the meanings and practices of ordinary men and women that constituted culture. Here, culture is lived experience: the tapestry of texts, practices and meanings generated by everybody as they conduct their lives. Williams' anthropological understanding of culture and its application to the lives and social organization of modern western industrialized cultures (rather than to the cultures of colonized peoples) has two important implications:

- The stress on the ordinariness of culture and the active, creative capacity of common people to construct shared meaningful practices suggests that we are all cultured. We all know 'how to go on' within our form of life.
- Within the context of English literary criticism, an anthropological definition of culture offered a critical and democratic edge. Comprehending culture as a 'whole way of life' had the pragmatic consequence of splitting off the concept from the 'arts', legitimizing popular culture and opening up television, newspapers, dancing, football and other everyday artefacts and practices to critical but sympathetic analysis.

While culture is concerned with tradition and social reproduction, it is also a matter of creativity and change. Williams was of course particularly engaged with questions of class culture, democracy and socialism in the context of the history of the British working class. As such, his view of culture is no less evaluative and political than the models held by his predecessors. To hold culture to be a whole way of life is not simply to express a more complex description or analytic category but to bring to the fore questions of democracy, education and the march of the working classes through institutions of contemporary life. This is 'the long revolution' (Williams, 1965) of the democratization of culture and politics.

Within Williams' schema, culture is located, for all intents and purposes, within flexible but sketchable boundaries. Williams no less than Thompson or Hoggart was concerned with the making of British, and particularly English, culture within the nation-state of the United Kingdom. Here culture is understood to be a facet of place; indeed it is constitutive of place. Williams' cultural materialism insists that culture be understood through the representations and practices of daily life in the context of the material conditions of their production. Hence the signifying performances of culture need to be understood as practices set within a material context in order to grasp culture as a 'realized signifying system'.

Raymond Williams was not of course the only writer to broaden the conception of culture or to link it with the study of working-class popular culture with an eye to the possibilities for social and cultural change. Nevertheless, he has become iconic in the narrative of cultural studies as the 'originator' of its first story: namely the move from perceiving culture as the 'arts' to seeing culture as being both 'ordinary' and 'political'. In asking questions about Williams' direction and pertinence to contemporary conditions, we are recomposing cultural studies.

Commodities are ordinary

The agenda that follows from defining culture as ordinary is one that supports the investigation of history and culture as productions 'from below'. This is the spirit of Thompson's celebration of 'the poor stockinger, the Luddite cropper, the "obsolete" hand-loom weaver, the "utopian" artisan, and even the deluded follower of Joanna Southcott', as he attempted to rescue them from the 'enormous condescension of posterity' (1963: 12). It is also the direction of Hoggart's (1957) identification of 'authentic' working-class culture as being in opposition to American commercial culture. Thus, Williams, Thompson and Hoggart have been banded together within the mythology of cultural studies because they stress the active, creative capacity of common people to construct shared meaningful practices. Yet, paradoxically, they all feared the impositions of capitalist consumer culture, in the face of which 'ordinary' people were apparently not to be trusted after all.

The legacy of locating authenticity in the 'people's culture' while juxtaposing it to the shallowness and manipulation of commercial or mass culture has dogged cultural studies for many years. Paper upon paper and author followed by author have sought to identify the 'bad' ideology within commercial culture and the 'good' spaces of resistance within authentic popular culture. However, at the start of the twenty-first century that which is popular turns out to be consumer culture. This is the case both in the mathematical sense of 'the majority' culture and in the more political interpretation of a culture of resistance. That is, culture is not only commercial in form but also 'cultural resistance' is located to some considerable extent within consumer culture.

The debates regarding the transformation of capitalism and the political character of consumer culture are discussed at greater length in Chapter 8. Nevertheless, we need to note here that there is a stream of contemporary writings that locates popular culture as commercial in origin. As Fiske argues, 'in capitalist societies there is no so-called authentic folk culture against which to measure the "inauthenticity" of mass culture' (1989a: 27). Rather, the meanings and practices that are generated by popular audiences at the moment of consumption constitute popular culture. This argument represents a reversal of the traditional question of how the culture industry turns people into commodities that serve its interests, in favour of exploring how people turn the products of industry into their popular culture serving their interests.

Chambers (1986, 1990), Fiske (1989a, 1989b), Hebdidge (1988), McRobbie (1989) and Willis (1990), amongst others, have shown us the creative meaning-producing activities of consumers as they become bricoleurs selecting and arranging elements of material commodities and meaningful signs. In general, after de Certeau (1984), it is argued that people range across a series of terrains and sites of meaning, actively producing sense within them, even though they are not of their own making. For de Certeau, as with Foucault (1980), there are no 'margins' outside of power from which to lay an assault on it or from which to claim authenticity. Instead, ambivalence and ambiguity occupy the space of resistance.

The end of authenticity

Thus, youth cultures, for example, can no longer be thought of as authentic and alternative spaces of resistance but are seen as places of negotiation where positions of resistance are strategic and themselves enabled by the structures of power (Best, 1997). This is so because the distinction between the media, the culture industries and an oppositional-authentic youth culture is no longer sustainable. While subculture theory perceived youth culture to be 'outside' of the media and opposed to them, contemporary theorists suggest that youth cultures are not only always 'inside' the media field but are dependent on it (Redhead, 1990; Thornton, 1995).

That youth fashion, style and music have their genesis in the culture and media industries does not reduce style to meaninglessness, nor does the end of authenticity mark the death of resistance. Thus the eclectic ransacking of history for items of dress involves the creative recombination of existing items to forge new meanings (McRobbie, 1989). This creativity takes place 'inside the whale' of postmodern consumer capitalism, where the binary divisions of inside–outside and authentic–manufactured collapse. Style is on the surface, culture is industry, subcultures are mainstream, high culture is a subculture, the avant-garde is commercial pop art, fashion is retro.

It may be that the location of resistance within consumer culture has led to a certain 'banality in cultural studies' by which the balance sheet of gains and losses wrought by commodity culture has been lost sight of (Morris, 1996). It may be that resistance in the work of Fiske and de Certeau does not distinguish sufficiently between types of resistance under sociologically and historically specific circumstances, that is, it is not sufficiently conjunctural (Bennett, 1998).

It may even be that cultural populism within cultural studies has led some writers to lose any conviction that there are grounds for criticizing the current order or for providing alternative visions (McGuigan, 1992).

However, what cannot be in doubt is that the 'ordinary' cannot be counterpoised to commodified culture as a source of authenticity or resistance. Soap opera and pop music are quite as ordinary as the working-class culture of miners or a day out by the seaside. Further, it is largely commodified culture that has been globalized and in the process deconstructs notions of the authentically local.

The ambiguity of resistance

I have argued that the phrase 'culture is ordinary' had a critical resonance in Williams' formulation because it recouped the meaningful practices of the 'popular' as valuable in the face of high cultural disdain. However, given that high culture has become just another subculture and that few people any longer feel oppressed by the devaluation of popular culture (indeed popular culture has become a celebrated object of its own attention), that cutting edge has been lost. However, politico-ethical cultural judgements need not be lost *per se* by the fact that the ordinary everyday culture of the contemporary West is a commodity culture. Everything turns on what we mean by resistance, on what is being resisted by whom under what circumstances and for what reasons. These questions are undecidable in the abstract and need to be established on an empirical case-by-case basis. Declarations that capitalist culture is all bad or culture from below is entirely good are of little use.

Resistance is a complex affair. Nevertheless, we may be sure that, however else it is to be characterized, its qualities will be measured against our values and purposes. All cultures may be regarded as equal in that they all form meaningful practices to their participants. All cultures may be held to be equal in that there are no universal criteria for aesthetic judgement that transcend cultural practices. Indeed, all cultures are equal in that there are no meta-cultural universal values that can provide the foundations on which to base cross-cultural cultural judgements. However, all cultures are decidedly not of equal virtue when measured against 'our' values. Thus, few people in cultural studies would mourn the passing of Nazi culture, racist culture, slave culture, the violence of a certain masculine culture or even the loss of Ur culture (see Rorty, 1998b). Indeed, the cultural politics of cultural studies has explicitly set out to eradicate certain cultural traits such as racism.

We all make judgements. Not only can we not escape this process, we should not seek to do so. A human culture without value judgements is simply unimaginable. Above all, our estimation of the merits of social formations, political arrangements, aesthetic styles and cultural habits depends on what values and practices we seek to promote or resist. Hence, clarifying the values we are prepared to support or decry is an important task for cultural studies for only then can we have a sense of what is or is not lost, recoverable, desirable and possible. This work becomes a necessity when we undergo the shift from truth to justification as the goal of intellectual inquiry and cultural criticism (Chapter 3). Thus, the 'popular' has intrinsic merit where democratization of culture is the primary goal. However, we might balk at justifying popular racism or widespread resistance to the advancement of women. Superiority or otherwise is always relative to the purpose to be served.

The whole divided

The direction of the discussion so far has been to suggest that the notion of culture as a whole way of life founded on authentic (class-based) norms, values and artefacts is at best problematic and at worst no longer viable in the face of commodification. Further issues arise when we realize that what was once regarded as a 'whole' is now held to be a discursive construction marked by multiple lines of difference. In this sense we are witnessing the *fragmentation* of culture where Williams had hoped to see it forged as a common whole.

There is an ambiguity about the notion of a 'common culture'. On the one hand, a common culture constitutes the collective (e.g. nation, youth group, class, etc.). On the other hand, a common democratic and participative culture is that which we have yet to build. Insofar as culture is a common whole way of life, its boundaries, at least in the work of Williams, are largely locked into those of nationality and ethnicity: for example, the culture of the English or perhaps the British. At the same time, culture is not 'one' in the sense that it is divided by class and other forms of 'difference'. As contemporary cultural theory has suggested, the whole way of life has now become fractured into a kaleidoscope of difference. That is, as cultural studies engaged with structuralism and post-structuralism, so it has been widely accepted that meaning is generated through the play of difference down a chain of signifiers. Further, subjects are formed through difference so that we are constituted in part by what we are not. In this context, there has been a growing emphasis on difference in the social and cultural fields, and in particular on questions of gender, race and ethnicity.

Not only is culture fractured along the lines of gender but also each sex is itself divided. Thus, it is doubtful if most women in the West would identify themselves as feminist and, in any case, feminism is a field of theory and politics that contains competing perspectives and prescriptions for action. Further, the very concept of patriarchy has been criticized for its treatment of the category of woman as undifferentiated so that all women are taken to share something fundamental in common in contrast to all men. This is an assumption continually challenged by, amongst others, black feminists who have argued that the movement has defined women as white and overlooked the differences between black and white women's experiences. Not only does race mark a line of cultural difference, but a contemporary emphasis in cultural studies on diaspora, hybridity and creolization suggests that cultures, languages and races are never presented in pure forms tied to place but are more mobile units of meaning operating on a global scale. Thus does culture begin to move 'out-of-place'.

Globalization, cultures and places

Globalization is the key dynamic that has increasingly problematized the idea of culture as a whole way of life located within definite boundaries. Globalization has important economic, political and military dimensions deriving from the institutions of modernity and instantiated in a variety of forms from militarized imperialism to disorganized capitalism. Here, we are mostly concerned with the cultural domain as people are increasingly involved in networks of practices and meanings that extend far beyond their immediate physical locations.

Globalization involves increasing multi-directional economic, social, cultural and political connections across the world and our awareness of them. A consequence of the dynamism of the institutions of modernity (Giddens, 1990) and time-space compression (Harvey, 1989), globalization is implicated in the global production of the local and the localization of the global. In particular, that which is considered to be local is produced within and by globalizing discourses, including corporate marketing strategies that orient themselves to differentiated 'local' markets. An emphasis on distinctiveness and diversity is part of an increasingly global discourse, so that much which is considered to be local, and counterposed to the global, is the outcome of translocal processes (Robertson, 1992). For example, nation-states were forged within a global system and the contemporary rise in nationalist sentiment can be regarded as an aspect of globalization.

Place is a socially constructed site or location in space marked by identification or emotional investment. That is, a specific place is a bounded manifestation of the production of cultural meaning in space. Giddens (1984) characterizes space and place in terms of absence–presence, where place is marked by face-to-face encounters and space by the relations between absent others. We may also distinguish between space and place on the grounds that the latter is the focus of human experience, memory, desire and identity. That is, places are discursive constructions that are the target of emotional identification or investment. For example, 'Home . . . is a manifestation of an investment of meaning in space. It is a claim we make about a place. It is constructed through social relations which are both internal and external and constantly shifting in their power relations' (Silverstone, 1994: 28).

Thus, both place and space, as meaningful terms, are cultural constructions with the specificities of place being endowed with our emotional investments. Of course, it is not only the *in situ* or 'original' population who make cultural investments in location. Place is now constructed by global forces by virtue of the movement of cultural elements from one location to another. This involves redefinition of the meaning of place, including the dislodging of long-standing authenticity claims whereby a place is considered to be solely local, natural, true and pure.

The days are gone when cultural practices could be claimed as 'authentic' because uncontaminated by invasion, tourism or consumer capitalism. There are no immaculate origins.

As a manifestation of globalization, facets of once-given local cultures have broken free, or become disembedded, from their location in a specific place and have been relocated elsewhere in space. Patterns of population movement and settlement established during colonialism and its aftermath, combined with the more recent acceleration of globalization, particularly of electronic communications, have enabled increased cultural juxtaposing, meeting and mixing. This suggests the need to escape from a model of culture as a locally bounded 'whole way of life'. Thus Clifford (1992) has argued that we should 're-place' culture by deploying metaphors of travel rather than those of location. The accelerated globalization of late modernity has increased the relevance of the metaphor of travel because all locales are now subject to the influences of distant places.

Unity and fragmentation

Although capitalist modernity does involve an element of cultural homogenization, the current phase of accelerated globalization is not uniform or one-directional. Rather it is a process of uneven development that both fragments and introduces new forms of world interdependence. Since mechanisms of both fragmentation and co-ordination are at work, it is a question neither of homogenization nor of heterogenization, but rather of the ways in which both are features of the contemporary world. Thus, Appadurai (1993) has argued that contemporary global conditions are usefully characterized in terms of disjunctive flows (of ethnoscapes, technoscapes, finanscapes, mediascapes and ideoscapes) that are not neatly determined by one harmonious 'master plan'. Rather, the speed, scope and impact of these flows are fractured and disconnected. Globalization is an uneven process in which modern and postmodern ideas about time, space, rationality, capitalism, consumerism, sexuality, family, gender, and so forth, are placed alongside older discourses, setting up discursive competition between them.

In this context, culture cannot be said to be located in one place nor can national and/or ethnic cultural identities be understood to be coterminous with state borders. Various global diasporas – African, Jewish, Indian, Chinese, Polish, English, Irish, and so forth – attest to national and ethnic cultural identities that span the borders of nation-states. Further, few states have ethnically homogeneous populations, so that over sixty nation-states are constituted by more than one national or ethnic culture (Smith, 1990). Consequently, cultures are not best grasped as static entities but need to be comprehended as constituted by changing meanings and practices. Thus, representations of national culture are simply snap-shots of symbols, habits and routines that have been foregrounded at specific historical conjunctures for particular purposes by distinctive groups of people. Here, national identity is a way of unifying cultural diversity so that, as Hall argues,

> instead of thinking of national cultures as unified, we should think of them as a discursive device that represents difference as unity or identity. National cultural identities are cross-cut by deep internal divisions and differences, and 'unified' only through the exercise of different forms of cultural power. (1992b: 297)

Diaspora and hybrid identities

Contemporary globalization has undermined the stability of tradition while increasing the range of resources available for identity construction. Thus, proliferation and diversification of contexts and sites of interaction prevent easy identification of particular subjects with a given, fixed identity. Consequently, in the context of the accelerated globalization of late modernity we have begun to talk about hybrid cultural identities rather than a homogeneous national or ethnic cultural identity. Indeed, the prominence given to difference in cultural theory has led many writers to think of culture, identities and identifications as always a place of borders and hybridity rather than of fixed stable entities (Bhabha, 1994).

The disembedding of cultural practices is manifested by, amongst other things, the journeys, border crossings and dispersion of ethnic disaporas, which, as networks of transnational identifications, are at once local and global. The concept of diaspora helps us to think about identities in terms of contingency, indeterminacy and conflict – identities in motion rather than absolutes of nature or culture; routes rather than roots: that is, a 'changing same' that involves 'creolized, syncretized, hybridized and chronically impure cultural forms' (Gilroy, 1997). Consequently, black identities cannot be understood, argues Gilroy (1993), in terms of being black *per se* or black American or black British or black West Indian. That is, they cannot be grasped in terms of ethnic absolutism or nationality but should be understood in terms of the diaspora of the 'Black Atlantic'. Here, cultural exchange within the Black Diaspora produces hybrid identities and cultural forms of similarity and difference within and between the various locales of the diaspora. For example, rap and hip-hop, American-Afro-Caribbean hybrids, have become the prominent musical forms of the Black Diaspora and a point of identification within the Black Atlantic.

The concept of hybridity has proved useful in highlighting cultural mixing and the emergence of new forms of identity. However, we need to differentiate between types of hybridity and to do so with reference to the specific circumstances of particular social groups. Thus Pieterse (1995) has suggested a distinction between structural and cultural hybridization. The former refers to a variety of social and institutional sites of hybridity, for example border zones or cities like Miami or Singapore. The latter distinguishes cultural responses that range from assimilation, through forms of separation, to hybrids that destabilize and blur cultural boundaries. Pieterse argues that structural hybridization, which increases the range of organizational options to people, and cultural hybridization, which involves the opening up of 'imagined communities', are signs of increased boundary crossing. However, they do not represent the erasure of boundaries, so that we need to be sensitive both to cultural difference and to forms of identification that involve recognition of similarity.

The notion of hybridity remains problematic insofar as it assumes or implies the meeting or mixing of completely separate and homogeneous cultural spheres. To think of Chinese Australian or Polish American hybrid forms as the mixing of two separate traditions is difficult because neither Chinese, Australian, Polish nor American culture is bounded and homogeneous. Each category is always already a hybrid form that is further divided along the lines of religion, class, gender, age, nationality, and so forth. Hybridization is the mixing of that which is already a hybrid. Hence the argument that all cultures are zones of shifting boundaries and hybridization. Nevertheless, the concept of hybridity or creolization has enabled us to recognize the production of new identities and cultural forms, for example 'British Asians' and British bhangra. Thus, the concept of hybridity is acceptable as a device to capture or temporarily freeze cultural change by way of a strategic cut or stabilization of cultural categories. The theory of hybridity is useful not because it accurately pictures an independent world but because it acts as a tool with which to capture the emergence of the 'new'.

The processes of globalization suggest that we would do well to understand culture less as a matter of locations and roots and more as hybrid and creolized cultural routes in global space. Cultures are not pure, authentic and locally bounded; rather, they are to be thought of as syncretic and hybridized products of interactions across space.

Unpredictable and elaborate over-determinations have led 'not to the creation of an ordered global village, but to the multiplication of points of conflict, antagonism and contradiction' (Ang, 1996: 165). Global culture is a chaos culture that, in principle, flows with no clear limits or single determinations. Yet there remains a value in locating culture in-place in order to say things like 'this is a valued and meaningful practice in Australian culture'. Or we may want to say that the cultural flows of the 'Black Atlantic' involve musical forms of 'West African origin' that have coursed through the 'USA' and 'Caribbean', where they have been hybridized with aspects of 'European' music before proceeding to Johannesburg, where rap and hip-hop have immense popular symbolic cultural and political significance. That is, we will want, for particular purposes, to see culture as both 'in-place' and as a flowing stream of disembedded meanings and practices.

Here the language of contemporary science can help us out. Thus, physics describes an undifferentiated reality with its own classificatory language that includes units of study held to perform in specific ways under definite conditions but which can be redescribed as holding alternative qualities for other purposes. Whereas classical physics holds the basic unit of analysis to be atoms that work 'as if' they were solid objects, quantum mechanics describes the universe at the sub-atomic level in terms of protons, neutrons, electrons, quarks, mesons, and so forth, that are best characterized not as entities but as forces and fields. Further, how one names an entity or field is less significant than what it enables scientists to predict and perform. Thus, by analogy, it may be temporarily useful for particular purposes to view cultures as linked to specific peoples and places. Here local culture can be thought of as a 'knot' in the global flows of culture – a 'constellation of temporary coherence' with 'lines of force' marking out nodal points within fluid 'cultural fields'.

Physicists suggest that for particular purposes light is best understood as constituted by particles whereas at other times for other purposes it is best considered as having a wave form. Metaphorically, culture partakes of particle and wave. The duality of culture lies in its being both 'in-place' and of 'no-place'. Global culture is a series of overlapping fields (or language-games) marked out with knots or nodal points. Further, culture has its own uncertainty principle by which we can never be sure of its location. Metaphors of uncertainty, contingency and chaos are replacing those of order, stability and systematicity.

Globalization and global cultural flows are not constituted through neat sets of linear determinations but are better comprehended as a series of overlapping, over-determined, complex and chaotic conditions that, at best, can be tracked in terms of a clustering into 'knots'. Under these circumstances it would be possible to shift the metaphor of culture as a 'whole way of life' from the level of the nation-state to that of the global (i.e. to the level of a species with human beings understood as a form of life) while simultaneously seeking to isolate and analyse culture as a part(icle) of a social formation and/or as a localized 'temporary coherence' in space. That is, phrases like 'a whole way of life' or a 'local culture' do not signify cultural entities but are expressions that mark out analytic boundaries – a temporary freezing of the flux of meaning and practice drawn for particular purposes.

Holism and levels of practice

If cultural studies' foundational story concerned the shift from culture as the 'arts' to culture as being 'ordinary' (encapsulating a whole way of life), then its second story concerned the place of culture in a social formation. This narrative was constituted through a series of debates regarding the relationship of culture to other social practices such as the economic and the political. In particular, cultural studies rejected the idea that culture was determined by economic forces in favour of understanding it as an autonomous set of meanings and practices with its own logic. This move had the great advantage of opening up culture to analysis within its own terms and in particular to an emphasis on language. In many ways this has been cultural studies' great achievement (see Chapter 2). However, this 'advance' has come at a price, namely the creation of isolated and to some extent arbitrary 'levels' of practice (e.g. culture or economics or ideology, etc.) that can appear to float off as independent activities or, worse still, as 'entities'.

For Williams, culture as a whole way of life represented the expressive totality of social relations. Thus, 'the theory of culture' is defined as 'the study of relationships between elements in a whole way of life' (Williams, 1965: 63). Williams rightly wants us to consider the indissociable character of meanings, practices and artefacts; the material processes of cultural production and the signifying practices of the symbolic. Yet he also requires us to explore the relationships between the elements of a whole way of life, which necessitates specification of analytical units that form parts of the whole. For example, Williams discusses the relations between the economic and the cultural (as elements of a totality) in terms of 'setting limits'. That is, the economic demarcates the boundaries of culture but does not determine it in a direct one-to-one relationship. Within Williams' schema, a crude base-superstructure model has been displaced in favour of a conception of society as an 'expressive totality' by which all practices – political, economic, ideological – interact, mediate and influence each other.

Nevertheless, Williams continued to hold the labour process to be the critical and dominant set of social relations, with other connections and practices set at 'variable distances' from this central set of activities. Thus, the closer cultural practices are to these central economic relations, the more they will be determined by them and vice versa. In accordance with Williams' reasoning, individually produced art is more autonomous than mass-produced television. However, while the production of television may be more embedded in capitalist production than painting, it is by no means certain that painting is any the less 'ideological' or political. Nor does 'setting limits' tell us much about the form that television takes and why it is different from painting.

Social formations as complex structures

For Hall (1992a), the moment of structuralism within cultural studies that followed Williams' influence is identified with forces that interrupted the search for underlying totalities. Instead, structuralism describes social formations as constituted by complex structures or regularities. These are analysed in terms of the various elements that make up structures and the way in which they are articulated or linked together. Here, the emphasis is on the irreducible character of the cultural as a set of distinct practices with their own internal organization or structuration.

Thus, Althusser (1969, 1971) conceived of a social formation not as a totality of which culture is an expression, but as a complex arrangement of instances (levels or practices) that are 'structured in dominance'. That is, the different instances of politics, economics and ideology are articulated together to form a unity that is the result not of a single one-way base–superstructure determination, but of determinations emanating from different levels. Consequently, a social formation is the outcome of 'over-determination'. By this is meant that any given practice or instance is the outcome of many different determinations. These distinct determinations are levels or types of practice with their own logic and specificity that cannot be reduced to, or explained by, other levels or practices.

This formulation was hailed by Hall (1972) as a 'seminal advance' because it enabled theorists to examine cultural phenomena as separate signifying systems with their own effects and determinations that were irreducible to the economic. Indeed, cultural practices can be seen as constitutive of that which the economic is understood to be. This is the foundation of Hall's formulation that 'we must "think" a society or social formation as ever and always constituted by a set of complex practices; each with its own specificity, its own modes of articulation; standing in an "uneven development" to other related practices' (1977: 237). That unity thought of as a 'society' is considered to be the unique historically specific temporary stabilization of the relations or articulation between different levels of a social formation.

The circuit of culture

More recently, Hall and his colleagues (du Gay et al., 1997) have deployed the metaphor of the 'circuit of culture'. Here, cultural meaning is produced and embedded at each level of the circuit – production, representation, identity, consumption and regulation – so that the production of significance is articulated to the next moment without determining what meanings will be taken up or produced at that level. Thus, culture is autonomous but articulated to other practices to form a whole – articulation being the form of connection that can, but need not, make a unity of diverse elements under specific conditions.

The advantage of the circuit of culture metaphor is that it allows us:

- to analyse the specificities of any given level of a social formation, for example culture;
- to consider the relations between culture and other sets of practices without predetermining how that relationship is constituted.

This model is more flexible, more useful and more sophisticated than Williams' concept of setting limits. However, it continually carries with it the serious danger of losing a sense of the inseparability of a whole way of life. Instead of seeing the idea of levels or practices as an heuristic device, critics start imagining that they represent organizational aspects of the 'real' world. Thus, while the concept of a whole way of life no longer works very well at the level of the nation, it does usefully remind us of the unity and inseparability of all aspects of human beings as a form of life.

Culture and methodological holism

Any act is multi-faceted in its meanings for it partakes of the multi-accentuality of the sign. Thus, buying flowers for one's partner is a commercial transaction enacted within a network of economic relations. However, within social relationships, buying flowers acts as a sign of affection (or apology or a strategy, etc.) implicated in gender relations and the politics of the family. Further, if culture is now held to be constitutive of other practices, that is, culture (as language or discourse) is the classificatory process that makes buying flowers meaningful (as an economic and romantic practice), then it is hardly a separate level of a social formation but permeates and constitutes the whole. Here, discourses mark out the boundaries of significance through their classificatory operations. Consequently, we need to grasp both the inseparable unity of forms of life and their cultural categorizing into parts.

Methodological holism argues that the best way to study a complex system is to treat it as a whole rather than be content with analysis of the structure and 'behaviour' of its component parts. Indeed, the inseparability inherent in holism suggests that the properties of the whole are not fully determined by the properties of its parts. In this view, a society always adds up to more than is stated by a description of the relationships of the parts or levels. While a methodological individualist maintains that to study society is to investigate the behaviour of individuals, a methodological holist argues that this will have limited value in illuminating the workings of the social and cultural whole.

Given the central place that language occupies in the study of culture, it is worth noting that the linguistic holism of Quine, Rorty and Davidson, amongst others, suggests that an understanding of language requires utterances to be put in the context of the entire network of language. Meaning is always relational and context-specific. Indeed, the philosophy of language espoused by those writers who have been influential in cultural studies – Derrida, Bakhtin, Foucault – shares an emphasis on the relational character of language and the contextual nature of truth. A language-oriented study of culture (which, with qualifications, was put forward in Chapter 2) must then seek to locate culture as a linguistic and cultural whole (way of life).

If culture is a level of a social formation, it is not in logic a whole way of life, and if it is a whole way of life, it cannot be separated into segments. However, we are dealing here with the languages of cultural analysis, not entities that possess hard-and-fast qualities. The notion of a cultural or economic level is an analytic tool, a metaphor by which to explore the relations between practices, and not a description of the 'real'. That is, in the context of methodological holism, one cannot meaningfully ascribe properties to a 'level' outside of a well-defined analytic arrangement or metaphor designed to achieve particular purposes.

A whole way of life remains a useful metaphor that eschews reductionism because it stresses the irreducibility of the whole. That is, conceiving of culture as a whole retains holism. On the other hand, Williams' concepts of expressive totality and setting limits threaten to reduce culture to other practices. Equally, the notion of a level or unit of analysis within the politics of articulation (e.g. the circuit of culture) endangers holism yet allows us to specify and analyse particular practices for specific purposes. For example, while in an holistic sense there are no signifying practices *per se* for all practices signify, the modelling of signifying practices as a level allows us to explore the mechanisms and specificities of signification. Thus, I am suggesting that while we still require the concept of a whole way of life in order to maintain holism, we will also need sub-divisions of the whole for analytic purposes.

Globalization has gone a long way towards breaking down the isolation of human cultures that allowed them to generate their own specific and identifiable language-games and practices. Consequently, a 'whole way of life' must be split off from the limitations of Williams' national parameters and may now be taken to operate at the level of global culture (Chapter 7). However, the notion of a global culture is an unmanageable level of analysis for most practical purposes (though it does carry the important ethical consideration that we are one interdependent human species living one interrelated human way of life). Further, a whole way of life might for specific analytic purposes be thought of as operating within almost any temporary lines of demarcation (hence culture→youth culture→punk culture).

Though such usage always carries with it the marks of arbitrary boundary formation, we do need a unit of analysis that can be located within the whole but which if added together or totalized is still short of being the whole. A number of candidates suggest themselves, for example discourse, language-game and practice. In Chapter 2, I explored the concept of 'performance' as a unit metaphor that can play this role set within overlapping language-games. That is, a 'performative language-game' is the basic unit of analysis (which, like the atom, can be split into yet still smaller units for other purposes, e.g. into signs). A local culture, which carries a sense of being in-place, is then treated as a set or knot of overlapping performative language-games located within the whole of the human form of life.

The concept of the performative holds signification and practice together as indissoluble and directs our attention to the simultaneous production of language-games and practices: the myths and rituals of our form of life. Here, culture would be understood to be a local performance that:

● is not tied to a place *per se* for it can move globally;
● may cluster with other performances around a certain 'knot' in a field to form a local culture; and
● may or may not survive across time and space as it proves useful/powerful.

In sum, I am suggesting that the concept of a whole way of life is most useful at the global level and that we treat the performative language-game as the local cultural unit. A local culture – which is never only local – is constituted as a configuration of performances, some of which are present in other local cultures and some of which are not (like language-games). The local is a knot in the flow of global culture whose particles are fluid and open to rearrangement. It is in this sense that local cultures can be understood as 'constellations of temporary coherence'.

Global chaos culture

Whether at the level of the local knot or the global field, culture is marked by regularities of meaning and practice. However, the concept of a global culture now faces the difficulties of other complex systems, that is, chaos. There is a sense in which global culture is an interconnected 'whole' – a human form of life. Nevertheless, it cannot safely be thought of as stable or predictable and thus open to planned change on a large scale. It was once argued that if you knew the 'laws' that held for the given parts of a whole, then you could predict its behaviour with certainty. Determination led to predictability. Thus, if you understood Newton's laws of physics, you could safely predict the outcomes of events at the level of the atom and above. However, while the fundamentals of classical Newtonian science still hold for particular purposes, from the viewpoint of sub-atomic quantum mechanics and complex system science, unpredictability or chaos can be the outcome of otherwise predictable events.

Chaos as persistent instability often arises when an 'object' feels the effect of more than one force, that is, it is over-determined (as we have noted culture must be). Thus, there are in-built limits to prediction at all levels of complexity and minute changes amplify rapidly through multi-dimensional feedback.

This is not to suggest that culture 'works' in the same way as quantum mechanics. However, the metaphors of a 'complex system' and of 'chaos' do have pertinence for the analysis of the global whole where instability is part of our environment and culture. This argument indicates limits to any cultural analysis, and in particular to modes of intervention, given increased levels of the unintended consequences of action. It will not be possible to intervene at the level of the whole without massive international co-operation and co-ordination, and, even in that highly unlikely event, the consequences will be volatile and unpredictable. Instead, analysis and intervention must follow the old adage 'think global act local'. That is, we are required to analyse the local performative language-game within the flow of world-wide culture while having an eye to its consequences at all 'levels'.

Culture and change

If we operate with a concept of culture as a bounded way of life, we tend to think that cultural change can be managed within those parameters. However, in the context of globalization, cultural policy and politics need to exercise some prudence in the face of the unpredictability of action. That is, though inspired by utopian impulses, a degree of pragmatism about the 'possible' together with wisdom regarding the reach of reform must be maintained. Cultural analysis and cultural politics are about as reliable as the movements of the stock exchange or forecasting the weather. Consequently, we might treat cultural policy with the same circumspection as we would if it was our personal money we were investing, or our family's picnic that was at risk from the rain clouds. This is not a recipe for inaction; it is a diagnosis that lends itself to the estimation of probabilities rather than certain determinations. It is a method that prescribes analysis of specific and local languages, performances, technologies, and so forth, in order to make cultural politics more effective.

Williams noted that culture is reproduced through acculturation and subject to the inventive change of human agency. Thus, culture is implicated in tradition and stasis as well as creativity and transformation. Cultural studies has been interested in the mechanisms that are implicated in the maintenance of the status quo insofar as they illuminate the possibilities for change. The rhetoric of post-structuralism in particular has stressed that deconstruction 'undoes' in order to open up a space for new thinking. Almost anything it seems can be deconstructed, and, we are asked to believe, this is necessarily a good thing. Further, almost every social arrangement and set of relationships in the current social order is held to be suspect, demanding swift but unspecified change.

We need to be reminded that Williams spoke of 'the long revolution' and the march of the working class (which must now be expanded to include other agents of cultural difference and social change) through the institutions of the social order. The era of wars and revolutions internal to western culture is largely over. There is no prospect of revolutionary change in the traditional sense of the word (i.e. radical, centralized and speedy overturning of the social order). Consequently, we need to consider more pragmatically how reform is to be achieved. Cultural maps of meaning and behaviour do not seem amenable to rapid change on a societal level let alone on a global scale. Rather, transformation is measured in decades, centuries and the *longue durée*. This is not an argument for quietism, complacency or the status quo but a call to put pragmatic assessment of the achievable before fantasy and wish fulfilment in a world that is not constituted as we might wish it to be (see Chapters 8 and 9).

Of course, social and cultural change has indeed occurred since Williams wrote *The Long Revolution* in the mid-1960s. However, the character of the contemporary scene in the West, and the changes it has undergone, are not supportive of planned revolutionary cultural transformation. For example, the alterations in the way that we speak about race and gender, including movements towards multiculturalism and gender justice (insufficient though we may feel them to be), have been at least forty years in the making (and a case could be made for a much longer period of time). Above all, the increasing speed and complexity of the global order at the dawn of the twenty-first century are making human performance, and therefore the unintended consequences of action, increasingly chaotic and unpredictable.

The modernist urge towards order, predictability and control linked to certain knowledge and planned change has reached its limit. In that context, we need to be a little more cautious about what we are seeking to change and for what purposes. We also need to pay close attention to how such change can be productively achieved. Let us remember as we contemplate the consequences of the Russian Revolution, from the Gulags to the Prague Spring, that Marxism was widely held to be an emancipatory philosophy and communism a new dawn for humanity. Similarly, changes in the family over the last thirty years have been hugely liberating for men and women. However, it is not unreasonable, or a sign of conversion to religious fundamentalism, to be concerned about the future of children without fathers and the association of that condition with crime, drug abuse, depression, and so forth, amongst young people (Daniels, 1998).

Conclusions

The concept of culture does not represent a fixed entity in an independent object world but is best thought of as a mobile signifier that denotes different ways of talking about human activity with divergent uses and purposes. Culture as a whole way of life; culture as like a language; culture as representation; culture as a tool; culture as practices; culture as artefacts; culture as spatial arrangements; culture as power; culture as a clustering or knot in a flow of meaning; high culture; popular culture; subculture; chaos culture; culture as administrative routines – these are among the multitudinous ways in which culture has been talked about. None of them are erroneous in the sense of being inaccurate, but they do achieve different purposes and may be more or less applicable in different times and places. The concept of culture is plastic, political and contingent. As such, cultural studies need not feel impelled to 'define' culture in any ultimate fashion, but may utilize the concept for a variety of purposes.

The institutionalized tradition of cultural studies opened its account of culture by describing it as a whole way of life. This had the merits of stressing culture as ordinary within an holistic analysis. However, the idea of culture as a whole way of life remains problematic for it weds culture to bounded places, notably those of the modern nation-state. In the era of globalization, diaspora and the politics of difference, diversity and solidarity, culture is best thought of not as a bounded unit but as a set of overlapping performative language-games that flow with no clear limits or determinations (chaos culture) within the global whole of human life.

Culture is less a matter of locations with roots than of hybrid and creolized cultural routes in global space. Cultures as syncretic and hybridized products of interactions across space are thought of as carving routes rather than possessing roots. They are constellations of temporary coherence or knots in the field of culture that is global in character. Of course, global interconnections are always imbued with power and the terms of cultural mixing are uneven. Indeed, cultural studies is distinguished by its focus on culture as the intersection of power, meaning and change for the purpose of improving the human condition. Here, given the unpredictability of human action within complex systems, we must counsel a watchful pragmatism of 'think global, act local'.

In this context, culture can be thought of as the continual hybridization of meaningful practices or performances in a global context. The marking out of intermediate categories between the performative unit and the global whole is a matter of pragmatic justification related to purpose, including demonstration of how the intermediate (e.g. the community, the nation, the race, the sex, etc.) is constituted by performative language-games. The duality of culture lies in its description as a whole and a part, as the global and the local, as in-place and placeless. In analytical terms, we are required to oscillate between the concept of culture as in-place and the notion of flows within a field of no-place.

5 Subjects, Agents and the Limits of Rational Action

Central problem:
How shall we talk about the actions of persons?

'I' is not the name of a person. (Wittgenstein, 1957 : 410)

The person is a conglomerate of independently functioning systems that in the main reflect non-verbal processing systems in the brain. (Gazzaniga, 1980: 689)

Introduction

This chapter is concerned with one of the most enduring and enigmatic paradoxes of human attempts to explore and explain their own social being, namely the problem of structure and agency or freedom and determination. Although this quandary is commonly posed through questions like 'What are human beings?' and/or 'Are human beings free to act?', I prefer to approach the issue by asking the question: 'How shall we talk about the actions of persons?' This is because we can never generate 'objective' knowledge of the conditions of our own actions but must be content with telling ourselves stories about the world (Chapter 3).

More specifically, we cannot step outside of the means by which we represent both ourselves and the conditions of our existence. Whatever we have to say about both is always already from within the boundaries of 'our' culture. Further, problems that revolve around binaries like structure and action are not problems of universal truth and reality but a case of different languages for different purposes. Thus, we can usefully stop inquiring about what structure or agency 'is' (as if we can observe it as an objective fact outside of representation), and ask instead about how we might best talk about them and for what purposes. That is, the criterion for judgement regarding the languages of subject and agent is not accuracy but usefulness as measured against our values.

We shall be exploring the languages of human determination and agency through three themes:

- We will investigate the constitution of the subject as conceived by cultural studies: that is, the manner in which cultural studies thinks of the subject as a discursive construction yet also proposes that we are cultural and political agents. I conclude that what is required is the capacity for switching between these languages as appropriate and according to our purposes.
- We will explore the limits of discussing human beings as rational animals. In particular, thinking within cultural studies continues to be captured by the language of rationality in relation to the subject. Only the import of psychoanalysis has pointed us towards the non-linear, arational, symbolic and emotionally driven aspects of human behaviour. Yet psychoanalysis has its own problems, not least its spurious claims to science and its phallocentricism, so that, I argue, cultural studies would benefit from engaging with other branches of psychology. In particular, cultural studies can learn from psychotherapy the need for 'alternative stories' to have an affective dimension.
- We will inquire about the plasticity of the cultural subject, its capacity for self-creation and/or its predetermination, through a juxtaposing of constructionism and the science of genetics/biochemistry. I propose that cultural studies' widespread unwillingness to engage with genetics necessarily entails a loss of perspective with regard to the malleability of human beings and thus leads to overly optimistic predictions about what can be achieved by cultural politics in a relatively short space of time. This general theme is picked again up in Chapter 6 in relation to issues of gender, while a fuller discussion of evolutionary biology/psychology can be found in Chapter 10.

The subject of cultural studies

There are a number of writers who stage the subject–object or agency–structure problem within their writing. For cultural studies, none has been more influential of late than Foucault. In his work the agency–structure tension is expressed as the strain between, on the one hand, the construction of persons by the subject positions embedded in discourse, and, on the other hand, the agency implied by the 'ethics of self-mastery', a phrase that Foucault later adopts to describe the means by which we are able to fashion ourselves.

The discursive construction of the subject

Foucault's 'genealogy of the modern subject' traces the derivation and lineage of subjects in and through history, laying down the ground for the claim that the subject is radically historized, that is, the subject is wholly and only the product of history. For Foucault, genealogy's task 'is to expose the body totally imprinted by history and the processes of history's destruction of the body' (1984a: 63).

Subsequently, he argues that we can locate particular kinds of 'regimes of the self' in specific historical and cultural conjunctures. That is, different types of subject are the outcome of specific historical and social formations. In particular, Foucault holds subjects to be discursive constructions, that is, they are said to be formed in discourse or regulated ways of 'speaking'. For Foucault (1972), discourse constructs, defines and produces objects of knowledge in an intelligible way while at the same time excluding other ways of reasoning as unintelligible. This includes the discursive production of subjects.

By way of example, Foucault (1973) explores discourses of madness, and, in particular, statements about madness which give us knowledge about it, the rules which prescribe what is 'sayable' or 'thinkable' about madness, and subjects who personify madness, namely the 'lunatic'. He also describes the manner in which discourses of madness acquire authority and truth at a given historical moment, the practices within institutions that deal with madness, and the idea that different discourses about madness will appear at later historical moments producing new knowledge and a new discursive formation.

Foucault attacks what he calls the 'great myth of the interior', arguing that the subject is an historically specific production of discourse with no transcendental continuity from one subject position to another. To speak is to take up a pre-existent subject position and to be subjected to the regulatory power of that discourse. In this conception, the speaking subject is not the author or originator of a statement but depends on the prior existence of discursive positions. These subject positions 'can be filled by virtually any individual when he formulates the statement; and in so far as one and the same individual may occupy in turn, in the same series of statements, different positions, and assume the role of different subjects' (Foucault, 1972: 94). In short, the process by which we are constituted as subjects is one in which we are 'subject to' social processes that bring us into being as 'subjects for' ourselves and others.

Central to Foucault's work is the subject who is the product of power and its capacity to individualize us. Here power is not simply a negative mechanism of constraint and control but is also understood to be productive of the self. The disciplinary power of schools, work organizations, prisons, hospitals, asylums and the proliferating discourses of sexuality produce subjectivity by bringing individuals into view. They fix them in writing via the discourses of, for example, medical science. Hence the body is a site of disciplinary practices that bring subjects into being, these practices being the consequences of specific historical discourses of crime, punishment, medicine, science, sexuality, and so forth. Thus is power held to be generative and productive of subjectivity.

Foucault concentrates on three disciplinary discourses:

- the 'sciences', which constitute the subject as an object of inquiry;
- technologies of the self, whereby individuals turn themselves into subjects;
- 'dividing practices' which separate the mad from the sane, the criminal from the law-abiding citizen, and friends from enemies.

Disciplinary technologies, which arose in a variety of sites, produce what Foucault called 'docile bodies' that could be 'subjected, used, transformed and improved' (1977: 198). Here, discipline involves the organization of the subject in space through dividing practices, training and standardization. It brings together knowledge, power and control to produce subjects by categorizing and naming them in an hierarchical order through a rationality of efficiency, productivity and 'normalization'. By 'normalization' is meant a normative system of graded and measurable categories and intervals around which individual subjects can be distributed. Classificatory systems are essential to the process of normalization and thus to the production of a range of subjects. For example, schools and universities not only demand that students be in certain places at specific times (classrooms and timetables), but they also supervise activities and grade people in relation to others by judging their (alleged) abilities (e.g. examinations).

Foucault and the problem of agency

Foucault's work concentrates the mind on issues of discourse, discipline and power. Subjects are understood as discursive constructions and the products of power where discourse regulates what can be said and done under determinate social and cultural conditions. As such, Foucault provides us with useful tools for understanding the connections between subjectivity/identity and the social order.

However, Foucault does not provide us with an understanding of how and why particular discourses are 'taken up' by some subjects and not by others or how a subject produced through disciplinary discursive practices can resist power (see Hall, 1996a). That is, he does not provide us with an understanding of the emotional investments by which subjects are attached to discourse, nor does he give us a theory of agency. In this context, Foucault's description of subjects as 'docile bodies', whereby subjects are the 'effect' of discourse, has been of concern to a range of social and cultural activists for he appears to deny subjects the agency that would be required for political action.

Though Foucault's work has inspired more studies of power as constraint and discipline than as the enabling 'power to', it is arguable that his later writing centred on 'techniques of the self' does reintroduce agency and the possibility of resistance and change. Here, Foucault explores how subjects are 'led to focus attention on themselves, to decipher, recognize and acknowledge themselves as subjects of desire' (1985: 5): that is, how the self recognizes him- or herself as a subject and becomes involved in practices of self-constitution, recognition and reflection. This concern with self-production as a discursive practice is centred on the question of ethics as a mode of 'care of the self'.

According to Foucault, while morality is concerned with systems of injunction and interdiction constructed in relation to formalized codes, ethics is concerned with practical advice as to how one should concern oneself with one-self in everyday life. Consequently, morality operates through a set of imposed rules and prohibitions whereas ethics is concerned with the actual practices of subjects in relation to the rules that are recommended to them. These rules are enacted with varying degrees of compliance and creativity. Thus ethics is con-cerned with the practices that are involved in being a good person, a self-disciplined person, a creative person, and so forth. It centres on the 'gov-ernment of others and the government of oneself' so that ethical discourses, which circulate independently of any given particular individual, are ways by which we constitute ourselves, bring ourselves into being (Foucault, 1979, 1984b, 1986).

Foucault goes on to explore the space between a system of laws and an indi-vidual's ethical practices that permits a degree of freedom to subjects in forming their singular behaviour. In particular, he points to an ethics of 'self-mastery' and 'stylization' that is drawn from the inner character of relationships themselves rather than from external rules of prohibition. Thus does Foucault attribute a degree of individual agency and autonomy to subjects even while pointing to the indissociability of subjectivity from social and cultural constraints. Here, ethical discourses construct the subject positions that enable agency to occur.

More broadly, one can argue that regulatory discourses themselves construct the subject positions of agency. That is, agency is a discursive construction exem-plifying the productive character of power. Nevertheless, in order to make Foucault's conception of ethics more workable, we would need to understand how subjects construct the language of ethics and agency, and how this empow-ers them to reflect upon their own actions even as that very language constitutes them as social subjects.

Structuration theory

An alternative conception of the structure–agency problem has been put for-ward by Giddens, who has been a steadfast critic of Foucault for what he takes to be the effacing of agents from the narratives of history. Giddens' structuration theory (Giddens, 1984) centres on the practices by which agents produce and reproduce social structure through their own actions. Regularized human activ-ity (i.e. structure) is not brought into being by individual actors as such, but is continually re-created by them via the very means whereby they express them-selves as actors. That is, in and through their activities, agents reproduce the conditions that make those activities possible. Hence, for Giddens, we are required to talk about the 'duality of structure', by which social organization is not only constraining but also enabling.

Giddens argues that the social order is constructed in and through the every-day activities and accounts of skilful and knowledgeable actors. The resources that actors draw on, and are constituted by, are social in character, and indeed social structure (or regular patterns of activity) distributes resources and competencies unevenly between actors. That is, regularities or structural properties of social systems constitute an actor as an actor so that individuals are shaped by social forces that lie beyond them as particular persons. However, those social structures also enable subjects to act.

Thus, subjectivity is posed as an issue of agency (the individual constructs a project) and of social determination (our projects are socially constructed).

For example, the patterns and practices associated with gender construct men and women differently as subjects. Subsequently, gendered subjectivity enables us to act in specific ways, for example as a mother or father, which itself reproduces and modifies structures of gender once more.

The social construction of agency

Although Giddens tends to stress agency while Foucault concentrates on discipline and determination, both writers require us to think of subjects both as being determined and as having agency. In order for this argument to be workable, we must differentiate between a metaphysical notion of the free self-constituting agent and a concept of agency as socially produced.

There is an important conceptual difference between agents who are held to be free in the sense of 'not determined' and agency as the socially constituted capacity to act. While the former concept makes no sense, for there can be no uncaused human acts, the latter asks us to consider agency as consisting of acts which make a pragmatic difference. Here, agency means the enactment of X rather than Y course of action. Of course, precisely because socially constructed agency involves differentially distributed social resources that give rise to various degrees of the ability to act in specific spaces, so some actors have more scope for action than others do and will consequently pursue different paths of activity.

Our ability to enact X rather than Y course of action does not mean that we have made an undetermined selection of activity. Rather, the basis for our choice has been determined or caused by the very way we are constituted as subjects; by where, when and how we came to be who we are. Indeed, a good deal of the actions of modern life are routine in character and are not thought about in a conscious discursive way but are part of our taken-for-granted acts of 'going on'. More often than not, we do not make self-conscious choices at all but follow a socially determined routinized path.

An important aspect of what psychology has to teach us is the idea that we act and choose in ways that are determined by psychic and emotional narratives that we cannot bring wholly to consciousness. That is, to a considerable degree the driving forces of acts have their source outside of the self-consciousness of the agent. Further, contemporary neuroscience suggests that our actions are structured by biochemical operations of the brain over which 'we' (i.e. the stream of language that brains produce and the processes of emotional identification with it) have no self-conscious control. That is, even when we are at our most rational and discursive, we act and think as a consequence of a set of brain processes of which we are not aware and over which we do not have self-conscious control. As far as the self-conscious self is concerned, thoughts simply appear in the space of the mind.

Agency is best understood as the socially and biochemically constructed capacity to act, where nobody is free in the sense of undetermined (in which event, one could not 'be' at all).

Nevertheless, agency is a culturally intelligible way of understanding ourselves and we clearly have the existential experience of facing and making choices. We do act even though social and biological forces that lie beyond us as individual subjects shape those choices and acts. Indeed, neither human freedom nor human action can consist of an escape from social determinants. Consequently, it is felicitous to consider freedom and determination as different modes of discourse or different languages for different purposes.

As such, it is a rather pointless metaphysical question to ask whether people are 'really' free or 'really' determined in any absolute sense. Rather, discourses of freedom and discourses of determination are different socially produced narratives about human beings that have different purposes and are applicable in different ways. Thus, our everyday practice and existential experience of decision making is not changed by the notion that we are the products of biochemical and cultural determination. Indeed, since the languages of freedom and determination are socially produced for different purposes in different realms, it makes sense to talk about freedom from political persecution or economic scarcity without the need to say that agents are free in some undetermined way. Rather, such discourses are comparing different social formations and determinations and judging one to be better than another on the basis of our culturally determined values.

Originality, innovation and change

To hold that subjectivity is contingent and determined does not mean that we are not 'original'. While subjectivity is a social and cultural accomplishment, our individuality can be understood in terms of the specific ways in which the resources of the self are arranged. That is, while we are all subject to the 'impress of history', the particular form that we take and the specific arrangements of discursive elements are unique to each individual, for we have all had singular patterns of biochemistry, family relations, friends, work and access to discursive resources.

The self is original in the manner of a matchless snowflake that has been constructed from the common ingredients of hydrogen and oxygen. Further, in the context of contemporary western societies it is intelligible to say that we can make ourselves singular by making new languages. This does not mean that we are not caused or determined, but rather that we produce new metaphors to describe ourselves with and expand our repertoire of alternative descriptions (Rorty, 1991a).

Nor does the determined or caused contingency of the self make the question of innovative acts especially problematic, for they can be understood as the practical outcomes of unique combinations of social structures, discourses and psychic arrangements. Innovation is not an intrinsic quality of an act but is a retrospective judgement made by us on the form and outcomes of that act in relation to other acts in specific historical and cultural conjunctures. Innovation can also be understood as a question of 'performance-in-context' insofar as innovative acts are the consequence of discourses formed in one sphere of cultural life that have been transported into another. For example, discourses of individuality and creativity formed in and through artistic practices or in the domain of leisure activities may have unexpected consequences in the context of discipline-oriented work organizations, schools or in families structured around parental authority and control. Innovation and change are possible because we are unique interdiscursive individuals and because the discourses that circulate throughout our culture are themselves contradictory.

Structure and agency: a problem of language

Our 'final vocabularies' (Rorty, 1989), that is, those explanations that we cannot currently do without, are always historically and culturally contingent. Consequently, cultural analysis cannot offer ultimate single resolutions of questions but instead substitutes one form of expression for another. There is no vocabulary that is universally 'true' in the sense of accurately representing structure and agency or what human beings 'really are' in any final or metaphysical sense. Rather, we tell a variety of constitutive stories and make a series of truth claims of and about ourselves whose purposes lie in the production of meaning and as signposts to action. Beyond language is that about which we cannot speak. Even if we can *be* in a world without signs that collapses the subject–object distinction, we are currently stuck with a dualist language.

Consequently, the 'problem' of structure and action is best tackled as a question of language and purpose rather than one of universal truth.

To investigate the problem of structure and agency, a riddle that has been set up by the very way we talk about ourselves in the first place, one must enter the realm of metaphors. The language of the individual subject is valuable when it provides the means to celebrate the cultural power and capacities of persons. Indeed, the language of agency encourages us to act and to seek improvement of the human condition. Additionally, it is deployed to persuade us to take responsibility for our actions or in circumstances where institutions, for example the courts, wish to hold persons accountable for specific acts.

However, it is also useful to point to the wider contours of discourse and cultural life that enable some courses of action while disempowering others. Here the purposes are solidarity and/or the alleviation of individual responsibility. Analytically, the language of determination helps to trace causality home while therapeutically it assists us in accepting that there are limits to the plasticity of the human condition and to our capacity to construct ourselves. This is the language of the dance in which we actively and creatively perform ourselves through the pre-ordained steps of a cosmic choreography that has no author.

As was argued in Chapter 2, the metaphor of 'language as a tool' that guides the notion of 'languages for purposes' should not be read as implying the rational intentionality of a pre-existent subject (i.e. one who wields the tool). Language speaks us as much as we speak language. Thus, it is not easy to shut off the flow of thoughts that bubble to the surface of the mind independently of self-conscious choice. Indeed, discussion of agency is consistently marred by the assumption that it consists in the premeditated acts of rational beings rather than lying in the simple capacity to enact X or Y, a province that for much of our lives is not driven by self-conscious reflection at all. Here psychoanalysis, psychology and biochemistry all point us to the limits of the rational.

The limits of the rational mind

Most of the stories spawned by western cultures assume that human life is explicable in terms of the rational choices of individual actors. The concept of rationality refers here to the grounds on which beliefs are held: namely that they are coherent, logical and compatible with experience. That is, beliefs and actions are the outcome of sound reasoning and valid inference. Since it is irrational to hold beliefs known to be false, then rationality implies that the grounds for holding beliefs are the foundations of truth. Here, both truth and rationality are grounded in the rule-governed social and cultural conventions of reason giving rather than in metaphysics.

Rationality, like truth, is a form of social commendation founded on cultural procedures rather than a universal given. Thus, within these terms, rational action is that which can be justified within a specific cultural context.

Of course, it is unlikely that thinkers associated with cultural studies would want to adopt the notion of the economically rational actor who calculates the means to maximize his or her interests. Nevertheless, there has been an implicit assumption not only that rationality could provide logical explanations for cultural phenomena, but also that the production and dissemination of rational analysis would further key cultural and political goals. For example, the common assumption made by many has been that racism and sexism would dwindle in the face of rational argument. This kind of thinking derives from two related sources:

- the everyday common-sense faith in rationality that pervades western culture;
- the primacy given to the systematic and logical analysis of language in the absence of any consideration of the role of emotion in speech and action.

Too often absent from analyses undertaken within cultural studies are the non-linear, non-rational and emotionally driven aspects of human behaviour. The exception to this observation is the import of psychoanalysis. For example, Hall (1990, 1992b, 1996a) and Butler (1993) have profitably explored Lacanian psychoanalysis to argue that identity is best understood as the suture of the 'inside' with the 'outside', that is, the processes by which our psychic identifications or emotional investments are attached to disciplinary discourses. At the same time, the psychoanalytic work of Mitchell, Chodorow, Kristeva, Irigaray and Rose has also made inroads into cultural studies, especially through feminist analyses.

Yet psychoanalysis has its own problems, not least in its spurious claims to objective science and its phallocentricism. Consequently, I shall be arguing that cultural studies would benefit from engaging with other branches of psychology and psychotherapy. Not only can these fields of practice assist us to explain the formation of subjectivity and cultural action, but they may enable us to intervene more effectively in cultural politics through the use of popular stories, images and myths that have an affective dimension.

Psychoanalysis in cultural studies

The main interest of cultural studies writers in psychoanalysis has centred on the formation of gendered subjectivity. For Hall (1996a), psychoanalysis has particular significance in shedding light on how discursively constructed subject positions are taken up (or otherwise) by concrete persons through their fantasy identifications and emotional 'investments'. This argument is Hall's response to what he sees as Foucault's weakness in not providing a description of the mechanisms by which subject positions are occupied or otherwise by living persons. Indeed, this contention is central to Hall's conceptualization of 'identity' as the point of suture, between on the one hand the discourses and practices which attempt to 'interpellate', speak to us or hail us into place as the social subjects of particular discourses, and on the other hand, the processes which produce subjectivities, which construct us as subjects which can be 'spoken'. Identities are thus the points of temporary attachment to the subject positions which discursive practices construct for us. (1996a: 5–6)

According to Freud (1977), the self is constituted in terms of an ego, or conscious rational mind, a superego, or social conscience, and the unconscious, the source and repository of the symbolic workings of the mind that functions with a different logic from reason. Since the self is by definition fractured into the ego, superego and unconscious, the unified narrative of the self can be understood as something we attain over time through entry into the symbolic order of language and culture. That is, through processes of identification with others and with social discourses we create an identity that embodies the chimera of wholeness.

The libido or sexual drive does not have any pre-given fixed aim or object. Rather, through fantasy, any object, which includes persons or parts of bodies, can be the target of desire. Thus, an almost infinite number of sexual objects and practices are within the domain of human sexuality. Subsequently, Freud's work is concerned to document and explain the regulation and repression of this 'polymorphous perversity' through the resolution (or not) of the Oedipus complex into the normative fate of heterosexual gendered relationships. Here, anatomy is destiny because bodily differences are signifiers of sexual and social differentiation, making it hard to escape the regulatory scripts that surround physical difference.

In Lacan's (1977) influential reading of Freud, the resolution of the Oedipus complex marks the formation of the unconscious as the realm of the repressed, and the very possibility of gendered subjects is established through entry into the symbolic order. The Oedipus complex involves a boy's desire for his mother as the primary love object, a desire that is prohibited by the symbolic order in the form of the incest taboo. Specifically, the father represents to boys the threat of castration that such prohibited desire brings forth. Consequently, boys shift their identification from the mother to the father, who is identified with the symbolic position of power and control (the Phallus). For girls, this process involves the acceptance that they have already been castrated. This leads to fury and partial identification with the mother as a gendered role together with the association of fathers with authority, domination and mastery.

For Lacan, the symbolic order is the over-arching structure of language and received social meanings. It is the domain of human law and culture whose composition is materialized in the very structure of language that forms the subject positions from which one may speak. Crucially, these are gendered subject positions as the Phallus serves to break up the mother–child dyad and stands for entry into the symbolic order. Indeed, it is the Phallus as 'transcendental signifier' that enables entry into language (for both sexes) and, by standing in for the fragmented subject, allows the construction of a narrative of wholeness.

The symbolic Phallus is the privileged and universal signifier because it is the law of the Name-of-the-Father that organizes the symbolic order and the infant's entry into it (since it is the symbolic father that prohibits desire for the mother). In addition, the unconscious is the site for the generation of meaningful representations that, in Lacanian terms, are structured 'like a language'. Not only is language the route to the unconscious, but the unconscious is a site of signification, that is, meaningful activity. In particular, the mechanisms of condensation and displacement, which Freud saw as the most important of the 'primary processes', are held by Lacan to be analogous to the linguistic functions of metaphor and metonymy.

Some problems with psychoanalysis

Although influential within cultural studies, the Lacanian reading of Freud poses a number of unanswered questions. For example:

- If gendered subjects are the outcome of subjection to the symbolic order, how can they be, at one and the same time, a necessary condition of the resolution of the Oedipus complex that itself marks entry into that very same symbolic order?
- How is it possible, once we are formed as gendered subjects, to struggle against and change the language of patriarchy – or are we forever formed in this way?
- Can psychoanalysis be cleansed of its phallocentricism?

Both Freud and Lacan have been attacked for being phallocentric. That is, their work is said to be a set of male-centred discourses in general and more specifically ones that are focused on the Phallus. For example, Freud's understanding of the Oedipal moment relies on the assertion that women would 'naturally' see their genitals as inferior and that heterosexual genital activity that stresses masculine power and feminine passivity is the normal form of sexuality. Further, for Lacan, it is the symbolic Phallus that serves as a 'transcendental signifier' that enables subject formation. Here the Phallus is that which covers over a sense of lack, allowing the subject to experience itself as a unity. For some critics (Irigaray, 1985a, 1985b), the centrality of the Phallus to Lacan's argument renders 'woman' an adjunct term. That is, in Lacanian psychoanalysis the feminine is always repressed and entry into the symbolic inevitably tied to the Father/Phallus.

More sympathetic critics (Chodorow, 1978, 1989; Mitchell, 1974; J. Rose, 1997) argue that Freud's patriarchal assumptions are an expression of *his* value system and not inherent to psychoanalysis *per se*. Psychoanalysis, they argue, could be

cleansed of these assumptions and the historical specificity of its categories rec-
ognized and reworked. Consequently, the particular kinds of psychic resolutions
that psychoanalysis describes are to be understood not as universals of the
human condition but as historically and culturally specific productions. Thus,
for its supporters, the great strength of psychoanalysis lies its rejection of the
fixed nature of subjects and sexuality, leading us to concentrate instead on the
construction and formation of subjectivity.

However, while psychoanalysis has proved useful in pointing us to the psychic and emotional aspects of human life, and in particular to the concept of
identification, there are numerous other ways to explore the historical and cultural formation of subjects. Why then should we be stuck with myths like the
Oedipus complex or the Phallus as transcendental signifier when we can do
without them? Ironically, the Oedipal myth underscores psychoanalysis's spurious claims to universal scientific truth. As was argued in Chapter 3, science is
best understood as a set of agreed procedures that give rise to regimes of truth.
Unfortunately, those of psychoanalysis are neither agreed nor for the most part
empirically testable and repeatable. Consequently, psychoanalysis should be
treated as a set of poetic, metaphorical and mythological stories with consequences. Its truths lie in its practice and its outcomes.

Further, as Nikolas Rose (1996) argues, psychoanalysis is an historically specific way of understanding persons that cannot be used as the basis for an
investigation of the historicity of being human. Indeed, insofar as psychoanalysis relies on linguistic and cultural processes that are deemed to be ahistorical
and universal, since they mark the psychic processes of humankind across history, then at the very least it sits uncomfortably within a cultural studies that
emphasizes the cultural construction of subjectivity. Indeed, the obscurity of its
language, its bogus science and its phallocentricism are real problems for psychoanalysis, particularly when other forms of psychotherapy can do its job more
effectively.

Constructionism as an alternative to psychoanalysis

It is somewhat surprising that cultural studies writers have not made more of
that strand of psychology that is embedded in social constructionism (e.g.
Gergen and Shotter) and/or that discursive psychology which emphasizes language in the constitution of persons (e.g. Billig, Potter, Edwards, etc.). Here, the
limits of language mark the edge of our cognitive understanding of the world,
for our acculturation in and through language is constitutive of our values,
meanings and knowledge. As such, there are no culturally transcendental or
ahistorical elements to what it is to be a human being. Indeed, the very notion of
what it is to be a person is a cultural variable.

Historical and cross-cultural work suggest that the resources that form the
material for personhood are the language and cultural practices of specific times

and places. Indeed, for Elias (1978, 1982), the very concept of 'I' as a self-aware object is a modern western conception that emerged out of science and the 'Age of Reason'. In short, we are constituted as individuals in a social process using culturally shared materials. Meaning is formed in the 'joint action' of social relationships, accounting practices and conversations (Shotter, 1993). Without language, not only would we not be persons as we commonly understand that concept, but the very notion of personhood and identity would be unintelligible to us. Consequently, our maps and constructs of the world are never simply matters of individual interpretation but are inevitably a part of the wider cultural repertoire of discursive explanations, resources and maps of meaning available to members of cultures.

In this vein, Potter and Wetherell (1987) have sought to demonstrate that fundamental psychological notions such as attitudes, emotions and the inner mind could be approached through the examination of a shared language. In particular, they argue that there are no 'things' that are called emotions or attitudes that lurk behind language. Emotions can, of course, be understood as biological functions of the nervous system (Chapter 10). However, this view is not incompatible with discursive psychology.

As William James (1890) argued, it is not so much that we run from a bear because we are afraid but that we are afraid because we are running. That is, our body reacts before our cognitive processes can label and assess the situation. In broad terms, contemporary brain research agrees with James that emotions are first and foremost to be understood as reactions generated by the brain before cognitive functions name and evaluate (LeDoux, 1998). In this sense, emotions are things that happen to us rather than something we will and control. Subsequently, the languages of emotion can be understood as convenient ways of talking about ourselves and guiding our self-conscious responses to our unconscious reactions.

As Potter and Wetherell (1987) argue, the constitutive nature and action-orientation of language mean that any state of affairs, for example, states of mind or emotions, can be described in different ways, giving rise to variability of accounts. In other words, events are put 'under description' by a variety of languages that constitute them in different ways (Davidson, 1984). Consequently, both cultural studies and psychology are required to examine the rhetorical organization of the linguistic and cultural repertoires by which we construct specific accounts of ourselves, including our emotions.

The logic of these arguments suggests that one isn't motivated or incited to action by emotions; rather, 'one *does* emotions, or participates in them as he or she would on a stage' (Gergen, 1994: 222). Concepts like anger, love, fear, sadness, and so forth do not have referents in identifiable and discrete mental conditions. The language of emotion gains its meaning not by reference to 'internal' states but by the way it operates within patterns of cultural relationships. Here we need to remind ourselves that phrases like 'inside the mind' or the 'inner self' are metaphors that guide us in action not references to literal places or entities. Thus, narratives of self-identity and the language of emotion can be understood as forms of social accounting or public discourse. In this context self-narratives act as 'a linguistic implement embedded within conventional sequences of action and employed in relationships in such a way as to sustain, enhance, or impede various forms of action' (Gergen, 1994: 188).

Here we have resources for an emergent 'cultural psychology' (Shweder, 1995) that collapses binaries like subject/object, form/content, person/environment, psyche/culture, and so forth. The fundamental premise of cultural psychology is that no socio-cultural environment exists independently of the way humans capture meanings and resources from it. Equally, every human being's subjectivity and mental life are constructed and altered through the processes of apprehending meanings and resources from the environment and using them. Thus,

> Cultural psychology aims to develop a principle of intentionality – action responsive to and directed at mental objects or representations – by which culturally constituted realities (intentional worlds) and reality-constituting psyches (intentional persons) continually and continuously make each other up, perturbing and disturbing each other, interpenetrating each other's identity, reciprocally conditioning each other's existence. (Shweder, 1995: 71)

In trying to find ways to talk about the psyche and culture so that neither is by nature intrinsic or extrinsic to each other, cultural psychology conceives of the world in terms of non-linear dynamic processes with circular or dialectical feedback loops between subject/object, person/environment, psyche /culture, and so on.

Constructionism and pragmatic therapy

While analysis should not attribute constructs to individuals as if they were self-originating unified and self-centred beings, nevertheless, our stories are performative in the sense that they enact and constitute that which they purport to describe. They are actions in the world that are to be evaluated according to their felicity within a procedure or social convention constituted by patterns of relationship. As such, it remains pragmatically and therapeutically useful to suggest that we can reflexively rewrite our scripts. Thus, it is a central assumption of psychotherapy that all constructs can be changed so that 'better' interpretations and predictions can be made. Here 'better' means the adoption of new stories and new languages that have consequences held to be an improvement in the lives of ourselves and others as measured against cultural values (which themselves may have been modified or re-prioritized). That is, the validity or pragmatic usefulness of stories is tested through performance in the context of social relationships, with different cultural constructions of the world generating divergent consequences.

In order to display and manifest ourselves as intelligible persons, we tell stories in the context of social relationships so that narratives are rationales for courses of action. In the therapeutic situation persons are in principle able to reconstruct the stories of the past, bringing them into line with the requirements of the present, thereby consolidating an emotional narrative with which they feel relatively content. This practice operates on the assumption that meaning is created by people who actively impose their constructs onto life events in the context of their purposes and goals. Here, therapy involves making reflexively explicit the constructs that are constitutive of ourselves and our actions, including the retelling of stories about the past and the generation of a range of alternative narratives in the context of a dynamic relationship between client and therapist.

According to Viney (1996), the assumptions of constructivist therapy include the idea that people use linguistic constructs, or personal meanings, to make sense of what happens to them. These constructs form a system that is forged through a series of interpretations and predictions that constitute a life-story. Exploring a person's constructs, which are deemed 'healthy' to the degree that they act as useful predictors and guides, enables understanding of his or her actions. Personal construct systems are 'locked into', indeed constitutive of, emotions so that confirmation of the usefulness and validity of one's construct system is intertwined with positive feelings, while more negative emotions are implicated in unsuccessful interpretation and prediction.

Thus, Rowe (1996) argues that to become 'depressed' one has to have acquired over the years a set of interlinked constructs that relate to the particular circumstances of one's life. These include a self-constituting description of the self as bad, evil and valueless while other people are to be feared, hated and envied. For such a person, life is terrible to the point where 'only bad things happened to me in the past and only bad things will happen to me in the future'. Above all, such a person feels unable to forgive anyone, least of all him- or herself. In a not dissimilar way, Seligman (1990) has explored the manner in which a gloomy world-view constituted by a learned vocabulary of pessimism underpins an array of 'affective disorders'. It is important at this stage to remind ourselves that emotional life is arational in the sense that we have not calculatedly chosen a particular mental vocabulary or rationally decided to be happy or miserable.

In so far as 'emotion' is taken to be a performance, a cultural dance, then self redescription implies, indeed requires, an affective shift in being. At some level there has to be a displacement in feeling simultaneous with the taking on of new maps of the meaning.

That is, rewriting a self-narrative involves an emotional shift that constitutes a transformation of one's whole being. An important implication for cultural studies is that personal and social change is never going to be a simple matter of argument and analysis. Yet, outside of the use of therapeutic drugs, language remains the primary means by which we seek to make alterations in our emotional identifications.

Constructionism and the language of biochemistry

As we have noted, the ascendant constructionist understanding of identity within cultural studies grasps it in terms of the suturing of the discursive 'outside' with the emotional or psychic 'inside'. There is, as I have indicated, much to be said in favour of social constructionism and its emphasis on the linguistic and cultural fashioning of subjectivity and identity. However, the 'inside' is not best understood in the psychoanalytic terms that Hall (1992b, 1996a) deploys; rather, emotion involves the stitching together of language with biochemical brain processes.

Of course there should be no question here of setting up biochemistry in opposition to the role of language and culture (or vice versa). Rather, we should be concerned with their mutual interdependence and interpenetration. After all, language itself is dependent on the functioning of the brain. Biochemistry and psychology are, in the final vocabulary currently available to us, not only inseparable but 'the same thing' (being otherwise describable as different languages for different purposes).

There is a considerable body of evidence to suggest that there are evolutionary, genetic and biochemical explanations for many of the differences between the emotional responses of persons. Thus, a tendency towards worry and anger, addiction and thrill seeking all have genetic ingredients that predispose subjects to particular kinds of behaviour. For example, one of the hallmarks of genetically influenced behavioural patterns is that they run in families, as evidenced by the study of twins. Here research has suggested that the separate symptoms of depression and anxiety are 33 per cent to 46 per cent heritable, while the coinheritance of the two conditions has been shown to be 99 per cent. That is, anxiety and depression have the same genetic root (Hamer and Copeland, 1998).

Thus, the anxiety and depression that psychotherapy attributes to our life scripts are widely thought by scientists and psychiatrists *also* to have biochemical and genetic components (LeDoux, 1998; Salmans, 1997). Some people have a greater predisposition than others towards emotional sensitivity and 'harm avoidance' strategies such as depression, anxiety, fear or hostility. This is likely to be the consequence of both genetic predisposition and an evolutionary strategy hard-wired into the brain. For example, depression is associated with an evolutionary strategy of 'realistic' appraisals of an actor's circumstances, including the acceptance of defeat so as to be able to live to fight another day (Buss, 1999a). Further, there is evidence that emotional responses involve differential brain activity on the left and right frontal lobes, with the right side more involved in controlling negative emotions and the left concerned with positive emotions.

LeDoux (1998), one of the world's leading investigators into the biochemical character of the 'emotional brain', argues that emotions are events that happen to us rather than things we will to occur. Consequently, we have little direct self-conscious control over our initial emotional reactions. The structure of the brain is such that external stimuli can provoke emotional responses at a level 'below' consciousness and before the cognitive aspects of our brain can name and attempt to control them. Further, the patterns of brain activity associated with fear and anxiety-provoking stimuli are 'burned' into the brain through the strengthening of repeatedly used synaptic connections. Hence, conditions like post-traumatic stress syndrome and obsessive-compulsive disorder are the outcome of fear conditioning.

Indeed, the examination of the capacities of the brain must be set in the context of human biological evolution (Chapter 10), whereby the reactive capacities of fear and anxiety predate the appearance of language and cognitive abilities. Further, the links that connect the emotional circuits of the brain to the cortex (responsible for cognitive capacities) are stronger than those running in the reverse direction, hence the relative ease with which our thoughts are flooded and overcome by emotion and the comparatively greater difficulty of using language and thought to control them.

Yet, a genetic predisposition towards, for example, depression and anxiety is just that, a predisposition and not an ironclad certainty, for these conditions also have social and cultural roots. The rise of depression to epidemic proportions in the western world cannot easily be attributed to genetics alone, for the time-scales involved are radically different. The evolution of genetic capacities is a slow process taking thousands of years, whereas the rise of depression has taken place over the last fifty years. One must conclude, then, that social and cultural conditions have increasingly triggered biochemical proclivities.

These cultural and environmental factors will include the rising expectations of material success allied to increased work stress and performance demands as well as the speed-up of daily life and the breakdown of community support networks, the family and meaningful belief systems found in various religions.

Today, we commonly generate emotional responses that were germane for our ancestors and their environment but that are inappropriate in the context of a contemporary human culture wherein we have cast ourselves to the winds of uncertainty, continually remaking ourselves as an ongoing project without foundations.

Perhaps this helps to explain our culture's growing interest in, and application of, psychotherapy.

Psychotherapy and biochemistry

Contemporary psychotherapeutic literature suggests that the low self-esteem and predilection for being emotionally wounded that lies at the base of depression is rooted in family life. Indeed, it is a bedrock argument of psychotherapy that adult personal attachments and relationships restage aspects of childhood encounters. Consequently, for many depressed and anxious people, life becomes a restless search to overcome their feelings of inadequacy rooted in the biochemical consequences of family experience. While the literature of psychotherapy often concentrates on trauma, it is frequently the less dramatic childhood injuries of meanness and neglect that take up residence in the mind. As much as physical violence, it is the lack of nurturing and guidance that leaves its mark.

A child's most common reaction in the face of family trauma is to take responsibility for the failing parent. In order to preserve the emotional attachment to the parent, and in a desperate attempt to maintain the sense of security that derives from being cared for by competent adults, children will tend to blame themselves.

> All of the abused child's psychological adaptations serve the fundamental purpose of preserving her primary attachment to her parents in the face of daily evidence of their malice. By developing a contaminated, stigmatized identity, the child victim takes the evil of the abuser into herself and thereby preserves her attachment. Because the inner sense of badness (shame) preserves a relationship, it is not readily given up even after the abuse has stopped; rather, it becomes a stable part of the child's personality structure. Similarly, adult survivors who have escaped from abusive situations continue to view themselves with contempt and to take upon themselves the shame and guilt of their abusers. The profound sense of inner badness becomes the core around which the abused child's identity is formed, and it persists into adult life. (Herman, 1992: 102)

Toxic parents come in many guises: there are the sexual abusers, the violent bashers, the verbal torturers, the silent neglecters, the active controllers and the plain incompetent. The outcome is that, 'at the core of every formerly mistreated adult – even high achievers – is a little child who feels powerless and afraid' (Forward, 1990: 16). In this context, the much-used therapeutic metaphor of the 'inner child' expresses the internalization of emotional language and behavioural maps associated with our early life. The stage is then set for the compulsive re-enactment of childhood routines that are broken only though a verbal declaration of emotional independence and responsibility. If the shackles of noxious parenting are not cast off, then further painful relationships and attempts at self-medication invariably follow.

Significantly, there is a growing consensus within the medical and therapeutic communities that the best results in the treatment of anxiety and depression are currently achieved through a combination of drugs and psychotherapy. The roots of depression are planted in genetic and biochemical dispositions inter-twined with family trauma. Indeed, one of the most fascinating aspects of current research is the evidence that personal experience, including the way we think, can alter the biochemistry of the brain. Thus, childhood trauma can have 'lifelong psycho-biological consequences' (Real, 1998: 103), with post-traumatic stress syndrome marking the extreme bio-psychological outcomes of dramatic events.

Thus, experiments with primates show that separation from the mother pro-motes changes in serotonin and adrenal enzyme levels, suggesting that social and cultural events can have biochemical consequences. For example, psy-chotherapy can be put 'under the description' of biochemistry. There is also evidence that learning or changing our patterns of thinking alters brain bio-chemistry (LeDoux, 1998). In this way, 'learned pessimism' as an explanatory style, which Seligman (1990) cites as the main cause of depression, and the acquisition of optimism that apparently relieves it, may well be implicated in changing biochemistry.

Certainly the evidence that Seligman cites to suggest that pessimism depletes the immune system while optimistic thinking boosts it suggests the ability of thought to amend the body. Seligman's work, along with the mounting evi-dence that cognitive and emotional states influence our probability of becoming ill and our capacities to heal (Kabat-Zinn, 1990), collapses the western cultural mind-body distinction. Thus, the rewriting of the self with which psychotherapy is implicated involves not just words but new conduct, and not just new conduct but alterations in biochemistry.

Language and culture dig deep down into the body (LeDoux, 1998; Pinker, 1994), so that what Goleman (1995) calls 'emotional intelligence' is not only culturally learned but simul-taneously etched into the biochemistry of the brain.

Biology and therapy agree that affective conditions like anxiety and depres-sion are the outcome of traumatic learning experiences in conjunction with genetic predispositions. In more general terms we can say that emotions are simultaneously linguistic, cultural and biochemical. Or, to put this differently, the language of emotions is put to linguistic, cultural and biochemical ends. Biochemistry, genetics and linguistics are constituted by a particular type of vocabulary deployed for the achievement of specific purposes. Their arguments should be understood not as the correspondence of language with an inde-pendent object world but as the practical achievements of agreed procedures. If they work for our particular purposes, then they are 'true' within that domain of knowledge.

We do not yet have a fully convincing vocabulary to describe the limits to behaviour that biochemistry may set, or how the interface between the bio-logical brain and consciousness works. Yet, in pragmatic terms, both drugs and psychotherapy can be successful in treating depression. The test is empirical and pragmatic, related to purposes and values not one of correspondence between the language of biochemistry or psychology and 'real' bodies. At the same time, what it *means* to be a person remains a cultural question. Consequently, we may say that the subject of biology and the subject of the discursive-performative are variable accounts of personhood deployed for different purposes. The language of biology enables us to make behavioural and bodily predictions and alterations through, for example, the use of drugs. The language of the discursive-performative helps to recast the symbolic, for example through psychotherapy, and to rethink the way we talk about and perform cultural identities.

In sum, cultural studies' concern with the formation of the subject and identity must move beyond conceptions of human beings as primarily rational language users and embrace the arational and emotional aspects of our existence. In doing so, we must overcome our aversion to science in general, and biochemistry in particular, while simultaneously looking beyond the obsession with psychoanalysis to more discursive forms of psychology. The outcome should be a more useful and less naïve model of human action that recognizes that there are limits not only to rational action but also to the plasticity of the human subject.

Conclusions

The work of contemporary cultural studies has centred on questions of subjectivity and identity. Subjectivity, that is, the condition of being a person, is argued to be an outcome of cultural processes, notably the acquisition of language, which bring us into being as 'subjects for' ourselves and others. Identity, it is said, is best understood not as a fixed entity but rather as an emotionally charged description of ourselves. Identities are discursive-performative, that is, identity is understood to be the 'effect' of discursive practice that enacts or produces that which it names.

After Foucault, cultural studies has seen the subject as the 'effect' of historically specific discourses and disciplinary practices. However, we observed that Foucault's work has difficulties explaining the mechanisms by which particular subjects 'take up' certain discourses, and thus how agency could be possible. Yet Foucault also proposed a form of agency through a discursively constructed ethics centred on the care of the self. Indeed, agency can be said to be a subject position within discourse. At the very least, agency is a matter not of premeditated and rational intentionality but of the socially constituted capacity to act. This is driven more by the unconscious processes of the brain and arational discourses of emotion than by discursive rationality.

We may understand identity in terms of those regulatory discourses to which we are attached through processes of identification or emotional investment. However, I have argued that psychoanalysis does not offer us the best route for understanding the emotional self. Rather, from discursive psychology we can learn about the constitution of emotion without assuming that states of mind lurk behind language. Further, through the study of language usage (discourse analysis and conversation analysis), we can explore the mechanisms by which identity claims are achieved in day-to-day linguistic encounters. As such, we can develop a more finely grained reflexive understanding of how personal and social change are possible. This is likely to lead to the conclusion that symbols, myths, novels, plays and other practices with an affective dimension are more effective politically than are rationally and logically constructed arguments. We need inspiration and faith as much as science and rationality.

Since cultural studies holds the subject to be historically and culturally specific, so cultural politics is concerned with the writing of new stories that define the world and the struggle to make those definitions stick. The plastic and changeable character of persons marks the cultural politics of subjectivity and identity as being concerned with the power to name and represent what it means to be male, female, black, white, young, old, and so forth. Consequently, cultural politics can be conceived of as a series of collective social struggles organized around the nodal points of class, gender, race, sexuality, age, and so forth, that seek to redescribe the social in terms of specific values and hoped-for consequences.

However, it is a mistaken assumption that flows from social constructionism that the human subject is entirely plastic and malleable. Rather, the human mind is the outcome of evolutionary and biochemical processes that, at any given moment, set limits to the humanly possible. This argument does not mean that we should not continue to struggle for change (in an imperfect world this will always happen anyway). However, it does ask us to recognize the complexity and limits of the task at hand when we have only restricted, if any (thoughts and actions happen on their own), self-conscious control over our minds and behaviour and where the biological body circumscribes the possible. Indeed, one of the most interesting questions of the hour is the mutual constitution, interdependence and interpenetration of language, culture and biochemistry (see Chapter 10).

6 Identity, Equality and Difference:
The politics of gender

Central problem:
Is gender equality possible and desirable?

[T]he work that cultural studies has to do is to mobilize everything that it can in terms of intellectual resources in order to understand what keeps making the lives we live, and the societies we live in, profoundly and deeply antihuman in their capacity to live with difference. (Hall, 1996d: 343)

I will be saddened if this book [*The Myth of Male Power*] is misused to attack the legitimate issues of the women's movement – issues for which I spent a decade of my life fighting. The challenge is both to go beyond feminism and to cherish its contributions. And feminism's contributions are many. (Farrell, 1993: 13)

Introduction

During the 1990s, cultural studies lent intellectual support, through its theorization of identity as discursive and without essence, to the political endeavours of feminists, gays, lesbians and others who commonly hold human sexuality and gender to be wholly malleable. The argument is that since sex and gender are social constructions, then they are entirely open to change. In turn, this position suggests that only the cultural power of men stands between women and social equality. In this chapter I want to explore some aspects of these debates. First, I want to ask about the meaning of 'equality' in the context of a conception of identity that stresses difference. Second, I want to investigate the argument that sex and gender are entirely plastic in the light of scientific evidence from the fields of genetics and biochemistry that suggests otherwise. Third, I want to inquire into the claim that men also suffer as a consequence of our culture's gender expectations.

Identity and difference

The common-sense cultural repertoire of the self that is available to us in the western world describes persons as having a true self, an identity that we possess and that can become known to us. Thus, our culture commonly takes identity to be expressed through forms of representation: that is, identity is an essence that can be signified through signs of taste, beliefs, attitudes and lifestyles. This argument is in direct contrast with the understanding of identity as it has developed within cultural studies, where subjectivity and identity are widely held to be contingent culturally specific productions. That is, identities are wholly social constructions and cannot 'exist' outside of cultural representations that constitute rather than express identity. Subsequently, it is from the plasticity of identity that its political significance flows, for contestation over identity and subjectivity concerns the kinds of people we are becoming. These questions are at the core of the essentialism vs anti-essentialism debates.

The anti-essentialist view of subjectivity and identity is dependent upon the anti-representationalist argument that language is not a mirror that reflects an independent object world (Chapter 2). Rather, meaning is understood to be generated by virtue of the differences between signifiers. Thus, black is not white, men are not women, Australians are not British, and so forth. Since there are no essences to which language refers, then there are no essential identities. In this vein, Hall's (1990, 1992, 1996a) influential account of identity draws on Derrida's concept of *différance* – 'difference and deferral' – by which meanings are continually supplemented or differed. Thus identity is understood as a becoming rather than a fixed entity. However, in order to stabilize identity, and in order to take action, a temporary closure of meaning is required. Consequently, 'identity' is said to represent a 'cut' or a snap-shot of unfolding meanings, a strategic positioning which makes meaning possible. Or, to put this another way:

Identity can be understood as a description of ourselves in language to which we are emotionally committed.

The claim that language is constitutive of identity is not simply an abstract philosophical argument but one located in the everyday social conversations of 'ordinary' life. Identities are achieved in the everyday flow of language and stabilized as categories through their embedding in the pragmatic narratives of our day-to-day social conduct. That is, the construction of identity is 'a fluid accomplishment, instantiated in the procedural flow of verbal interaction' (Widdicombe and Wooffitt, 1995: 218). This suggests that debates about essentialism and anti-essentialism are something of a distraction since, after Wittgenstein, it can be said that the meanings of language are forged in use and embedded in pragmatic narratives. Thus, the stabilizing 'cut' in language which

Hall holds to be the operation of hegemonic power can also be described as the routine operation of pragmatic narratives in social practice.

Gender and difference

The concern with difference in the field of language and identity has under-pinned a growing emphasis within cultural studies on the operation of difference in the domain of culture, and on questions of gender and ethnicity (as forms of difference) in particular. My interest in this chapter is with the former as an exemplar of the politics of difference. Here, feminism is centrally con-cerned with sex as an organizing principle of social life that is thoroughly saturated with power relations subordinating women to men. As a movement, feminism is concerned to construct political strategies by which to intervene in social life in pursuit of the interests of women. However, at this point two cru-cial questions arise: 'What is a woman?' and 'What is in women's interests?'

What is a woman?

One line of feminist argument stresses women's difference from men and their similarity with each other. Thus, Collard and Contrucci (1988) argue that all women are linked by childbearing bodies and innate ties to the natural earth, and that this supports egalitarian, nurturance-based values. Likewise, Rich (1986) celebrates women's difference from men, locating its source in mother-hood. This is condemned in its historical modes of oppression but celebrated for its female power and potentialities. A more culturally founded argument for women's difference comes from Gilligan (1982) and her study of moral reason-ing. She argues that while men are concerned with an abstract 'ethics of justice', women are more centred on a context-specific 'ethics of care'.

Irigaray (1985a, 1985b, 1993) has been amongst those to have spearheaded 'difference feminism' through her attempts to inscribe the feminine by way of *écriture féminine* (woman's writing) and *le parler femme* (womanspeak). She asserts the specificity of the feminine and celebrates the indefinable *jouissance* of women. She speculates on the 'otherness' of the feminine; in particular she turns to the mother–daughter relationship of the pre-Oedipal imaginary as the source of a feminine that cannot be symbolized because it precedes entry into the symbolic order and the Law of the Father. For Irigaray, woman is outside of representation (i.e. of the symbolic order) and is not so much an essence as that which is excluded.

By contrast, much cultural feminist writing has sought to challenge what it takes to be essentialism and biological determinism through the conceptual division between a biological sex and a culturally formed gender. Subsequently, it is argued that no fundamental sex differences exist and that those that are apparent are insignificant in relation to arguments for social equality. Rather, it is the social, cultural and political discourses and practices of gender that are held to lie at the root of women's subordination. Thus Mackinnon (1987, 1991) argues that women's subordination is a matter of social power founded on men's dominance of institutionalized heterosexuality.

However, the sex–gender distinction upon which this argument is based has itself become the subject of criticism. The differentiation between sex as biology and gender as a cultural construction is broken down on the grounds that there is in principle no access to biological 'truths' that lie outside of cultural discourses and therefore no 'sex' which is not already cultural. Thus, sexed bodies are always already represented as the production of regulatory discourses. Judith Butler has been at the cutting edge of this argument by suggesting that 'the category of "sex" is, from the start, normative; it is what Foucault has called a "regulatory ideal". In this sense, then, "sex" not only functions as a norm, but is part of a regulatory practice that produces the bodies it governs' (1993: 1–2). Thus, discourses of sex are ones that, through repetition of the acts they guide, bring sex into view as a necessary norm. Here, while sex is held to be a social construction, it is an indispensable one that forms subjects and governs the materialization of bodies. This does not mean that 'everything is discourse'; rather, as Butler argues, discourse and the materiality of bodies are indissoluble.

Butler's work is emblematic of a wider body of thought produced by feminists who have been influenced by poststructuralist and postmodern thought (e.g. Nicholson, 1990; Weedon, 1997). These writers have argued not only that sex and gender are social and cultural constructions, but also that there are multiple modes of femininity (and masculinity) that are enacted not only by different women, but potentially by the same woman under different circumstances. For Kristeva, 'the very dichotomy man/woman as an opposition between two rival entities may be understood as belonging to *metaphysics*' (1986a: 209).

Here, rather than a conflict between two opposing male–female 'masses', sexual identity concerns the balance of masculinity and femininity within specific men and women. This struggle, Kristeva (1986b) suggests, could result in the deconstruction of sexual and gendered identities understood in terms of marginality within the symbolic order. This argument stresses the singularity and multiplicity of persons as well as the relativity of symbolic and biological existence. Yet, if there is no such thing as a woman, how then can women possess collective interests?

What are women's interests?

The cultural variations that exist between women, based not only on differences of class, ethnicity, age, and so forth, but also on differences about what it means to be a woman, suggest to many cultural theorists that there is no universal cross-cultural category of 'woman' that is shared by all women. Thus, there can be no universal feminism based on 'women's interests' either for there is no metalanguage of translation nor is there a single common cause. For Nicholson, the conclusion to be drawn favours the 'replacement of claims about women as such or even women in patriarchal societies with claims about women in particular contexts' (1995: 59). Nicholson goes on to argue that we should regard the meaning of the word 'woman' not in the singular but as part of a language-game of different and overlapping meanings. Consequently, feminism is conceived of as a coalition politics formed amongst women who come to believe that they share particular interests in specific contexts. The meaning of 'woman' in feminist politics has to be forged rather than taken as a given. The politics of identity has to be *made* rather than found.

As such, feminism does not need essentialism at all, but rather a 'new language' in which the claims of coalitions of women come to be accepted as 'true' (in the sense of a social commendation). Feminism forges a moral identity for women as women by gaining linguistic authority over themselves rather than assuming that there is an essential identity for women waiting to be found. Consequently, feminism is best thought of not as the discovery of truth or less distorted perception, but as the development of a language that seeks to serve particular purposes and values. The emergence of such a language is part of an evolutionary struggle that has no immanent teleology, that is, no future predetermined destiny to which it must evolve (Rorty, 1995). Accordingly,

---

Universal essentialist answers to the questions 'What is a woman?' and 'What is in women's interests?' are not required in order to forge an alliance of some women who perceive there to be shared interests amongst them for specific purposes. This is an aspect of the 'necessary fictions' of identity politics.

Thus, feminism can lay claim to take 'woman' to be a quasi-essential category for tactical reasons while needing to remain attentive to the exclusions that *any* identity category enacts. Feminism is about power, languages, identifications and consequences. That is, feminism is a politics not a metaphysics of truth.

Equality, difference and gender justice

As a consequence of the above, the theoretical debates about essentialism and anti-essentialism are becoming irrelevant since in practice what counts is the tactical line that becomes drawn around a coalition of diverse persons. On the one hand, we do not need recourse to essentialism in order to pursue gender politics; indeed it is useful to combat the idea that gender is a universally fixed substance in order to open the door to cultural experimentation. On the other hand, we do not need the excesses of anti-essentialism either, whereby it is claimed that sex and gender are wholly malleable, for this flies in the face of the evidence (discussed below). Much of our gendered capacities and behaviour is plastic and changeable, but there is also a significant aspect of sexed being that is not open to transformation (at least not within a humanly manageable time-scale). In this context, the question of which values or ends to pursue and which practices to develop in the context of the possible is rather more signifi-cant than the question of identity *per se*.

Broadly speaking, the liberal and poststructuralist lines of feminist thought seek the achievement for women of social 'equality' with men, while 'difference' feminists (such as Irigaray and Rich) argue for the pursuit and development of women's creative capacities and the celebration of their fundamental difference from men. However, the equality–difference debate relies on a misleading and unnecessary binary since it is conceivable that equality and difference can co-exist. Indeed, the principle of equality is best realized through a respect for difference and a reverence for all human life: that is, an equally applied sensi-bility of acceptance, solidarity and compassion towards all difference and all suffering. Since difference is the condition for all identities, so the very meaning of equality is not sameness but the similar application of principles of classifi-cation and treatment to all persons regardless of difference. This is one way of understanding the concept of justice. We may struggle for equal opportunities but we should not expect or hope for sameness of outcome. Difference will remain and should be celebrated.

However, I think we need to go further than this by investigating what it is we mean by equality. The modernist conception of equality is commonly read as 'sameness', that is, identical outcomes, thereby seeking to eradicate difference. By contrast, a respect for difference is supportive of a pragmatic cultural plural-ism based on a diverse public sphere of citizens engaged in continual dialogue. Further, the values of equality, liberty, solidarity, tolerance, difference, diversity and justice should underpin a reverence for individual difference along with forms of sharing and co-operation that are genuine and not enforced.

Thus, our best chance of maintaining difference and pursuing a private iden-tity project lies in the development of a culture that prides itself on being heterogeneous. Consequently, where we acknowledge that there are differences between men and women (and within the categories of male and female), then our objective is not equality of outcome (as sameness) but equivalence under the sign of justice. That is, divergent manifestations of inequality and disparate forms of oppression are by a logic of comparison put on the same footing. This stance seeks to maintain solidarity and widen the circle of the 'we' who are part of the community of justice.

When we replace the impossible idea of equality of outcome with equality of opportunity, we will certainly find that a particular person or cultural group is not in a position to take full and equal advantage of the opportunities that face them because of previously existing inequalities and injustices. For example, even if we fantasized that we could have equal educational opportunities or equal possibilities for making a good livelihood, then it is arguable that women, people of colour and the poverty-stricken are not entering that field from the same starting position as privileged white men. In fact, *nobody* is entering the field at the same point as any other person. This argument makes the notion of equality of opportunity problematic unless one can trace difference back to a pristine state of original equality and maintain it from then onwards. This is not possible in principle and in the case of gender there are sound genetic arguments that place difference of capabilities and qualities at the very core of our being, that is, within our very cells.

The solution to this problem, I would propose, is to drop the ideas of both equality of outcome and equality of opportunity, replacing them with the concept of gender justice. Needless to say, we then require a workable understanding of the concept of justice. On the one hand, the basis for justice lies in the application of agreed principles and procedures to all persons irrespective of difference. On the other hand, justice must also involve *compassion* and the notion that we should 'do unto others as we would be done by'. As such, justice may sometimes require the differential application of principles and laws as a consequence of divergent 'starting points'. Indeed, we are required to oscillate between these two conceptions, that is, justice as similar treatment and justice as differential treatment. Either way, justice will be relational and context-specific. It may even be, as Irigaray argues, that we need to find different kinds of juridical codes in order to 'offer justice to *two genders that differ* in their needs, their desires, their properties' (1993: 4).

Further conceptual clarification is clearly required. However, I think that shifting the focus of the debates to one centred on justice rather than on equality is a step in the right direction. Under current cultural conditions this would seem to require the development of a 'voice' for women outside of the male binding and justifying world-views that predominate in western culture. However, it also suggests the need to look a little harder at the gender-specific problems faced by men.

Amongst the implications of a turn to the concept of gender justice is that we need no longer be afraid of male–female difference and the scientific evidence for genetic variance between the sexes.

Many writers within cultural studies reject the 'science of sex' because they fear that in the absence of the total cultural construction and plasticity of gender full equality will not be possible. However, neither equality of outcome nor equality of opportunity is perfectly possible. Nor do we want the kind of equality that values sameness over difference. By contrast, the concept of justice embraces difference, including genetic difference.

The science of sex

Most writers within cultural studies have adopted the view that sex and gender are cultural constructions and that biology has little of value to say on the subject (other than to be demonized). The reason why this view is so popular within cultural studies is not difficult to discern: it leaves the door open to unlimited changes in gender and the possibility of full equality (as sameness) of the sexes. However, intellectual inquiry must remain open to continual reflexivity and questioning. Thus, feminist psychologist Diane Halpern began her review of the literature holding the opinion that socialization practices were solely responsible for apparent sex differences in thinking patterns, but came, as I did, to a different conclusion.

> After reviewing a pile of journal articles that stood several feet high and numerous books and book chapters that dwarfed the stack of journal articles, I changed my mind . . . there are real, and in some cases sizeable, sex differences with respect to some cognitive abilities. Socialization practices are undoubtedly important, there is also good evidence that biological sex differences play a role in establishing and maintaining cognitive sex differences, a conclusion I wasn't prepared to make when I began reviewing the relevant literature. (1992: xi)

In any case, cross-cultural diversity and the evidence for a genetic core to sexual difference are not contradictory stances. Biochemical similarity amongst women (and difference from men) is able to co-exist with cross-cultural divergence. This is for two reasons:

- Cultural difference operates 'on top of' genetic similarity.
- Similar genetic predispositions can have widely different outcomes within divergent contexts.

The languages of science and sex

In my view, contemporary evolutionary biology and psychology account for the background picture to any discussion of the human body and sexuality in particular (see Chapter 10). Darwin's story tells us that human beings are best understood as animals that walk the earth adapting and changing themselves in the context of their environment. This naturalistic and holistic description is an evolutionary tale that explains human organisms in terms of relationships, causes and consequences, with 'development' being contingent on the outcome of numerous acts of chance and environmental adaptation. One such acclimatization was the emergence of language as the primary human tool that forms the bedrock of culture. That is, the play of both DNA and cognitive brain modules in human evolution pre-dates a language-based culture.

Having said that, biochemistry and genetics are themselves languages and forms of cultural classification. This means that there can be no access to bio-logical truth from a position that is external to culture and language. The way out of this apparent cul-de-sac or fly-bottle is to consider the purposes and con-sequences of the vocabularies we use rather than their adequacy to the real. For example, we do not ask about the 'true' way to ride a bike. If I ride my bike from home to my place of work arriving unscathed and on time, I have ridden suc-cessfully, given my purpose. It makes no sense to say I have ridden my bike truthfully. If, by contrast, I wobble and fall off and as a consequence I am late for work, I have not ridden my bike untruthfully but have done so badly for the purposes I had in mind.

The argument here is that the particular vocabularies that constitute bio-chemistry and genetics are deployed for the achievement of specific purposes. The justifications of these sciences should be understood not as the revelation of objective truth, but as the achievements of agreed procedures that have enabled us to produce higher levels of predictability within specific domains of knowl-edge and action.

Of course, such achievements are themselves always provisional, for science proceeds by error and the methodology of doubt. Paradigm shifts in scientific thinking mean that the truths of today's ordinary science are revised and even overturned by tomorrow's conceptual revolution. The test for science, and indeed any causal story, is pragmatic. Hence hormone treatment is a necessary and central plank in sex-changes that operates in tandem with rethinking one's place in the cultural world, including styles of dress, speech and bodily move-ments. Neither path requires access to universal truth (see Chapter 3). Rather, the language of biology enables us to make behavioural and bodily predictions and alterations through, for example, the use of drugs. At the same time, what it *means* to be gendered remains a cultural question. On the one hand, there is evi-dence that points to the *predictability* of a range of male and female capabilities and behaviour that derives from genetics. On the other hand, there are also clear indications that cultural attitudes about masculinity and femininity have changed over time. Thus, biochemistry should not be used as an excuse for test-ing the limits of sexed behaviour, but equally, the evidence for genetic determination should not be overlooked in favour of wishful thinking.

It is tempting to argue that the biological and evolutionary features of human beings constitute only the broadest of constraints on human behaviour and on the differences between men and women in particular. This is the position adopted by those teachers, researchers and writers from within the humanities and social sciences who want to acknowledge biology but effectively banish it to the periphery of their vision. Not only is this something of an evasion of the issue, but it also fails to specify what the character of the pertinent constraints actually is. I think we need to acknowledge that at this point in human evolution there is evidence that biology plays a significant part in human sexed behaviour and that this is sometimes quite specific in character.

This does not mean that all sexed behaviours are biologically driven rather than culturally formed. Nor does it mean that biological predispositions are acted out in the same way under different cultural circumstances. For example, even if men were predisposed by their genes towards 'aggressive behaviour' (itself a cultural category), not only are there a variety of men with different degrees of predisposition, but also changes in the cultural environment (e.g. normative sanctions against violent behaviour) will still alter the outcomes involved. Though human beings may have a genetically formed temperament that predisposes them to certain styles of behaviour, everyone has the ability to grow and to change using the resources of our cultural environment.

Nevertheless, the importance of biochemistry and genetics means that we are not blank sheets at birth and we cannot remake ourselves into anything we want to. Some aspects of being can be changed and some cannot. As the old saying goes: wisdom lies in knowing the difference.

Evidence for the genetic determination of sexed behaviour

I want to open this account of sex and genetics by noting an assumption that I make in my discussion: namely that what counts here is not what a gene 'really is' but what the science of genetics allows us to predict. In that context, and for my purposes, genes are taken to be chemicals that direct the combination of other chemicals, notably DNA. DNA builds the brain and the body, with apparently minor differences accounting for the divergent character of human individuals' inherited temperaments. It is responsible for the unique chemical structure of individual brains as they develop within singular environments.

It is the reliability of its predictions that makes genetic science of value. Through the studies of twins – especially identical twins and those separated at birth – it is possible to carry out a mathematical calculation that 'measures' how much 'difference' is the consequence of inherited factors, that is, heritability. In this context, we are led to understand that every foetus is initially brought into being as 'female' until a single gene switches on and begins the cascade of chemical reactions that turns roughly half of the human species into men and the other half into women. It is argued that this affects not only our physical characteristics but also our mental ones. I accept that, in a sense, the scientific discourses of sex contribute to the production of 'sex', as Foucauldian-influenced writers want to argue (e.g. Butler, 1993; Harding, 1998). However, this does not invalidate claims for the usefulness of genetic science to understanding and predicting the actions and life-choices of human bodies that have taken on the cultural identities of male and female.

Here I would make a distinction between identity as a social construction, a representation with which we emotionally identify, and those human capacities and behaviours that correlate highly with certain biochemical structures of the brain. To attach identity categories to human capabilities and behaviour is a function of cultural classification, expectation and evaluation. Wilfully to ignore the evidence for biochemically structured differences between male and female brain capacities and the divergent behaviour that follows from this does seem to be a combination of myopia and fantasy.

Hamer and Copeland (1998) re-present the arguments that heterosexual men and women have different optimal reproductive strategies that underpin the male requirement for multiple sexual partners and women's need for a man who will commit time and resources to the raising of children within a stable environment. They further argue that men seek fertile partners, as indicated to them by certain physical features of women's bodies that are culturally described as 'attractive'. By contrast, women are said to be drawn to signs of status and power. These authors cautiously suggest that the gene structures that might explain such differences are not clearly understood. However, they do suggest that the cross-cultural prevalence of such behaviour and the apparent evolutionary conservation of similar features amongst other species does undermine a purely cultural account. Indeed, Buss (1999a) puts forward evolutionary psychological explanations based on mating and survival strategies developed across evolutionary time and structured into the functioning of the brain.

Hamer and Copeland (1998) argue that they are on much stronger ground with regard to genetic determination of male sexual orientation, in relation to which the evidence is said to be compelling. The argument is that men's sexual orientation is more dichotomous than that of women. Men are largely gay or straight, while a larger proportion of women show a degree of bisexuality. Male sexual orientation has many of the features of genetic influence in being consistent, stable and dichotomous. Averaging all the studies to date, the heritability of male sexual orientation is said to be 50 per cent, with further data suggesting a higher genetic link and predictability amongst gay men.

Moir and Moir (1998) argue that a baseline figure of some 4 per cent of the male population being gay is stable over time and across societies, suggesting biological rather than cultural forces as the primary determination. They suggest that a so-called 'gay gene' might predispose certain men to other biochemical processes, notably the degree and timing of testosterone washing of the foetal brain. Further, they cite LeVay's research findings that the structures of heterosexual and homosexual male brains are different. They also point to a variety of studies suggesting that female foetal exposure to certain hormones – for example, androgens – alters their sexual orientation and spatial abilities in adult life in ways that have more in common with men than other women.

The core of the argument that biochemistry determines male and female behaviour lies in the evidence for differential male and female brain structures and capabilities (Christen, 1991; Moir and Jessel, 1991; Moir and Moir, 1998). For example, over thirty world-wide studies show that girls who are born with congenital adrenal hyperplasia (CAH) as a consequence of exposure to high levels of 'male hormones' in the womb exhibit styles of play more commonly seen amongst boys. Greater levels of testosterone and lower levels of serotonin appear to pre-dispose boys to be greater risk takers with fewer inhibitions than girls. The consequence, or so it is said, is that men have a higher propensity to find multiple partners whereas women are inclined to look for stability. Men are also disposed more to anger and less to empathy than are women, while women have greater ability to verbalize emotions. It should also come as no surprise that women are thought to be hard-wired for a greater inclination toward bonding with babies as a consequence of hormone production (of oxytocin) during pregnancy.

There is also considerable evidence that women and men have other divergent capacities and capabilities, with the former more verbal, co-operative and organized and the latter having greater spatial, mathematical and motor skills. These tendencies have been repeatedly demonstrated amongst both humans and animals. As Doreen Kimura argues,

> Scientific evidence for consistent sex differences in cognitive function between men and women has accumulated for well over fifty years. A solid body of research, carried out primarily in North America and Western Europe, has established that men, on average, excel on spatial tasks (particularly those tapping ability to imaginably rotate a figure), perception of the vertical and horizontal, mathematical reasoning and spatio-motor targeting ability. Women, on average, excel on tasks of verbal fluency (where words must be generated with constraints on the letters they contain), perceptual speed (in which rapid pattern-identity matches are made), verbal and item memory, and some fine motor skills. (1996: 259)

It is argued that the brains of the two sexes are organized in distinct ways, giving rise to differences in a range of abilities. Thus, women have more of their brain dedicated to verbal matters (e.g. the larger corpus callosum region of the brain in women) while men with higher verbal skills commonly possess brains that are organized in more 'female' ways. Men and women also use their brains in different ways. Men specialize their key brain functions on one side of their cerebral matter (e.g. verbal performance on the left and spatial skills on the right) while women are more able to communicate across the two hemispheres of the brain. For men, this has the advantage of concentrated focus on specific tasks but the disadvantage of lower levels of integration and cross-referencing, where women excel: for example, connecting the emotional and reasoning aspects of the mind. Much of this argument is confirmed by functional MRI scans that locate the active parts of the brain while subjects carry out specific tasks.

Scientific evidence confirms many school-teachers' common-sense observations, namely that girls and boys have different learning styles, with the former being more verbal, co-operative and organized and the latter having less concentration, being more active and restless. This, it is argued, is the outcome of differential brain structure in that, to put it crudely, men have lower 'arousal thresholds' than women, who are able to pay greater focused attention to events and more swiftly than are men. Further, girls would appear to have greater frontal lobe (i.e. rational) control over their 'fight or flight' responses than do boys, who more quickly become unsettled, distracted and aggressive.

The consequence, given current educational practices, is that boys, being in need of further active stimulation, become distracted and troublesome to teachers more easily than do girls. Boys are suspended from school more than are girls, they are more likely to be involved in risk taking and accidents, they find it harder to sit still and require a more competitive environment to challenge and stimulate them. So alarming is the disparity between boys' needs and the educational system that 33 per cent of young boys in the USA are, according to a survey of parents and teachers, considered excessively hyperactive or hyper-distractable, with 10 per cent of boys between the ages of 9 and 13 being treated with ritalin. Boys are four times more likely to suffer from a learning disorder and they are consistently underachieving in schools ('The Gender Project', *Sunday Telegraph*, Sydney, Australia, 09/07/00).

Of course these arguments are generalizations: many boys who have learned to concentrate and channel their energy do very well at school. However, gender justice may require different styles of schooling for boys and girls. Indeed, there is considerable evidence that most girls (and some boys) perform better academically in single-sex lessons. Better still, we might wish for individualized learning so that different persons can learn in different ways, though there seems little prospect of the increased resources being made available for such a project.

The predominance of evidence suggests that different kinds of brain organization are the result of hormone exposure in the womb rather than of cultural training. Thus, CAH girls have better spatial and mathematical skills than the average girl does, while other experimental evidence suggests that the level of spatial skills found in female children correlates with exposure to testosterone in the womb. Indeed, Moir and Moir argue that 'testosterone is the architect of the sex difference in brain organization. The male brain begins as a female brain, but foetal testosterone changes its structure' (1998: 125). These differences are enhanced when more hormones come on stream during puberty.

At this stage, it is important to say that a genetic predisposition to certain capacities and behaviour does not in itself mean that particular actions are inevitable. Genes operate within an environment that conditions their significance and consequences. Change the environment and we see alterations in the end result of biochemistry. For example, if we are able to alter aspects of the education system, we may see improvement in the learning outcomes for boys. However, since biochemistry sets limits to the possible, so only *specific kinds* of changes to teaching and learning styles would benefit boys. Further, it is clear that many boys love verbal learning and adopt 'feminine' styles of understanding, and growing numbers of women are active, restless and/or scientific. Nor does a general tendency amongst men to orient to sex and children in different ways from women mean that some men cannot develop loving monogamous relationships and care for children or some women become multiple-partner sex addicts and child abusers.

Since it is the interpenetration and mutual constitution of bodies and the environment that counts, paying attention to our cultural conditioning remains an important and viable project. Experimentation, judgement and changing values are inscribed in a human history that lacks certainty – either genetic or cultural. Indeed, we can never be sure about the outcomes of our behaviour since it is continually marked by the unintentional consequences of action. Too often we try to control a destiny that is not in our hands – indeed it is not in any hands at all. To some extent, then, we have to accept 'what is' in relation to the biology of sex while experimenting with the limits of gender plasticity in the name of compassion and justice.

Genetics offers us a general picture of patterns of predictable performance, some of which relate to sex difference. Nevertheless, what it *means* to be a woman or a man is historically and culturally flexible and specific. In neither case are they reducible to each other. Equally, not all men are Men and not all women are Women – but women are not men. In this context, the imperative of gender justice requires that we pay attention to how people articulate their needs and to consider how best they can be met. For example, clichéd though it sounds, we really do need to try to educate people according to their capacities and inclinations, which may or may not show a certain fissure along gender lines. Indeed, while for many years girls have been the object of study in relation to educational underachievement, today that concern is also, and increasingly, being directed towards boys and men.

The conclusion that we can draw from this is that we need, above all, to develop respect for difference and to engage in dialogue between the sexes and between individuals.

Man trouble

The study of gender throughout the history of institutionalized cultural studies has for the most part meant the investigation of women by women within an explicitly feminist framework. However, the contemporary perception of masculinity as a 'social problem' has put men on the research agenda. For Farrell (1993), men are the 'disposable gender': not only do they die in war and from suicide more often than do women, but they are the most common victims of violence, overwork and mental illness. Of course, men also commit over 90 per cent of convicted acts of violence and comprise over 90 per cent of the inmates of jails (Biddulph, 1994). Either way, according to Biddulph, there are very few happy men. This awareness has prompted an expanding literature centred on men and masculinity (e.g. Biddulph, 1994; Connell 1995; Farrell, 1993; Johnson and Meinhof, 1997; Nixon, 1997; Pfeil, 1995; Seidler, 1989).

This growing interest in men is further signified by the regular appearance of features on masculinity in the supplements of the Sunday papers and within 'women's' magazines. This new-found attention for men is, as is so often the case in the schoolroom, a result of the apparent destructiveness of contemporary masculinity – from naughty boys to bad men. However, bad men often turn out to be better described as 'sad men', the damaged goods of industrial society. Thus, in Australia the press (*The Sun Herald*, 29.08.99) reported a government health survey's findings that represent an enormous cost to the state and a human tragedy of vast proportions. The report suggests that men are more likely than women to:

- be obese;
- be diagnosed as having 'mental disorders' as a child (e.g. attention deficit disorder);
- be diagnosed as HIV positive (ten times higher);
- have an accident (five times higher);
- engage in high-risk behaviour (e.g. dangerous levels of drinking or drug taking);
- be a victim of suicide (six times higher, with 80 per cent of suicide victims being male and death rates highest among men aged 20–24 or 80 and above).

Our modern fathers

In Andrew O'Hagen's novel *Our Fathers* (1999) a recurrent motif is that 'Our Fathers were made for grief'. O'Hagen's fathers are the post-war generation of toughened Scottish men schooled in poverty, war and industrial graft. Hard drinking and hard hitting, some of these men sought solutions in collective unionism and socialist housing, others at the bottom of a liquor bottle. Our fathers share aspects of a modernist masculinity forged under specific historical, social and cultural circumstances that is both constituted and expressed by the metaphors of manliness that circulate in our culture. In particular, the contemporary male concern with metaphors of reason, control and distance (see Barker and Galasinski, 2001) is an instantiation of wider discourses of masculinity.

As Seidler (1989) has argued, since the Enlightenment, men have traditionally associated masculinity with metaphors of reason. Enlightenment philosophy and the discourses of modernity have championed 'reason' as the source of progress and knowledge, manifested in science and increased levels of material production. At the same time, the price of industrial growth and the rise of rational decision-making procedures based on calculability, rules and expert knowledge was that people submitted to a rigorous discipline and urban anonymity. Hence the new society produced new forms of subjectivity. Factories, now run by clock time rather than on the basis of seasonal rhythms, demanded discipline and control while the division of labour gave men the role of providing the wages of survival and women the domestic duties of childrearing and housekeeping. Meanwhile, managers and bureaucrats, mainly men, were to operate with impersonal task-oriented hierarchical rules. Thus, modernity is an epoch not just of external domination but also of self-control. 'As men it is difficult not to be "control freaks". This is the history we inherit' (Seidler, 1989: 63).

Reason, control and distance are central metaphors of contemporary masculinity: control over other people and control over ourselves; distance from other people and distance from ourselves. In particular, the association of rationality with masculinity involves the self-discipline of, and distance from, the language of emotions. While it is part of contemporary common sense that men 'suppress' feelings, this is better put as the failure to learn a productive language of emotion. Instead, men's relationships are often inscribed by spatial metaphors – including emotional 'distance' and 'controlling their own space' – that mark a lack of communication. The male imperative to control emotion, allied to men's lack of experience with the language of feelings, including their inability to name emotions and recognize them as such, can lead to confrontational incidents. Thus emotions like anger can be controlled, metaphorically held within, only to burst out in an explosive moment.

The language of modernity stresses the gulf between the feminine coded private world and the masculine coded public world where men are acculturated to seek esteem through public performance and the recognition of achievement. This can take many forms, from violence, through sport, to educational qualifications and occupational status. It also lends itself to hyper-individualism, competitiveness and separation from the relational, for it is 'I' who must perform and 'I' who will take the glittering prize. Performance orientation of this kind – from work to sexuality – is manifested in grandiosity, on the one hand, and deep feelings of inadequacy and depression, on the other (for the performances are never outstanding enough to satisfy the internal parents).

Stiffed: The Betrayal of the Modern Man

Even Susan Faludi, author of a radical critique of masculinity as a 'bedrock of misogyny' (Faludi, 1991), is now giving more sympathetic observance to men's lives (Faludi, 1999). Her story centres on the 'promise of postwar manhood' and its subsequent 'betrayal'. Through a series of men's stories she relates an array of strategies that men have adopted in order to live with the loss of the unstated covenant that they had presumed gave them a valued place in the social order. Forged through war and work, argues Faludi, the modern man was acculturated to value being *useful* at work, to his family and to the community at large. A man, especially the American man, was expected to be in control, the master of his destiny, a person who makes things happen. Further, as a man he was able to develop and rely on solidarity with other men.

Today, the 'very paradigm of modern masculinity – that it is all about being the master of the universe – prevents men from thinking their way out of their dilemma, from taking active political steps to resolve their crisis' (Faludi, 1999: 14). This is so because men fail to acknowledge that they are shaped, boxed in, by social and cultural forces beyond their individual control: that is, they are not and never have been the masters of their destiny. 'Even the most powerful man has had at least as much happen to him as he has made happen' (Faludi, 1999: 16). In particular, World War II proved to be the 'last gasp' of the useful and dutiful male as the ideal of manhood. The post-war American baby boomer generation was offered a 'mission to manhood' that revolved around the conquest of space, the defeat of communism, a brotherhood of organizational men and a family to provide for and protect. However,

> The frontier, the enemy, the institutions of brotherhood, the women in need of protection – all the elements of the old formula for attaining manhood had vanished in short order. The boy who had been told he was going to be the master of the universe and all that was in it found himself master of nothing. (Faludi, 1999: 30)

Downsizing, unemployment, the Vietnam and Korean wars, feminism and a decline in public concern with space travel all undermined the confidence and security of post-war American men. In particular, what Faludi calls 'ornamental culture' signalled the end of a utilitarian role for men. Ornamental culture is rooted in no kind of society at all, let alone one in which men are called upon to be useful. Instead of a culture founded in utility, this is a culture of celebrity, image, entertainment and marketing, all underpinned by consumerism. In this context, masculinity becomes a matter of personal display rather than the demonstration of the internal qualities of inner strength, confidence and purpose. Manhood has become a performance game to be won in the marketplace, where, amongst the more merchandisable poses of contemporary manhood, we find the 'bad-boy' image laced with hostility and violence. Here, raw dominance emerges without being harnessed to any social good, and appearance – of youth, money and aggression – comes to define manhood.

In the absence of an alternative vision of manhood that could provide a new sense of meaning and purpose in the world, Faludi documents a series of 'men in trouble':

- shipyard workers who have lost not only their source of income but also their craftsmanship, pride and solidarity;
- corporate executives and middle mangers who watch their consumer dream of the house, the pool, the car and the cozy family threatened by the onset of recession;
- young men – both black and white – who seek purpose in celebrity and, failing to find either, turn instead to crime;
- Christian men who look to reassert their symbolic status as head of the

family even as their wives pack up and leave;
- disillusioned casualties of the Vietnam war who, expecting to return as heroes, find themselves to be social pariahs, leaving them wounded once more even after the bullets have ceased flying.

All these and more appear as the distressed and confused men who inhabit the ghostly landscape of the contemporary USA.

According to Faludi, the model of confrontation that revolved around an enemy that could be 'identified, contested, and defeated' has served most counter-cultural movements well enough. This included a feminism that could oppose men and 'patriarchy'. However, she argues that this model is not suited to the predicaments of contemporary men. Instead,

---

Men need to find new ways of being men or rather, new ways to be human that bestow masculinity as a side-effect of doing and living in a manner that brings respect, esteem and self-worth. Masculinity is not an ornamental 'thing' to be or a set of traits to possess, but the emblem of a socially approved virtue. The need for men, as for women, is a struggle for human liberty, happiness and solidarity that encompasses us all.

Fathers and sons

For both Susan Faludi (1999) and the authors of the 'men's movement' such as Robert Bly (1991), Steve Biddulph (1994) and John Lee (1991), post-war men have been devastatingly unfathered, unnourished and unprepared by the men who sired them. For many men, their fathers are not complex human beings but are reduced to being symbols of virtue, that is, 'what it is to be a man', and/or the embodiment of abusive power, cruelty and lovelessness. For men, comprehension of their fathers, and if needs be a coming to a peace with them, is a necessary aspect of mental health and autonomous self-development. 'All men are sons and, whether they know it or not, most sons are loyal' (Real, 1998: 21). Consequently, sons internalize their father's voice as the representation of 'true' manhood, even as he may also be the hand that wields the stick that is beating them for their alleged failings. One way or another, fathers are a part of their sons, and, it is argued, if men are at war with Him, they are divided against themselves and feel themselves to be inadequate as human beings (Biddulph, 1994).

As Forward (1990) suggests, we are not responsible for what is done to us as a defenceless child, but, if we are to 'recover', then we must take responsibility for positive actions to rectify the damage. A start for many men is to enter into a dialogue with the figure of the father. The sign of our fathers is marked by ambivalence. 'Father' represents an all-powerful protector but also the omnipotent lawmaker who wields the rod of punishment. 'Our Father who art in heaven' is the Lord: the power and the glory, the provider whose will must be done even as he is the fount of love and forgiveness. In psychoanalytic terms, the father is signed as the symbolic Phallus, the breaker of the mother–child dyad, the castrator, the abjector and the 'transcendental signifier' of the law, culture and language. The power of the father is the authority of patriarchy, with all its suggestions of mastery and masculine control. He is the one with whom boys identify and wish to emulate. He is the one whom heterosexual girls long for in the 'quest romance'.

Biddulph (1994) argues that the central problems of men's lives as he sees them – loneliness, compulsive competition and lifelong emotional timidity – are rooted in the adoption of impossible images of masculinity that men try, but fail, to live up to. These idealized images are formed in the absence of a loving father to act as a living male role model. Biddulph locates a father-hunger or father wound at the heart of contemporary men, who mourn lost contact and love with their fathers, expressing it in the form of anger. 'Fixing it with your father' and 'loving the father in your self' are, according to Biddulph, necessary steps towards becoming a man rather than simply being a bigger boy.

These arguments are echoed by John Lee, whose book opens with the claim that 'our fathers were not there for us emotionally, physically, or spiritually – or at all' (1991: xv). Without the guidance and training that a loving father can give, men don't learn enough of the skills required for living, including the ability to give and receive. Instead, they are offered a range of more negative fathering styles: 'the Man Who Would be King', 'the Critical Father', 'the Passive Father' and 'the Absentee Father'. The consequence, for Lee, is an absence, a hole and an emptiness at the core of men's being that is filled by the demons of over-work, drugs, sex and unsatisfactory relationships with both men and women. While I do not necessarily agree with all the prescriptions that the so-called 'men's movement' offers, there is plenty of evidence to suggest that if the shackles of noxious parenting are not cast off, then further painful relationships and attempts at self-medication invariably follow.

Family life and the roots of male addiction

The other side of the performance of control and the medallion of achievement is the need to take flight from the pressures of constant reflexivity and self-interrogation. This is commonly sought after through compulsive behaviours (addictions) centred on work and drugs. That is, the achievement orientation of 'successful' men and the drug abuse of social 'failures' are two sides of the same coin. Both have their roots in the scripts of contemporary masculinity and familial relations. Real (1998) argues that 48 per cent of men in the USA are at some point in their lives implicated in depression, suicide, alcoholism, drug abuse, violence and crime. In Australia, a recent survey suggested that:

- over 35 per cent of boys in school year 10 had been 'binge drinking' in the previous two weeks;
- at least 45 per cent of the male population under 24 drink to a degree hazardous or harmful to them (National Drug Strategy, 1995).

Much psychotherapeutic work (e.g. McLean et al., 1996; Rowe, 1996) suggests that low self-esteem (itself an outcome of family life), along with the self-perceived failure to meet cultural expectations of achievement, lies at the root of depression and drug abuse amongst men. Indeed, there is a case to suggest that personal pain, anxiety and depression underpin much male behaviour that appears to the 'outsider' as needless self-destruction. For Real (1998), men's violence, sex addiction, gambling, alcohol and drug abuse is a form of self-medication, an attempted defence (achieved through 'merging' or self-elevation) against covert depression stemming from shame and 'toxic' family relationships. For many men, life becomes a restless search for love and the overcoming of feelings of inadequacy rooted in the biochemical consequences of family experience.

Though sexual abuse and post-traumatic stress syndrome mark the currently understood outer limits of psychological pain and damage, for most men it is the less dramatic childhood injuries of 'petty' violence and neglect that do the damage. Either way, in order to maintain his attachments and relationship with his parents, and his father in particular, a boy, though feeling traumatized or abandoned, will take responsibility for the failing parent. That is, the child will take on the mantle of blame, assuming that he deserves the treatment he is receiving for being a bad person. Since this inner sense of badness (shame) preserves a relationship, so it is not readily given up even after the abuse has stopped. Rather, it becomes a stable part of the child's personality structure and the core around which the abused child's identity is formed (Herman, 1992). Further, through a process of projective identification or 'carried feeling' (Mellody, 1987), the child may take on the feelings of rage, shame and sadness that have driven the parent. The stage is then set for the compulsive re-enactment of childhood routines in adult life.

Addiction and other forms of compulsive behaviour, including the 'workaholism' of high achievers, offer a source of comfort and a defence against anxiety, so that failure to engage in them produces an upsurge of dread and/or depression. Thus Giddens argues that addictions – as compulsive behaviour – are narcotic-like 'time-outs' that blunt the pain and anxiety of other needs or longings that cannot be directly controlled. Addiction is the 'other side' of the choice and responsibility that goes with the autonomous development of a self-narrative (or identity). In circumstances in which traditional guidance (e.g. about what it is to be a man) has collapsed, these lifestyle decisions become a potentially 'dread-full' process of 'making oneself'.

That is, the addictive experience is a search for that 'high', and giving up of the self, which acts as a release from anxiety, marking a temporary abandonment of the reflexivity generic to contemporary western life. This suspension of the self is frequently followed by feelings of shame and remorse. Since addictions signal an incapacity to cope with certain anxieties, they tend to be functionally interchangeable. That is, one may overthrow one addiction only to replace it with another. We may use alcohol to ameliorate the pain of toxic fathers, but unless we deal with the source of the pain the struggle to stop drinking may only result in a shift to sex, cannabis, heroin, violence, endorphins or over-work.

Men's apparent predilection for addiction and self-destruction at the dawn of the twenty-first century needs to be understood within the context of modern life and its increasing stress on the self-regulation of emotions. According to Giddens (1992), men's predominance in the public domain and their association with 'reason' has been accomplished at the cost of their exclusion from the 'transformation of intimacy'. Intimacy is largely a matter of emotional communication, and the evident difficulties men have talking about relationships, which requires emotional security and language skills, is rooted in a culturally constructed and historically specific form of masculinity. From birth, boys are treated by parents as independent and outgoing beings, leading to a framework of masculinity that stresses externally oriented activity (e.g. work and sport) at the price of a masked emotional dependence on women and weak skills of emotional communication.

What many men repress, or fail to acquire, is the autonomy necessary for the development of emotional closeness. That is, lacking competency in the vocabulary of intimacy, many men are unable to name and speak about feelings or take responsibility for their own emotions. Instead, they seek to uphold the basic trust that forestalls anxiety and sustains ontological security through mastery and control of themselves, others (both women and male subordinates) and their environment. For example, a good deal of contemporary male violence can be regarded as a kind of hyper-mastery born out of anxiety that self-assured routine competence and intimacy cannot assuage because they have not been attained. Alternatively, self-medication in the form of violence, drug use or over-work masks the pain. Put in this way,

---

Every addiction is a defensive reaction, and an escape, a recognition of lack of autonomy that casts a shadow over the competence of the self. (Giddens, 1992: 76)

Conclusions

This chapter began with the argument that identity is constituted by representations with which we emotionally identify. Subsequently, it was suggested that identity is rooted in difference to the degree that signification is so grounded. Indeed, given the instability of meaning in language, identity is taken to be a becoming rather than a stable entity. At this point it is usually argued that identity, being a question of representation, is wholly a cultural construction. I agreed with this suggestion with regard to cultural identity. However, there is a distinction to be made between identity, which is wholly cultural in its formation, and certain embodied capacities and behaviours that are not culturally forged.

Thus, given the growing scientific evidence from the fields of genetics and bio-chemistry, I questioned the claims that sex and gender are entirely malleable. I agreed that biological science is itself a culturally produced language. However, while our descriptions of the body and behaviour are cultural, the make-up of the body itself is not, nor is the effect of biochemistry on the brain. The 'truth' of this assertion, and of science in general, lies in its ability to predict outcomes rather than in the construction of representations that lie outside of signification and that accord with an independent object world. Subsequently, I cited evidence to suggest that genetic science is able to offer testable predications about gendered behaviour. In other words, there are aspects of male and female activities that are rooted in bio-chemistry and which are not going to change in anything like the foreseeable future.

To suggest that there are some differences between men and women that are not open to change does not have to undermine women and the project of feminism. Rather, it is to accept and respect difference in the pursuit of gender justice. I drew on the concept of justice as being more useful to us than notions of equality. While we may continue to pursue equal opportunity as a useful but unrealizable goal, the pursuit of equality cannot, and should not, lie in achievement of 'samenesss'. Finally, in the context of the need for gender justice, I argued that the gender expectations of our culture have detrimental consequence for men as well as for women. However, the politics of gender justice for men cannot and should not be pursued by constructing women as 'the enemy'; rather, all of us as men and women must be engaged together in the struggle for liberty, happiness and solidarity. In more theoretical terms, the posing of debates in terms of essentialism vs anti-essentialism is now more of a hindrance than a help. Instead, we need to consider more carefully what it is about men and women that cannot be changed, what can be altered, and with what purposes in mind.

7 Global Culture/Media Culture

Central problem:
How should we assess global media culture?

> [Rap is] a hybrid form rooted in the syncretic social relations of the South Bronx where Jamaican sound-system culture, transplanted during the 1970s, put down new roots. (Gilroy, 1993: 144)

> For the people of Irian Jaya, Indonesianisation may be more worrisome than Americanisation, as Japanisation may be for Koreans, Indianisation for Sri Lankans, Vietnamisation for Cambodians, Russianisation for the people of Soviet Armenia and the Baltic Republics. (Appadurai, 1993: 328)

Introduction

The topic of this chapter is the globalization of media culture with specific reference to television as the primary disseminator of popular texts. In particular, we shall be concerned with the question of how to assess and name these developments. This 'problem' breaks down into a number of pertinent questions, namely:

- To what degree has television been globalized?
- What do we know about how audiences respond to media culture?
- What kinds of identities are being formed in the era of globalized media?

The answers to these questions shape our response to the theoretical issue of whether the concept of cultural imperialism, still commonplace in the literature, is the best way to characterize contemporary global cultural flows.

Globalization and cultural imperialism

According to Robertson (1992), the concept of globalization refers us to an intensified compression of the world and our increasing consciousness of it: that is, the ever-increasing abundance of global connections and our understanding of them. This 'compression of the world' can be understood in terms of the power and efficacy of the institutions of modernity, while the reflexive 'intensification of consciousness of the world' can be beneficially perceived in cultural terms.

The dynamism of the institutions of modernity are said by Giddens (1990) to be inherently globalizing because they allow for the separation of time-space and the 'disembedding', or lifting out, of social relations developed in one locale and their re-embedding in another. Subsequently, globalization is to be grasped in terms of the world capitalist economy, the global information system, the nation-state system and the world military order.

Giddens likens the institutions of modernity to an uncontrollable juggernaut of enormous power that sweeps away all that stands before it. In this view, modernity originated in western Europe and subsequently rolled out across the globe. However, this characterization of the relationship between modernity and globalization has been subject to the criticism that it is Eurocentric, envisaging only one kind of modernity, that of the West. Thus, Featherstone (1995) argues that modernity should be seen not only in temporal terms (i.e. as an epochal social transformation), but also in spatial and relational terms. That is, he argues, different spatial zones of the globe have become modern in a variety of ways, requiring us to speak of global modern*ities* in the plural.

Many of the processes of contemporary globalization can be described as being economic in character. For example, during the 1970s the bid to escape from recession hastened renewed levels of world economic activity, involving the speed-up of production and consumption turnover assisted by the use of information and communication technology (Harvey, 1989). Thus, 'accelerated globalization' refers to a set of related economic activities understood as the practices of capitalism in its 'disorganized' era. Indeed, contemporary globalization is marked by the predominance of transnational corporations in the marketplace, especially amongst the automobile, chemical and construction industries. We should also note the significance of semi-conductor production, information technology and twenty-four-hour world-wide financial transactions in creating an interconnected though unevenly developed world economy as an aspect of the processes of globalization (see Chapter 8).

For Lash and Urry (1987), this era of 'disorganized capitalism' involves a world-wide deconcentration of capital through globalized production, financing and distribution. In addition, the expansion of capitalism in the 'developing world' has led to increased competition for the West in the extractive and manufacturing industries. Thus, western economies have experienced a decline in these sectors as their economies are deindustrialized. This has led directly to a decrease in the absolute and relative size of the core working class as the occupational structure of First World economies has shifted towards the 'service' sector. However, it is one thing to document the institutional rise of global capitalism and another to grasp its complex cultural significance. Indeed, my central concern here is to counteract the erroneous equating of the institutional spread of television and western consumer culture with the inevitability of cultural homogenization and imperialism.

The shadow of cultural imperialism

The cultural homogenization thesis proposes that the globalization of consumer capitalism has led to a loss of cultural diversity. This argument stresses the growth of 'sameness' and a presumed loss of cultural autonomy that is cast as a form of cultural imperialism. This form of reasoning centres on the alleged domination of one culture by another and is usually conceived of in national terms. However, the principal agents of cultural synchronization are said to be transnational corporations. Consequently, cultural imperialism is regarded as the outcome of a set of economic and cultural processes implicated in the reproduction of global capitalism. In this context, Robins argues that, '[f]or all that it has projected itself as transhistorical and transnational, as the transcendent and universalizing force of modernization and modernity, global capitalism has in reality been about westernization – the export of western commodities, values, priorities, ways of life' (1991: 25).

In a similar vein, Herbert Schiller (1969, 1985), a leading proponent of the cultural imperialism thesis, argues that the global communications industries are dominated by US-controlled corporations. He points to the interlocking network that connects US television, defence sub-contractors and the Federal government. Schiller's case is that the mass media fit into the world capitalist system by providing ideological support for capitalism in general and transnational corporations in particular. That is, they are said to act as vehicles for corporate marketing along with a general 'ideological effect' that purportedly produces and reinforces locals' attachment to US capitalism.

There are three central difficulties with the 'globalization as cultural imperialism' argument:

- It is no longer the case, if it ever was, that the global flows of cultural discourses are constituted as one-way traffic.
- Insofar as the predominant flow of cultural discourse remains from West to East and North to South, this is not *necessarily* a form of domination.
- It is unclear that globalization is a simple process of homogenization since the forces of fragmentation and hybridity are equally as strong.

There can be little doubt that the first waves of economic, military and cultural globalization were part of the dynamic spread of capitalist modernity. Given that these institutions originated in Europe, we would have to say that modernity is a western project (Giddens, 1990). The early phases of globalization certainly involved western interrogation of the non-western 'Other', while colonial control manifested itself as military dominance, cultural ascendancy and the origins of economic dependency. Today, however, though the economies of the world are integrated into the world economic order, with developing nations occupying subordinate positions, cultural homogenization is not the inevitable consequence.

While the values and meanings attached to place remain significant, we are increasingly involved in networks which extend far beyond our immediate physical locations. Though we are not yet part of a world state or unitary world culture, we can identify global cultural processes, of cultural integration and dis-integration, which are independent of inter-state relations. In this context, Appadurai (1993) has argued that contemporary global conditions are best char-acterized in terms of the disjunctive flows of ethnoscapes, technoscapes, finanscapes, mediascapes and ideoscapes. That is, globalization involves the dynamic movements of ethnic groups, technology, financial transactions, media images and ideological conflicts that are not neatly determined by one harmo-nious 'master plan'. Rather, the speed, scope and impact of these flows are fractured and disconnected.

Metaphors of uncertainty, contingency and chaos are replacing those of order, stability and systematicity. Global cultural flows cannot be understood through neat sets of linear deter-minations but are better comprehended as a series of overlapping, over-determined, complex and chaotic conditions.

Indeed, I shall be arguing that the disjunctive cultural flows that mark glob-alization are characterizable less in terms of domination and more as forms of cultural hybridity. However, we need first to identify the patterns that constitute the culture industries and their accompanying cultural flows, even though it remains unclear what the consequences of this are going to be.

Globalizing the television market

There is little doubt that television is a global phenomenon in its production, dis-semination and viewing patterns – and one that grows daily. For example, in 1995 *Screen Digest* (February issue) estimated the number of television sets world-wide to be approximately 850 million distributed across more than 160 countries and watched by 2.5 billion people per day. Three years later the same journal placed the number of television sets globally in the order of one billion plus (*Screen Digest*, May 1998).

Since the mid-1980s the fastest growth area for television set ownership has been the 'developing world', with marginal growth in Europe and America in comparison with Africa and Asia, where the number of television sets trebled, or Central America, where the figure doubled. Thus, although the USA has the highest density of televisions per head of population, with 99 per cent of American households owning a television and 74 per cent of these having two

Table 7.1 *Global television households (millions)*

Country	TV households	Cable TV households	Satellite TV households
China	340	57	0.80
USA	98	66	8
India	79	19	2.5
Russia	45	14.5	0.35
Japan	41	14	12
Germany	37	19	11
Brazil	36	1.3	2.4
Britain	24	2.3	4.3
Indonesia	20	0.02	3
Italy	19	0.01	0.76

Original source: *Screen Digest*, May 1998; modified from Thussu, 2000: 132

or more sets (Nielsen Media Research, 1999), it is actually China that can claim the most number of television households (see Table 7.1). Indeed, Asia now claims some 34 per cent of the global television market, as does Europe, with the USA taking 21 per cent of this business. Of course, the crucial growth area for terrestrial television in the immediate future is going to be digital television, where the USA and UK hold a substantial 'lead'. Thus, it is estimated (*Screen Digest*, February 2000) that by 2005 there will be 11.2 million digital TV homes in the USA (11.5 per cent of the market) and some 8.4 million digital households in the UK (8.4 per cent of the market).

In this context, television may be considered to be global in terms of:

- the various configurations of public and commercial television that are regulated, funded and viewed within the boundaries of nation-states;
- the technology, ownership, programme distribution and audiences for television that operate across the boundaries of nation-states;
- the world-wide circulation by television of similar narrative forms and discourses (see Barker, 1997, 1999).

Synergy and convergence in global television

Exploration of contemporary television technology and ownership needs to be placed in the context of wider changes in the communications industries. Here a combination of technological developments and market change has contributed to the convergence (or erosion of boundaries) between organizational sectors and hence to the creation of global communications giants. Technological developments such as the unfolding of fibre-optic cable, satellite technology and digital switching technology have opened up commercial possibilities that have led telecommunications to be hailed by corporation and state alike as the industry of the future. Of particular significance are the processes of *synergy, convergence* and *deregulation.*

In recent years there has been a good deal of diversification by financial, computer and data-processing companies into telecommunications, creating multi-media giants that dominate sectors of the market. For example, between April 1997 and March 1998 there were at least 333 mergers involving media and communications companies world-wide. Of these, 133 were identified as 100 per cent acquisitions and 106 involved 'foreign' investors. Corporations based in the USA (139) and the UK (42) were responsible for largest part of the mergers and acquisitions noted (*Screen Digest*, April 1998).

This process has been driven by the corporate need for the financial power that can come from mergers and which enables them to undertake the massive investment needed to be a player in the global market. For example, the 1989 merger of Time and Warner created the largest media group in the world with a market capitalization of $25 billion. This was followed in 1995 by Time-Warner's acquisition of Turner Broadcasting (CNN) and in 2000 by its merger with the major Internet company America On-Line. Similarly, the acquisition by News Corporation of the Hong Kong-based Star TV for $525 million has given Rupert Murdoch a satellite television footprint over Asia and the Middle East with a potential audience of 4.5 billion viewers. When allied to his other television interests, primarily Sky TV (UK) and Fox TV (USA), News Coporation's television interests alone have a global reach of some two-thirds of the planet.

One of the prime reasons for these developments is the search for synergy. In effect, synergy means the bringing together of the various elements of television and other media at the levels of both production and distribution so that they fit together and complement each other in order to produce lower costs and higher profits. Consequently, what is significant in looking at the News Corporation dominion is not just the spatial breadth of ownership but also the potential link-ups between its various elements. For example, in Twentieth Century Fox and Star TV Murdoch acquired a huge library of film and television product that he can channel through his network of distribution outlets. He clearly hopes to create a lucrative global advertising market. At the same time, Murdoch can use his newspapers to promote his television interests by giving space in his press holdings to the sporting activities covered by his television channels. Thus does News Corporation make the gains accruing to synergy whose intertextual link-ups are paralleled by technological and organizational convergence.

It has been estimated that by 2005 there will be 25 million interactive cable households in the USA and some 22 million in Europe (*Screen Digest*, October 1994). More recent estimates place the European digital cable market at 18 million by 2003, a forty-four-fold increase on the 1999 figure (*Screen Digest*, January 2001). This expansion of the Internet and interactive cable is said to be laying the foundations for a 'super information highway': that is, television sets with built-in computers that are linked to cable, enabling us to order and pay for shopping, transfer e-money, keep an eye on our bank accounts, call up a selection of films, and search the World-Wide Web for information.

The idea of PC-TV highlights the issue of technological convergence: that is, technologies that had once been produced and used separately are beginning to merge into one. To a considerable degree, technological convergence is enabled by digital technology that permits information to be electronically organized into bytes, or discrete bundles of information, that can be compressed during transmission and decompressed on arrival. This allows a good deal more information to travel down any given conduit, be that cable, satellite or terrestrial signals (it also opens up previously unusable zones of the spectrum) and at greater speed over larger distances. Indeed, the impact of new technologies in general, and digital processes in particular, can be summed up in terms of speed, volume and distance: that is, more information at greater speed over larger distances.

Alongside the development of digital television, it is becoming apparent that the technologies having the most impact are those concerned with distribution, that is, cable and satellite. Thus, organizations that control the distribution mechanisms are eclipsing the power of producers because no one wants to commit expensive resources to a project that has not secured a distribution agreement. Indeed, distributors are becoming producers and vice versa.

The impact of satellite technology has of course been distinct in different parts of the world. In India, the development of commercial satellite television threatens the dominance of state-owned television (Doordarshan), (thus forcing the government to entertain commercial broadcasting), whereas in Britain, though the satellite-distributed channels of Sky TV have had some success in creating a niche for themselves, especially in relation to sport, their audience share of 8 per cent has some way to go before they can even conceive of dislodging the BBC or ITV stations. A similar contrast can be made between Holland, where the Luxembourg-based RTL4 satellite station has made decisive inroads into the Dutch market, and the USA, where Direct Satellite Broadcasting (DBS) has had little impact, having been eclipsed by cable (though News Corporation's intervention in the market may change this).

Unsurprisingly, there is also extremely unequal distribution of the quarter of a billion cabled households across the globe. For example, nearly 70 per cent of television households have access to cable in North America, some 23 per cent in the European Union, 20 per cent in Asia and only 7 per cent in South America. World levels of cable penetration of television households stand at about 23 per cent (*Screen Digest*, April 1995). The USA has about 66 million cabled households compared to 57 million in China, 19 million in India, 1.3 million in Brazil and 0.02 in Indonesia (see Table 7.1). In the USA, cable expanded at a considerable rate during the early 1980s (indeed Fox TV is effectively a fourth network), though the latter part of the decade saw a considerable slowing of penetration rates. In contrast, cable struggled in the UK, which has one of the lowest cable density rates in Europe, despite government attempts to encourage

its development. However, during the 1990s a new wave of American investment in British cable, combined with its use as a carrier for satellite programmes,
prompted a gradual expansion of cable, though it is a long way from the 95 per
cent penetration level enjoyed by the Netherlands – the most densely cabled
country in Europe.

Deregulation and reregulation

The kinds of synergy and convergence described above have been made to
happen by the captains of industry and allowed to happen by politicians.
Though multi-media conglomerates have been with us for many years, the
scope of their activities has been permitted to widen by governments who have
relaxed the regulations that restricted cross-media ownership and the entry of
new players. In particular, during the mid-1980s and early 1990s we witnessed
a significant period of deregulation or, to be more accurate, reregulation in
European and North American television. These new regulations are consider-
ably less stringent than their predecessors and prompted widespread discussion
about the emerging shape of the new tele-landscapes.

In Europe, the 'old order' was marked by the subordination of broadcasting
to public service goals set in the context of a broadly political process of regulation. Television was of a largely national character and was generally
non-commercial in principle. By contrast, the television order that emerged
during the 1980s was marked by the co-existence of public and commercial
broadcasting, the deregulation of commercial television, the increasing emergence of multi-media transnational companies and pressure on public service
television to operate with a commercial logic (McQuail et al., 1992). While there
has been some decline in the viewing figures for public television in Europe, this
has not as yet proved to be terminal. Indeed, public service broadcasting has
proved surprisingly resilient in the face of competition.

For example, in Australia the nationally funded ABC has achieved its highest ratings for decades and in Britain the BBC looks set to remain a major
player for the foreseeable future. In Italy the public RAI channels rate better
than their combined commercial rivals, while in India the state-owned
Doordarshan is fighting back against commercial opposition. However,
though they have survived, public service organizations are now simply one
player, instead of being *the* player, in the more plural and fragmented global
television landscape that sedimented itself during the 1990s and looks set to
grow into the new century.

---

*In sum, the processes of synergy, convergence and deregulation have seen the creation and
growth of multi-media corporations that span the globe. While public television continues to
survive, growth in global television has been fuelled by commercial concerns.*

Programme flows in global television

Mapping global electronic culture, in this instance through the example of television, requires us to consider not only the political economy of the industry, but
also the evidence regarding the flow and distribution of television texts. Thus,
concerns about media imperialism have been fuelled by a very limited number
of somewhat out-dated studies of the global television trade. The authors of
these studies concluded that international programming flows are dominated by
the USA (Varis, 1974, 1984). Certainly America is the world's major exporter of
television programmes, a position enabled by the economics of the industry,
which allows US producers to cover much of their costs in the domestic market,
leaving exports as profit. This enables American producers to sell their programmes abroad at a level borne by the market rather than by the production
costs of a given programme. Thus, an episode of a popular programme costing
$1.5 million to produce can be sold in France for $50,000 and in Zimbabwe for
$500. Of course the world-wide familiarity with, and popularity of, Hollywood
narrative techniques also plays its part.

While, in the late 1980s, 44 per cent of all imported television hours to
Western Europe came from the USA, Sepstrup (1989) argues that what is more
relevant is that 73 per cent of the total national supply in all of Western Europe
was domestically produced. Some critics argue that the USA can claim at least 75
per cent of world-wide television programme exports (Hoskins et al., 1995). Yet
a growing number of nations are producing an increasing proportion of their
own programming and a significant number of them are 'doing over half of their
own programming, both in the total broadcast day and during primetime'
(Straubhaar, 1997: 293).

Indeed, there has been a distinct move towards *regionalization* of markets on
the basis of shared language, culture and historical trade links. Thus Straubhaar
(1997) argues that there are a number of 'geo-cultural' markets emerging, including those based on Western Europe, Latin America, the Francophone world of
France and its former colonies, an Arabic world market, a Chinese market and
a South Asian market. Further, these markets are not necessarily bounded by
geographical space, but involve diaspora populations distributed world-wide.
For example, the Indian film industry serves not only the Indian sub-continent
but also areas of Africa, Malaysia, Indonesia and Europe.

Television texts: the global and the local

Television has become a globalized cultural form through its circulation of similar narrative styles around the world: soap opera, news, sport, quiz shows and
music videos can be found in most countries. Soap opera, for example, is a
global form in two senses: it is a narrative mode produced in a variety of countries across the globe, and it is one of the most exported forms of television,

viewed in a range of cultural contexts. The global attraction of soap opera can be partly attributed to the apparently universal appeal of open-ended narrative forms, the centrality of personal and kinship relations, and in some circumstances the emergence of an international style embedded in the traditions of Hollywood. However, the success of the soap opera also reflects the possibilities offered to audiences of engaging in local or regional issues and problems located in recognizable places. For example, while South African television screens a good deal of American and Australian soap opera, it is also possible to watch the locally produced *Generations*.

The tensions between the poles of the global and the local are highlighted by, on the one hand, the enormous global popularity of soaps like *Neighbours* and *Dallas*, and, on the other, the failure of these very same soaps in particular countries (e.g. *Neighbours* in America, *Dallas* in Japan). As Crofts (1995) has pointed out, the global successes, and failures, of soap opera depend on both the specificities of soap opera as a televisual form and the particularities of its conditions of reception. While we have witnessed the emergence of an international prime-time soap opera style, including high production values, pleasing visual appearances and fast-paced action-oriented narrative modes, many soaps still retain local settings, regional language audiences and slow-paced melodramatic story telling.

Similar arguments can be put in relation to the genre of news, which shows both global similarities and local differences. The general case for regarding news as a global phenomenon rests on the establishment of news exchange arrangements whereby subscribing news organizations have organized a reciprocal trade in news material with a particular emphasis on the sharing of visual footage. Consequently, Straubhaar (1992) concluded (based on a cross-cultural study involving the USA, USSR, Japan, West Germany, Italy, India, Columbia and China) that 'what is news' is 'fairly consistent' from country to country, and that the format of twenty- to forty-minute programmes anchored by presenters was a common feature. Likewise, data collected by Gurevitch et al. (1991) about the Eurovision News Exchange and the thirty-six countries which regularly use it suggest that the availability of common news footage and a shared professional culture has led to 'substantial, but not complete' convergence of news stories.

That Straubhaar should have found similarity over difference may reflect 'the drift towards an international standardization of basic journalistic discourses' (Dahlgren, 1995: 49) and the domination of global news agendas by western news agencies. The raw material of international news is gathered, selected and controlled by western transnational corporations that treat news as a commodity to be bought and sold. For example, two large western services, Visnews and WTN, are powerful forces within television news. Further, there is an emerging direct supply of finished news product offered to audiences via satellite television, most notably by CNN, the BBC and News Corporation. However, the fact that western news agencies tend to supply 'spot news' and visual reports without commentary still allows different verbal interpretations of events to be dubbed over the pictures. This has led to what Gurevitch et al. (1991) call the 'domestication' of global news, which they regard as a 'counter-vailing force to the pull of globalization'.

Global postmodern culture

In addition to the circulation of specific genres like soap opera and news, the global multiplication of communications technologies has created an increasingly complex semiotic environment in which television produces and circulates an explosive display of competing signs and meanings. This creates a flow of images that fuses news, views, drama and reportage so that the juxtapositions of a variety of images and meanings form an electronic bricolage. Thus, the globalization of television is at the heart of the image production and circulation which forms that collage of stitched-together images which is core to postmodern cultural style. This is both an outcome of the flow of a given channel and a reflection of multi-channel diversity by which viewers are able to zip and zap, channel change and fast forward. In doing so they create a 'strip text' (Newcombe, 1988) of their own, adopting the 'appropriate' reading attitudes and competencies as required.

The stylistic markers of the postmodern in television have been seen as:

- aesthetic self-consciousness/self-reflexiveness;
- juxtaposition/montage;
- paradox, ambiguity and uncertainty;
- the blurring of the boundaries of genre, style and history.

Techniques include montage, rapid cutting, non-linear narrative techniques and the de-contextualization of images, so that programmes that have commonly been identified with the postmodern decentre the importance of linear narrative in favour of a new look and feel in which image takes precedence over story-telling (Kellner, 1992).

The American TV cartoons *The Simpsons* and *South Park* are widely regarded as being indicative of a postmodern televisual style. The former has made a 'dysfunctional' American family the ironic heroes of a series that is double-coded in its appeal to children and adults. It is both entertainment and a subtle reflection on American cultural life. Here, in accordance with contemporary culture, the television set is at the heart of the Simpsons' life as well as that of its audience. Further, the programme requires us to have a self-conscious awareness of other television and film genres as it makes a range of intertextual references. For example, *Itchy and Scratchy*, the Simpson children's favourite cartoon, parodies *Tom and Jerry*, mocking the double standard by which television violence is simultaneously condemned and enjoyed.

The postmodern markers of ambivalence, irony and intertextuality are equally evident in the popular show *South Park*, which parodies a series of cultural stereotypes. Here we are presented with a range of small-minded racist and sexist characters in conjunction with a series of stereotypes of race, gender, age, body size, and so on. Yet the show manages to undermine the stereotypes by making us laugh at them. For example, the representation of the African-American chef as the sexy black soul singer, the Barry White of *South Park*, parodies the 'original' image as itself a stereotype. This is given an added intertextual dimension and ironic twist by the voice of Isaac Hayes, known for the theme song to the blaxploitation *Shaft* movies. Overall, the show walks the thin line between offending everyone and undermining the offence. It takes nothing seriously while making serious statements about, for example, the use of television as a child-minder.

Promo culture

The development of global television in a fundamentally commercial form has placed that core activity of consumer culture, visual-based advertising, in the forefront of its activities. Consequently, television is pivotal to the production and reproduction of a promotional culture focused on the use of visual imagery to create value-added brands or commodity-signs. Indeed, Wernick argues that cultural phenomena which serve to communicate a promotional message of some type or another have become 'virtually co-extensive with our produced symbolic world' (1991: 184). The phrase 'Coca-Cola culture' encapsulates the global reach of this promotional phenomenon and highlights the alleged link between global capitalism, advertising and cultural homogenization. That is, global processes are argued to represent a form of cultural homogenization, particularly in the field of consumer culture, so that Coca-Cola, McDonald's, Nike and Microsoft's Windows circulate world-wide.

For some critics, contemporary consumer culture is depthless and meaningless, while for others it is to be welcomed as a new and popular form of transgressive culture. Thus, for Baudrillard, postmodern culture is constituted through a continual flow of images that establishes no connotational hierarchy. Rather, it is argued to be flat and one-dimensional, literally and metaphorically 'superficial'.

By way of contrast, Kaplan (1987) claims a transgressive and progressive role for postmodern culture and its collapsing of established cultural boundaries. Thus, she argues that the postmodern music video offers, in deconstructionist mode, no assured narrative position for the viewer, undermining the status of representation as real or true. Further, for Chambers (1986, 1990), consumers construct multiple identities thorough selecting and arranging elements of material commodities and meaningful signs into a personal style. Indeed,

---

The ways in which audiences make use of the competing meanings embodied in texts, including those of television, become the touchstone of arguments about globalization and cultural imperialism.

Global audiences and creative consumption

The argument that globalization is a form of cultural imperialism in which western-produced texts dominate and destroy other cultures has implicitly relied on the so-called 'hypodermic model' of audience response. That is, it has been assumed that the meanings that critics identify as being embodied in a text are also those that audiences activate and take up. If, for example, the world of Disney films represents American capitalism as the desirable highpoint of human civilization, then this is what the apparently passive and mindless viewers of film and TV will adopt as their own values.

However, it is now widely held that television audiences are active producers of meaning and do not simply and uncritically accept 'official' textual meanings. Rather, they bring previously acquired cultural competencies to bear on texts, enabling them to generate an array of meanings. Further, since texts do not embody one set of unambiguous meanings but are polysemic, that is, they are carriers of multiple meanings, differently constituted audiences will work with different textual meanings. In this context, there is now a good deal of mutually supportive work on television audiences within the cultural studies tradition from which the following conclusions can be drawn:

- Audiences are conceived of as active and knowledgeable producers of meaning not products of a structured text.
- Meanings are bounded by the way the text is organized and by the domestic and cultural circumstances under which they are viewed.
- Audiences need to be understood in the contexts in which they watch television, in terms of both meaning construction and the routines of daily life.
- Audiences are easily able to distinguish between fiction and reality; indeed they actively play with the boundaries between them.
- The processes of meaning construction, and the place of television in the routines of daily life, alter from culture to culture and in terms of ethnicity, gender and class within the same cultural community.

As such, television and other cultural texts are best seen as *resources* that we draw on in a variety of different ways. Thus, we should talk not of an audience so much as audiences who use television to construct a range of meanings in the context of the wider circumstances of their lives. This will include their engagement with discourses found in other cultural sites. However, to simply associate the active audience with an inevitable resistance to 'ideology' or cultural homogenization is as mistaken as the previous reliance on the hypodermic model of audience response. Indeed, the construction of multiple audience positions is entirely compatible with a wider consumer culture of niche marketing, while the adoption of any ideology or identity, be it critical or conservative, *requires* audiences to be actively engaged with texts.

Audiences are *always active* in relation to decoding texts, whose meanings are continually unstable and in flux. Hence, the critical questions do not surround whether audiences are active as such but what the consequences of their activity are. That is, how, in the over-determined and chaotic play of audiences' discursive competencies and television's preferred encodings, does meaning come to be stabilized into those representations with which audiences identify and from which they construct their identities? Indeed, the argument presented below suggests that television plays a role in the creation of hybrid identities rather than the reproduction of western identities, as the cultural imperialism thesis argues. However, this contention continues to credit television with an impact amongst audiences through the provision of alternative resources. It is just that this role is now understood to be less clear-cut than implied by hypodermic audience models and the premises of the cultural imperialism thesis.

In this context, watching television is both constitutive of and constituted by forms of cultural identity. In other words, television forms a symbolic resource for the construction of cultural identity, just as audiences draw from their own sedimented cultural identities and cultural competencies to decode programmes in their own specific ways. Whether audience decodings constitute 'resistance' to cultural homogenization is a case-by-case empirical question.

Television audiences and cultural identity

Perhaps the most distinguished empirical study of national and ethnic cultural identity and television fiction viewing is Liebes and Katz's (1991) focus group exploration of the reception of *Dallas* amongst viewers from a range of cultural and ethnic backgrounds. What makes the Liebes/Katz *Dallas* project of particular interest is its exploration of the cross-cultural dimensions of viewing. Their study, which assumed that members of the groups would discuss the text with each other and develop interpretations together based on mutual cultural awareness, was looking for evidence of different readings of *Dallas* in terms of comprehension and critical ability. Liebes and Katz argue that their study does indeed provide evidence of divergent readings of the narrative founded in different cultural backgrounds.

In particular, they explore the differences between 'referential' and 'critical' approaches to the programme across a range of ethnically based focus groups. By 'referential', they mean an understanding of *Dallas* that takes the programme to be referring to 'reality' and discusses it as if it were real. By 'critical', they mean an awareness of the fabricated character of the text as evidenced by group discussions of the mechanisms of narrative construction and the economics of the television industry. Liebes and Katz argue there were distinct differences between ethnic groups in the levels of each type of statement, and conclude that Americans and Russians were particularly critical.

However, the critical awareness displayed by Americans was centred on questions of form and production context, based on their greater understanding of the business of television. Americans were less critical in terms of content and tended to assume *Dallas* has no themes and 'ideology' but is merely entertainment. In contrast, the Russians were more critical of the 'politics' of Dallas, seeing it as a distorted representation of the capitalist West, while Arab groups had a high sensitivity to the 'dangers' of Western culture and of western 'moral degeneracy'.

Significantly, we can draw the conclusion that audiences use their own sense of national and ethnic identity as a position from which to decode programmes, so that, for example, American programmes are not always uncritically consumed by audiences with the destruction of 'indigenous' cultural identities as the inevitable outcome. Indeed, the very deployment of their own cultural identifications as a point of resistance to 'foreign' texts and values also helps to constitute that very cultural identity through its enunciation.

Thus, Miller (1995) argues in his study of television in Trinidad that we would be mistaken in regarding the US soap *The Young and the Restless* simply as the export and consumption of American culture or as the unproblematic carrier of modernity and consumer culture. Instead, he recounts the ways in which the soap opera is 'localized', made sense of and absorbed into local practices and meanings.

Miller demonstrates the social and participatory nature of soap opera viewing alongside a sense of the relevance of the narrative content for moral issues in Trinidad. In particular, the gossip and scandal (specifically that of a sexual nature) which are core concerns of the soap opera's narrative resonate with the Trinidadian concept of 'bacchanal', which, according to Miller, is a deeply rooted folk concept that fuses ideas of confusion, gossip, scandal and truth. The concern of the soap thus 'colludes with the local sense of truth as exposure and scandal' (Miller, 1995: 223). Miller's work is significant because it suggests that the study of the formal characteristics of narratives is insufficient and stresses the need to understand local processes of absorption and transformation that, by their very nature, will be specific, contingent and unpredictable.

That television is uneven and contradictory in its impact is further illustrated by research work undertaken in China. Here, according to Lull (1991, 1997), is a television system introduced by a government that was keen to use it as a form of social control and cultural homogenization. However, it has turned out to have quite the opposite consequence. Although the Chinese government have attempted to use television to re-establish social stability after Tiananmen Square, and preserve the authority of the Communist Party, it has instead become a central agent of popular resistance. Television has amplified and intensified the diversity of cultural and political sentiments in China by presenting alternative views of life. For example, commercial and imported dramas have been juxtaposed with China's own economic difficulties as television, driven by the need to attract larger audiences, becomes a cultural forum of competing ideas. Further, not only are programmes themselves polysemic, but audiences have become adept at reading between the lines of official pronouncements. For Lull, the challenge to autocratic rule raised by the Chinese resistance movement, with its stress on freedom and democracy, could not have happened without television.

In short, though television may circulate discourse on a global scale, its consumption and use as a resource for the construction of cultural identities always take place in a local context.

Resistance and creative consumption

The argument that audiences are not cultural dopes but active producers of meaning who operate from within their own cultural contexts forms a part of a larger discourse about creative consumption (see Chapter 8). For example, Willis (1990) argues that young people have an active, creative and symbolically productive relation to the commodities that are constitutive of youth culture. Meaning, he suggests, is not inherent in the commodity but is produced through actual usage. This he calls 'grounded aesthetics':

> the specifically creative and dynamic moments of a whole process of cultural life, of cultural birth and rebirth . . . This is a making specific of the ways in which the received natural and social world is made human *to them* and made, to however small a degree (even if finally symbolic), controllable by them. (Willis, 1990: 22)

Hence, for Willis, contemporary culture is not meaningless or superficial but involves the active creation of meaning by all people as cultural producers. Indeed he argues that it is the very expansion of consumer capitalism that has provided the symbolic resources for young people's creative work.

Traditionally, the resources required for cultural 'resistance' have been located in some measure outside of the dominating culture. However, when consumer capitalism is the stated target for resistance, there is virtually no aspect of contemporary culture that can be said to be external to it. If resistance is taking place, it is taking place within commodity culture and is not best understood as a simple reversal of the order of high and low, of power and its absence. This is the kind of resistance that de Certeau (1984) has in mind when he distinguishes between the *strategies* of power, which mark out spaces for power that are distinct from its environs (through which it can operate as a subject of will), and the *tactics* of the poacher (see Chapter 8). Here, for example, young people take the commodities of record companies, clothes manufacturers and magazines and, in the spaces of clubs, pubs and streets, make them their own, investing them with their own meanings.

Yet such resistance is always limited in the scope of its challenge, which can only ever be partial (see Chapter 8). Resistance is always a matter of degree and within the eye of the beholder. It is to be evaluated, on the one hand, in terms of our values and, on the other, in relation to our judgement as to what is possible. There is no rulebook and there are no guarantees. For example, what are we to make of an emergent global youth culture that is implicated in consumer capitalism?

Syncretic global youth culture

For some critics, the emergence of brands like Nike, Levi, Playstation, Coca-Cola and MTV in tandem with the promotion of international pop stars represents the commodification and subsequent homogenization of youth culture. For other writers, global youth culture is understood as more chaotic and syncretic in character, representing the forging of creative and hybrid cultural forms. For example, as American, Jamaican, West African, South African, British, Indian, German and Icelandic (amongst others), rap music cannot be said to have any single point of origin or authenticity. Rap is always already a cultural hybridization.

Consider the prevalence and popularity of American inspired hip-hop and rap music on South African television and amongst black South Africans. South African rappers take an apparently non-African musical form and give it an African twist to create a form of hybridization that is now being exported back to the West. Further, rap, which is commonly described as American, can be said to have travelled to the USA from the Caribbean and can trace its roots/routes back to the influence of West African music and the impact of slavery. Thus, any idea of clear-cut lines of demarcation between the 'internal' and 'external' are swept away. Rap has no obvious point of 'origin' and its American form is indebted to Africa. Consequently, its popularity in Soweto cannot justifiably be called cultural imperialism.

In Britain, Asian youth have produced their own hybrid forms of ragga-bhangra-reggae-rap cross-overs. Indeed, African-American and black British fashion, music and dance styles are appropriated by Asian youth and absorbed into their own lifestyles (Gillespie, 1995). For Mercer, these 'emerging cultures of hybridity, forged among the overlapping African, Asian and Caribbean diaspora' (1994: 3), are a challenge to white western authority as well as being ways of living with and in 'conditions of crisis and transition'.

Massey (1998) highlights some of the issues raised by the emergence of a global youth culture. She recounts how, after interviewing a group of Mayan women in the Yucatán (Mexico), she turned away from this picture of apparently authentic and indigenous culture to be confronted by a dozen young people playing computer games and listening to western music. 'Electronic noises, American slang and bits of Western music floated off into the night-time jungle' (Massey, 1998: 121). She argues that while this youth culture of Yucatán Maya is not a closed 'local' culture, it is not an undifferentiatedly global (or American) one either. It is a product of interaction in which the terms 'local' and 'global' are themselves in dispute. In each particular youth culture the mix of the global and the local will be different. Indeed, what is or is not a global status symbol for youth will vary by location.

What is at stake here is not just an understanding of youth but the place of culture. Culture is a matter less of locations with roots than of hybrid and cre-olized cultural routes in global space (see Chapters 4 and 8). Youth cultures are not pure, authentic and locally bounded; rather, they are syncretic and hybridized products of interactions across space. Of course, global intercon-nections are always imbued with power and the terms of cultural mixing are uneven. It is commonly American popular culture that is valued by global youth as the symbol of international status. However, the traffic is not all one-way. For example, the impact of 'world music' and 'Eastern' philosophies such as Hinduism and Buddhism amongst young people mark the impact of non-western culture within the West. These developments are commonly heightened by contact with diaspora populations located in the heart of the West. Thus Afro-Caribbean-originated reggae and the 'red, green and gold' of Rastafarianism became a sign of resistance and solidarity for First World Blacks within Britain.

Diaspora and hybrid identities

The concept of diaspora focuses our attention on travel, journeys, dispersion, homes and borders in the context of questions about who travels, where, when, how and under what circumstances. Thus diaspora identities are at once local and global, being formed through networks of transnational identifications. The concept of the diaspora is a relational one involving arrangements of power that differentiate them internally as well as situating them in relation to one another. Thus,

> Diaspora space as a conceptual category is 'inhabited' not only by those who have migrated and their descendants, but equally by those who are constructed and repre-sented as indigenous. In other words, the concept of *diaspora space* . . . includes the entanglement, the intertwining of the genealogies of dispersion with those 'staying put'. The diaspora space is the site where *the native is as much a diasporian as the dias-porian is a native*. (Brah, 1996: 209)

The concept of diaspora directs our attention to the contingent and indeter-minate character of identities. That is to say, the continual construction and deconstruction of cultural identities across space is emphasized rather than a sense of their being absolutes of nature, culture and place (see Chapter 4). By way of example, Gilroy (1993) introduces the concept of the Black Atlantic. Black identities cannot be understood in terms of being American or British or West Indian, he argues. Nor can they be grasped in terms of ethnic absolutism. Rather, they should be understood in terms of the black diaspora of the Atlantic. Here, cultural exchange produces hybrid identities and cultural forms of similarity and difference within and between the various locales of the diaspora wherein black 'self-definitions and cultural expressions draw on a plurality of black histories and politics' (Gilroy, 1987).

Hybridization and creolization

The physical meeting and mixing of peoples across the globe, as exemplified by the Black Atlantic and other diaspora formations, throws the whole notion of national or ethnic culture and literature into doubt. Thus, the hybridization and creolization of language, literature and cultural identities is a common theme of postcolonial literature and theory, marking a certain meeting of minds with postmodernism. For example, increasing significance has attached to the idea of the 'Creole continuum': that is, a series of overlapping language uses and code-switching that not only deploys the specific modes of other languages, say English and French, but also invents forms peculiar to itself.

Creolization stresses language as a cultural practice over and against the abstractions of grammar or any notions of 'correct' language usage. Here, dialogue with the values and customs of the past allows traditions to be transformed into the midwives of the new so that the meanings of old words are changed and fresh ones brought into being. At the same time, neither the colonial nor the colonized cultures and languages can be presented in 'pure' form, nor can they be separated from each other. This gives rise to a hybridity that challenges not only the centrality of colonial culture and the marginalization of the colonized, but also the very idea of centre and margin as being anything other than 'representational effects'.

The concept of hybridity has proved useful in highlighting cultural mixing and the emergence of new forms of identity. However, we need to differentiate between types of hybridity and to do so with reference to the specific circumstances of particular social groups. This requires us to recognize the range of cultural and national identities that are formed and unformed over time and across a variety of spaces. We might in theory think of at least six different kinds of cultural juxtaposing (Barker, 1997):

- Two distinct cultural traditions are kept separate in time and/or space. We would define ourselves as Asian *or* British, Mexican *or* American. This is the domain of nationalism and ethnic absolutism.
- Two separate cultural traditions are juxtaposed in time and space. We would

define ourselves as Asian *and* British, Mexican *and* American, moving between them as situationally appropriate.
- Cultures are translocal and involve global flows. Hybridization occurs out of recognition of difference and produces something new. We are 'British Asian' or 'Mexican American'.
- Cultural traditions develop in separate locales but develop identifications based on perceived similarity and commonalty of tradition and circumstance: for example, an essentialist version of pan-global black or Hispanic nationalism.
- One cultural tradition absorbs or obliterates the other and creates effective similarity. This could involve assimilation ('My parents are Asian but I am British') or cultural domination and imperialism (one tradition is wiped out).
- New forms of identity are forged out of shared concerns along the axes of class, ethnicity, gender, age, and so forth. This is an anti-essentialist position in which similarity is forged strategically. For example, a strategic alliance in which black and Asian people share a common anti-racist strategy. Equally, strategic identifications and alliances occur on other axes, such as gender so that a shared feminism might be more significant for some people than ethnic difference.

As was argued in Chapter 4, the concept of hybridity remains problematic insofar as it assumes or implies the meeting or mixing of completely separate and homogeneous cultural spheres. To think of British Asian or Polish American hybrid forms as the mixing of two separate traditions is problematic because none of the component parts are bounded and homogeneous. Each category is always already a hybrid form that is also divided along the lines of religion, class, gender, age, nationality, and so forth.

Hybridization is the mixing of that which is already a hybrid, so that all cultural practices are hybrids. There is no pure cultural practice that belongs in one place or to one people.

Nevertheless, the theory of hybridity has enabled us to recognize the production of new identities and cultural forms, for example 'British Asians' and British bhangra. Thus, the concept of hybridity is acceptable as a device to capture cultural change by way of a strategic cut or temporary stabilization of cultural categories.

Hybridity and British Asians

In the UK, the position of Asian cultures and identities in relation to Anglo and Afro-Caribbean Britons has raised issues of purity and hybridity. In particular, the emergence of British-born young 'Asians' gave rise to a generation that was much more deeply involved in transactions across ethnic boundaries than were the original migrants. Young British Asians went to school with white and Afro-Caribbean Britons, shared leisure sites, watched television and were frequently bilingual. Consequently, British Asian young people have developed their own home-grown syncretic or hybrid cultural forms along with political and cultural discourses of 'British Asianness'.

In her study of Asian youth in Southall (London), Gillespie (1995) shows how young people constitute themselves, to varying degrees, as British Asian. Under some circumstances she describes identification with Britishness, whereas at other times identification is with aspects of Asian culture (neither being homogeneous). For example, the circumstances of the Gulf War opened up ambiguities and insecurities around those questions of belonging. On the one hand, some young Asians identified with an Islamic 'developing nation' in conflict with the West. On the other hand, they wanted to remain within the boundaries of Britishness, the place of their birth and upbringing. Consequently, these young people shifted from one subject position to another as they determined it to be situationally appropriate. This shifting within and between the discourses of Britishness and Asianness was further complicated by religious and geographical differences within Asian culture and by age, gender and class. Contemporary events surrounding the so-called 'War on Terrorism' raise similar identity dilemmas for young British Muslims.

In my own study (Barker, 1999) I explored the way in which young British Asian girls enunciated identities in the context of everyday talk about television soap operas. Issues of globalization formed a background to the study in two ways:

- Soap opera is one of the prime genres of global television; there are few television systems that do not produce and/or import soap operas.
- These girls are the second- and third-generation children of migrants from India whose arrival in Britain is an aspect of global economic and political forces.

The position of British Asian girls in British culture is significant and special by virtue of living across cultural boundaries – at its simplest, Asian, Afro-Caribbean and white – and also, as girls, being somewhat marginalized within male-dominated cultures. These girls need to be able to reflect across the range of their identity experiences to 'make sense' of their lives and are arguably in a unique position to construct hybrid identities reflexively. They are aware of themselves as operating across discourses and sites of activity and offer some insights into their own circumstances. Further, the kinds of Asian identities constructed by these girls were not 'pure' or essentialist Asian identities; rather, they were British Asian hybrids cross-cut by considerations of gender. Through an active engagement with soap opera, and in particular through collective talk, the girls defined themselves as Asian at the same time as they reworked the meaning of Asianness to encompass their own British Asian hybrid identities.

Globalization and power

There is little doubt that capitalist modernity does involve an element of cultural homogenization for it increases the levels and amount of global co-ordination. However, mechanisms of fragmentation, heterogenization and hybridity are also at work, so that it is 'not a question of *either* homogenization or heterogenization, but rather of the ways in which both of these two tendencies have become features of life across much of the contemporary world' (Robertson, 1992: 27). Thus, the valorizing of bounded cultures, ethnic resilience and the re-emergence of powerful nationalistic sentiments co-exist with cultures as 'trans-local learning processes' (Pieterse, 1995).

In this context, much of what is cast as cultural imperialism is better understood as the creation of a layer of western capitalist modernity which overlays, but does not necessarily obliterate, pre-existing cultural forms. Modern and postmodern ideas about time, space, rationality, capitalism, consumerism, sexuality, family, gender, and so forth, are placed alongside older discourses, setting up 'ideological' competition between them. The outcome may be both a range of hybrid forms of identity *and* the production of traditional, 'fundamentalist' and nationalist identities. Nationalism and the nation-state continue to co-exist with cosmopolitanism and the weakening of national identities. The processes of reverse flow, fragmentation and hybridization are quite as strong as the push towards homogenization.

Though the concepts of globalization and hybridity are more adequate than that of cultural imperialism, because they suggest a less coherent, unified and directed process, this should not lead us to abandon the exploration of power and inequality. The fact that power is diffused, or that commodities are subversively used to produce new hybrid identities, does not displace our need to examine it. As Pieterse argues:

> Relations of power and hegemony are inscribed and reproduced *within* hybridity for wherever we look closely enough we find the traces of asymmetry in culture, place, descent. Hence hybridity raises the question of the terms of the mixture, the conditions of mixing and mélange. At the same time it's important to note the ways in which hegemony is not merely reproduced but *refigured* in the process of hybridization. (1995: 57)

For example, the cultural hybridity produced by the black diaspora does not obscure the power that was embedded in the moment of slavery or the economic push–pull of migration. As Hall argues, diaspora identities are constructed within and by cultural power. 'This power', he suggests, 'has become a constitutive element in our own identities' (Hall, 1992b: 233). Thus, the cultural identities of rich white men in New York are of a very different order to those of poor Asian women in rural India. While we are all part of a global society whose consequences no one can escape, we remain unequal participants in it.

Globalization is spatially, culturally and politically an uneven set of processes. Consequently, one of the tasks of cultural studies in the era of glob-alization is to work out how and where the lines of power within contemporary culture are emerging and with what consequences. As I have suggested, one such domain of study is the role that television plays in the construction of hybrid identities. Here, we should be aware that while we are right to credit audiences with an active role in interpreting television, nevertheless, the fact that the discourses of an international medium are partially incorporated into hybrid identities does suggest that television has an impact within non-western cul-tures, though this is not best understood as a form of imperialism.

Is a global conversation possible?

The exchange of cultural goods and meanings of which television forms a part can be regarded as contributing to a global cosmopolitan 'conversation'. However, both practical and theoretical considerations warn against excessive optimism. For example, continued conflict in the Middle East, the day-to-day racism of western cities and the simple fact of global differences in wealth, power and tradition do not meet the criteria for sensible negotiation let alone a conversation between equals. On a theoretical level, Lyotard has argued that 'there is no unity of language, but rather islets of language, each governed by a system of rules untranslatable into those of others' (1984: 61). In this view, truth and meaning are constituted by their place in specific local language-games and cannot be universal in character. In Lyotard's interpretation, this implies the 'incommensurability' or untranslatability of languages and cultures. That is, since all knowledge is postional or culture-bound, cultural and political discourses are incommensurable for there is no metalanguage of translation. Hence it is said that we cannot bridge cultures but must be satisfied with being specific to times and places.

However, Rorty (1991a) argues that we should see language as a *practice* that utilizes skills. Though exact translation of languages or cultures is not feasible, we can learn the skills of language. If we consider languages (and thus culture) as constituted not by untranslatable and incompatible rules but by learnable *skills*, then incommensurable languages could only be unlearnable languages (which Davidson [1984] argues is not possible). This would encourage *dialogue* and the attempt to reach pragmatic agreements. There is no *a priori* reason why this should succeed – agreement may never be reached – but there is no *a priori* reason why it should fail either.

Given that the alternatives to talking are violence and/or isolationism, seeking practical agreements based on continual dialogue remains the urgent task.

Conclusions

In this chapter it has been argued that globalization is not best understood in terms of cultural imperialism and the homogenization of world culture. Rather, it was suggested that while the forces of homogenization are certainly in evidence, of equal significance is the place of heterogenization and localization. The processes of localizing the global are in part an outcome of audiences' capacities to create their own meanings from texts. Here it was suggested that audiences are active creators of meaning and not simpletons who swallow whole everything television has to offer. Rather, television provides us with resources that we draw on to construct our identities in a variety of different ways. This does not mean that audiences can create any intelligible meanings from cultural texts. Indeed, the critical issue is not whether audiences are active but rather what the outcomes of that activity are.

The relationship between globalization, television and cultural identities is a complex one that gives rise to a variety of outcomes. These include absolutist ethnic identities, fundamentalist religious identities, hybrid cross-cultural identities, fragmented multiple identities, postmodern neo-tribes, 'third cultures' of trans-global workers and intellectuals and a paradoxical understanding that while our planet is a finite bounded space, it is composed of diverse cultures and peoples with complex local and global cultural identities. This intricacy and diversity suggest that globalization and hybridity are preferred concepts to imperialism and homogeneity as we enter the twenty-first century. Nevertheless, it was also suggested that de-centring conceptions of cultural imperialism in favour of the idea of globalization did not negate the necessity to explore issues of economic and cultural power. Indeed, hybrid cultures and identities are themselves embroiled in questions of might and mastery. Over all, the whole domain of culture and globalization is best thought of not in terms of binaries – i.e. homogeneity or heterogeneity; active or passive – but through their blending and supersedence.

8 Transforming Capitalism

Central problem:
The persistence of capitalism and the rise of consumer culture

---

To be modern is to find ourselves in an environment that promises us adventure, power, joy, growth, transformation of ourselves and our world – and at the same time, that threatens to destroy everything we have, everything we know, everything we are. (Berman, 1982: 15)

Introduction

In this chapter we will be concerned with the theoretical problems that the growth and transformation of capitalism pose for cultural studies. There is no doubt that we in the West (along with most of the people on our planet) live in social formations organized along capitalist lines. Consequently, they are marked by deep class divisions manifested in work, wages, housing, education and health. Further, cultural practices are heavily commodified by large corporate culture industries so that ours is a consumer culture. However, and this is the central problem for cultural studies, capitalism has demonstrated a stubborn refusal to collapse in crisis or be overthrown by working-class revolution, as Marxists had hoped for and expected.

Cultural studies has been troubled by capitalism for a number of reasons:

- As it developed, the field inherited the 'problem of capitalism' from Marxism, a stream of thought that can, along with structuralism, make strong claims to be a major source and progenitor of the cultural studies tradition.
- Capitalism is the structural force behind the greater part of human inequalities as a consequence of an exploitative class system that not only yields economic disparities but also underpins inequities in the domain of culture. Thus, a politics concerned with equality, liberty, solidarity, difference, diversity and justice (Chapter 3) must address the inequities and injustices of capitalism, and appraise the possibilities for its transformation.
- The cultures of the developed capitalist world, and increasingly those of all

nations, are essentially commodity cultures. Indeed, they are consumer cultures supervised by commodity signs. In this context, any domain of study concerned with culture must explore the characteristics of consumer capitalism and the degree to which a challenge to it is desirable and possible.

British cultural studies of the 1970s and early 1980s was much concerned with explaining the persistence of capitalism while continuing to maintain that its demise could still be brought about. In part, cultural studies writers have attributed the continued stability of capitalism to the winning of consent by ruling groups at the level of culture. Hence, in its engagement with Marxism, cultural studies has been particularly concerned with issues of economic determinism, ideology and hegemony. These concepts have been deployed to illustrate how resistance to capitalism has been muted as well as explaining the continued rumbling of discontent beneath the surface of contemporary culture. However, in addition to the problems that surround questions of political economy/culture, ideology and hegemony (see Chapters 3 and 4), we are faced with the simple empirical truism that capitalism has not disappeared but has continued to thrive. Indeed, the persistence and transformation of global capitalism has left humanity with no clear and viable alternative mode of economic production and distribution. In this context, we will need to ask about what resistance might possibly mean.

The Transformation of Capitalism

Capitalism is a dynamic system whose profit-driven mechanisms lead to the continual revolutionizing of the means of production and the forging of new markets. For Marx, this was its great merit in relation to feudalism, for it heralded a massive expansion in the productive capacities of European societies. Capitalism dragged Europe into the modern world of railways, mass production, cities and a formally equitable and free set of human relations in which people were not, in a legal sense, the property of others.

However, the mechanisms of capitalism were also thought to give rise to perennial crises and ultimately, or so Marx argued, to its supersedence by socialism. The intrinsic problems that would result in the collapse of capitalism were said to include a falling rate of profit, cycles of boom and bust, increasing monopoly, and, most decisively, the creation of a proletariat that is set to become the system's grave digger. Marx expected that capitalism would be rift asunder by class conflict, with the proletariat's organizations of defence, trade unions and political parties overthrowing it and replacing it with a mode of production based on communal ownership, equitable distribution and ultimately the end of class division.

Today, capitalism is still a world-transforming force. However, there is now neither a real contemporary alternative to global capitalism for large-scale mass societies nor any immediate prospect of finding one. However useful Marx's analysis of nineteenth-century capitalism might have been, his vision of its revolutionary overthrow now appears as so much wishful thinking. Capitalism is firmly entrenched as the mode of organization by which human societies produce and distribute material goods and services and there is no evidence that it will be replaced. Indeed, capitalism is the driving force of a renewed globalization. This is a reorganized capitalism in which multinational corporations manage the commanding heights of the world economy as they refashion the spatial distribution of their networks to become more geo-global. This involves turning London, New York, Los Angeles, Tokyo, Singapore, and so forth, into global cities that operate as the command and control points of an unevenly developed but interconnected world economy.

These developments do not mean that capitalism is completely unavailable for reform and reregulation. However, it does suggest that abolition of the central capitalist principles and mechanisms by which global and national economies work is not yet on the cards. Indeed, insofar as we have witnessed revolutionary transformations of human societies, these have been brought about by the reorganization of capitalism rather than through its supersedence.

From Fordism to post-Fordism

There are a number of explications available to us of the post-war transformation of capitalism. Perhaps the most influential account within cultural studies has been the post-Fordist model as presented by Hall and Jacques (1989). Here, Fordism and post-Fordism are more than simply 'economic' models for they are said to constitute the organizing principles and cultural relations of an entire social formation. The broad parameters of Fordism/Keynesianism included large-scale production of standardized goods in the context of mass consumption requiring relatively high wages, at least for core workers, in order to sustain the purchasing of large-volume production. Central to the mass production and mass consumption of consumer goods was a developing culture of promotion and advertising that supported the selling process.

Keynesianism was also marked by a corporate state that played an interventionist role as the manager of social welfare provisions, in industrial conflict resolution, and as a significant direct employer. Here, full employment strategies were pursued not just as a social 'good', but as a means of keeping spending power at levels that met the capacity for production. In this context, the labour movement was able to take successful industrial action to push up wages. Indeed, some critics hailed a process of 'embourgeoisement' (see Goldthorpe and Lockwood, 1968) marked by the acquisition of incomes comparable to the middle class by manual workers and the adoption by them of middle-class lifestyles and values.

On an international level, stability was maintained through US domination of the currency markets and a degree of inter-state co-operation. Indeed, so solid did this picture of industrial stability and prosperity appear that some commentators held it to represent the very logic of industrialization for all societies world-wide (Kerr et al., 1973). Certainly Fordism yielded very little prospect of social revolution leading to the abolition of capitalism.

As described by Harvey (1989), the Fordist regime began to experience problems that came to a head during the early 1970s. In particular, a system geared towards mass production and consumption faced the difficulties of saturated western markets with a consequent crisis of over-production. In addition, western economies were facing increased price competition from Japan and the Newly Industrialized Countries (NICs), including Taiwan, Korea and Singapore. This, combined with the success of the Oil-Producing and -Exporting Countries (OPEC) in pushing up world oil prices, and the failure to stabilize the world financial markets as US ascendancy weakened, led to economies blighted by stagflation (economies with nil growth but high inflation levels). The global recession that followed proved difficult to escape, not least because of the very structure of Fordist production, that is:

- the rigidity of Fordism in relation to long-term and large-scale fixed capital investments carried out on the assumption of stable mass markets;
- the organization of labour markets in terms of job specialization and demarcation; and
- state commitments to welfare spending involving large budget deficits.

This situation could reasonably be characterized as a 'crisis of capitalism'. However, rather than precipitate a revolutionary scenario, capitalism successfully reorganized itself yet again. In particular, corporations sought to reintroduce growth and increase the rate of profit through more flexible production techniques involving new technology, the reorganization of labour and a speed-up of production/consumption turnover times. On the level of production, the move from Fordism to post-Fordism involved a shift from the mass production of homogeneous goods to small-batch customization. That is, economic production was transformed from a basic concern with uniformity and standardization to more flexible and variable manufacture for niche markets. This was enabled by Just-in-Time stock management, the use of information technology to manage variable production runs, and the large-scale sub-contracting out of domains of manufacture to horizontally related 'independent' companies. Of course, to characterize these changes with the concept of post-Fordism does not imply that all production or cultural forms follow this model; rather, it suggests that these changes represent the leading edge of economy and culture.

It is commonly argued by Marxists that if the working class can be made to pay the price of capitalism's crisis, then the 'system' can go on reorganizing itself for ever. Certainly the western world saw industrial strife and working-class resistance (e.g. the British miners' strikes of the 1970s and 1980s) during this period of capitalist restructuring, but at no time was the supplanting of capitalism a realistic prospect. Instead it was the labour force that was either laid off or restructured. In particular, post-Fordism involves a reorganization of the labour process that includes multi-skilling and the elimination of rigid job demarcation lines to create a more horizontally organized workforce. For example, quality control shifts from post-production testing into the very process of manufacturing. This demands that the labour force take greater responsibility for quality and 'continuous improvement' as one of their central tasks.

In theory, the expensive labour training required for multi-skilling leads companies to offer the core workforce greater long-term job security rather than waste their investment through high worker turnover. In the classical imagery of post-Fordism/Japanization, this investment in training is epitomized by the Nissan or Toyota life-long company worker. However, even if this is the case for the core workforce, about which there is considerable doubt, such privileges do not extend to the large periphery workforce upon which post-Fordism depends. Thus, a good deal of the production process, particularly in the horizontally related supplier companies, is handled by part-time, short-contract, low-paid temporary workers. Women, people of colour and young people are over-represented in the 'peripheral' labour force.

The regulation school and 'New Times'

The concept of post-Fordism refers not just to the working practices of flexible specialization but also to a new 'regime of accumulation' and an associated 'mode of social and political regulation': that is, a stabilizing of the relationship between consumption and accumulation, or how much companies retain and how much consumers spend. Such an analysis implies an affinity between the conditions of production and social/political relations and lifestyles, so that what occurred was not just an economic restructuring but also involved changes in our everyday culture. This argument follows the 'regulationist' approach of Aglietta (1979), which stresses the role of social and cultural relations, rather than the 'hidden hand' of the free market, in stabilizing the advanced capitalist economies.

The new configuration of production, politics, consumption, lifestyles, identities and aspects of everyday private life constitutes a condition which has been dubbed 'New Times' (Hall and Jacques, 1989). The 'New Times' approach explored a wide-ranging set of cultural, social and economic issues and the connections between them. These included the global emergence of flexible manufacturing systems linked to the customization of design and quality for niche markets within the framework of consumer lifestyles. Politically, post-Fordism was associated with the rise of new social and political movements and the deregulation and privatization of welfare provision against a background of reconfigured class relations, notably a decline in the traditional manual working class and its political allies.

Scholars continue to discuss and dispute the specificities of the contemporary transformation of capitalism. For example, many would consider neo-Fordism a better characterization of the workings of capitalism than post-Fordism. That is, as an extension of Fordist practices aimed at giving capitalism new life through economies of scale, internationalization (in search of new markets), diversification (into new products) and the intensification of the labour process by means of new technology and automation.

We can surely accept that post-Fordist and neo-Fordist modes of organization co-exist within the same social formation. In any case, what is not in dispute is that capitalism has not only continued to survive, but has also evolved and transformed the central relationships between economy, class and culture.

The recomposition of class and culture

Patterns of consumption and the reconfiguration of class

A transformation in the structure of industrial capitalism is of course related to shifts in its occupational structures. Though theorists of the post-industrial society (e.g. Bell, 1973) commonly present their arguments through an erroneous form of technological determinism and overstate the scale, scope and range of the change, they have nevertheless put their finger on a number of significant contemporary shifts in the patterns of class organization. To a considerable extent these transformations are implicated in the displacement of industrial manufacturing by service industries centred on information technology and by a more general shift of emphasis from production to consumption. In particular, information exchange and cultural production are held to be displacing heavy industry at the heart of western economies.

There has been both a sectoral redistribution of labour from the primary and secondary sectors to the service sector and a shift in the make-up of labour towards white-collar work increasingly organized on craft rather than industrial lines. Thus, the proportion of administrative, professional and technical workers in the USA and the UK steadily rose until it formed nearly a third of the total workforce (Bell, 1973; Goldthorpe, 1982). This service class is not primarily involved in the direct production of commodities. Rather, its members sell their skills and depend on their market power. In addition, they usually have a high degree of autonomy, working either as professional 'experts' or as managers directing the labour of others. Though they do not own the means of production, they may be shareholders and/or possess the ability, at least at the highest levels, to manage the strategic direction of powerful companies.

In this context, the old certainties that linked economy, culture and politics together through the figure of class have been put into doubt. For example, it has been argued by Hall and Jacques (1989) that we are witnessing a radical decline in the manual working class, a rise in service and white-collar work, and an increase in part-time and 'flexible' labour leading to new social divisions that have been expressed as the two-thirds/one-third society. That is, two-thirds of the population are relatively well-off while one third is either engaged in de-skilled part-time work or forms a new 'underclass' of the unemployed and unemployable. Others, for example Bell, describe a class structure constituted by a professional class, a technical and semi-professional class, a clerical and sales class and a class of semi-skilled and craft workers.

Increasingly absent from this picture is the traditional manual working class, to whom critics such as Gorz (1982) have said their metaphorical 'farewells'. Here, the identities of class factions are understood to be increasingly unpre-dictable in the face of class fragmentation and the consumer orientation of the working class. That is, the increased productivity of capitalism has meant that the majority of the populations of western societies have sufficient housing, transportation and income to be in a 'post-scarcity' situation. This has con-tributed to an increased consumption-centredness amongst the working class that has led to its fragmentation as its members' differential incomes and con-sumption capabilities are expressed in the market. Further, as its relative prosperity has risen, so the employed working class has become dislocated from the unemployed urban underclass.

With this reconstruction of class relations has come a new uncertainty regard-ing the relationship between class position and political allegiance. According to Crook et al., since the late 1960s, 'studies of voting behaviour and political activism showed a steady decline in allegiance between the major classes or occupational categories on the one hand and the major political parties on the other. . . . [and] the class voting index has been in steady decline' (1992: 139). It is also argued that there has been a reduction in trust in the major political par-ties expressed as both a decline in voting and an interest in more direct forms of political action. More generally, we have witnessed the demise of a revolutionary working-class politics that could realize an alternative social order. This is marked by the decline of the working class as a numerical and political force allied to the degeneration of socialism as an alternative systemic world-view that carries explanatory authority.

The end of history?

Though overstated in somewhat hyperbolic terms as the 'end of history', there is nevertheless merit in Fukuyama's argument that liberal democracy and capital-ism have finally triumphed. This is characterized as 'the end-point of mankind's ideological evolution and the universalization of Western liberal democracy as the final form of human government' (Fukuyama, 1989: 3). By this is meant not the end of events, but the universal triumph of the *idea* of liberal democracy as the only viable political system (Fukuyama, 1992). The end of history is the end of ideological competition to liberal democracy. Though Fukuyama does not expect social conflict to disappear, he does argue that grand political ideologies will give way to economic management and technical problem solving in the context of liberal democratic states and capitalist economic and social relations.

By contrast, Held (1992) suggests that global economic inequalities, along with national, ethnic, religious and political ideologies, will continue to generate conflict that *could* give rise to new mass-mobilizing forces capable of legitimating new kinds of regime. However, it is difficult to see from where alternative economic and political *systems* are going to be generated either ideologically or in terms of social actors capable of bringing about systemic change. Held's criticisms of Fukuyama do not disrupt the claim that liberal democracy and global capitalism have triumphed as ideas.

This is not to suggest that all societies will follow the western path. There will no doubt be regional variations as the character of capitalism and its political forces take on different configurations in different parts of the world. However, it is to suggest that capitalism has achieved global ascendancy and that liberal democracy has largely triumphed in the West. This directs political activity to reformist changes, including social democratic regulatory tinkering and/or to new social movements as pressure groups.

The argument here is not that class has miraculously disappeared so that we no longer need concern ourselves with it. Rather, I am suggesting that western societies are not in a position to generate a radical working-class political movement that is able and willing to replace capitalism with a viable alternative.

Class: the return of the repressed

In tandem with the loosening of the empirical connections between class, culture and political allegiance, cultural studies has carried out a theoretical disengagement of economy and culture that has an 'elective affinity' with the changing character of class as a predictor of politics, beliefs and cultural behaviour. The rejection of economic and class determinism from the study of culture is to be welcomed. Economic relations do not determine cultural meanings (which can be articulated together in a variety of ways), nor does history have a prime agent of social change springing from one central point of antagonism (i.e. class conflict). However, the eclipse of the category of class from cultural studies, allied to the loss of a political economy of culture, does seem to have been the undesirable consequence of the turn away from Marxism and economic determinism. Thus the metaphorical baby is in danger of being lost along with the bath-water.

Without a political economy of culture, cultural studies has difficulty expressing the full range of material circumstances and power relations that pertain between people (McGuigan, 1996). Further, though the category of class can no longer occupy the centre of cultural analysis, it does retain a powerful and important place in social life that should not be ignored. There are still inequalities in educational access and outcome that are underpinned by social class; there are still differences in cultural tastes and practices that mark out class boundaries; and there are still many millions of people world-wide whose lives are blighted by poverty and unemployment together with the associated social problems of violence, crime, drug abuse and neglect.

The new urban inequalities

The increasing globalization of capitalism gives rise to the need for command, control and co-ordination centres that constitute the core of 'global cities', including New York, London and Los Angeles. Here contemporary class inequalities are clearly visible. For Sassen (1996), the contrast between the homogeneity of the high-rise offices of the Central Business District and the diversity of the urban forms that mark immigrant communities reveals how power inscribes itself in the urban landscape. This is manifested spatially and architecturally in the high-rise, high-density office developments of downtown areas that, because they require servicing by suppliers and sub-contractors, are surrounded by layers of unregulated economic activity, including the small firms and labour force of separate ethnic communities.

The de-industrialization and re-industrialization of major American cities has typically involved the development of high-technology and/or leisure industries alongside the growth of low-skill, labour-intensive and design-sensitive industries (Soja, 1989). Together with the growth of the finance, insurance and real estate businesses, these developments have reorganized not only the economic substructure of urban areas but also the residential zones. This has included the emptying out of the centre and the urbanization of suburbia, involving a degree of 'white flight' from the city to the suburbs and edge cities. This emptying out of the inner city can be seen at its most extreme in a city like Detroit (USA), which contains a poor black inner zone whole sections of which are not even supplied with basic services like electricity and water.

The kind of urban change typically seen in the USA, and to some extent the UK and Australia, involves the abandonment of an 'underclass' to mass unemployment, drug trafficking, poverty and homelessness. Here are the conditions for the urban rioting witnessed in the UK during the 1980s, more recently still in 2001, and of course in LA in 1992. Thus, new patterns of social fragmentation, segregation and polarization are implicated in new patterns of social, economic and cultural inequality. In particular, an enlarging managerial technocracy, a shrinking middle class and a growing base of the homeless, welfare dependants and cheap labour now mark a social landscape that has become increasingly difficult to govern. The consequence has been walled-in estates, armed guards, patrolled shopping centres, surveillance cameras and wire fences, all aimed at keeping the threatening spectre of crime, violence and ethnic difference at bay.

The paradigm case is Mike Davis's nightmarish vision of Fortress-LA, where 'the defence of luxury lifestyles is translated into a proliferation of new repressions in space and movement, undergirded by the ubiquitous "armed response"' (1990: 223). For example, Davis cites the redesign and rebuilding of the Downtown area, in which street frontage is denuded, pedestrians carefully channelled, 'undesirable' sectors cut off from access and certain 'types of people' (notably people of colour and the poor) 'discouraged' and excluded. In parallel with this 'cleansing' of Downtown there has, he argues, been a deliberate strategy of 'containment' of the poor into designated spaces where they can be policed and harassed. This has included banning cardboard shelters and even avoiding the erection of public toilets in designated areas.

According to Rorty (1998a), the Left is, or should be, the symbol of hope in the struggle for social justice. However, it is his contention that to a major extent the cultural Left has become 'a spectator Left' more interested in theorizing than in the practical politics of material change. The cultural Left, he suggests, prefers theoretical knowledge to pragmatic and applicable hope. It imagines that it can somehow 'get it right' on the level of theory and has given up on the practical task of making democratic institutions once again serve social justice. Thus, as a matter of balance, cultural studies would do well to re-explore class relations in the light of the turn to identity as the central category of its politics, where 'identity' seems to have meant gender and race. Cultural politics needs to re-engage with class politics in a world that currently has no viable alternative to global capitalism.

In doing so we will need to maintain a delicate balance between saying that class is of declining significance as a predictor of political and cultural practices but nevertheless retains a critical importance to the study of culture. On the one hand, we must reject economic and class reductionism, but, on the other, we need to keep political economy in view. Politically, it will be important to gauge the degree to which social democratic parties are in a position to offer new solutions to reforming the tiger of capitalism. However, because this is a book about cultural studies rather than political processes *per se*, I am not going to discus this question. Instead, I want to explore some of the manifestations of the regeneration of capitalism in the domain of culture.

The problem of consumer culture

The post-war period has witnessed the rise of consumer culture across western societies and beyond. Fordism, of course, was based on mass advertising, selling and the consumption of standardized goods, while post-Fordism is marked by customization and niche marketing. Consequently, the surface of western culture is now constituted by visual-based consumer images and meanings. That this is a promotional culture plastered with the signs of Coca-Cola, Nike, Marlboro, Microsoft, and so forth, is not in doubt.

The question remains: what does this all mean for individuals and for our culture in general?

- On the one hand, cultural studies writers have expressed the fear that consumer culture generates meanings that serve to justify and reproduce the power of capitalist domination.
- On the other hand, a series of studies of consumption have stressed the productive role played by commodities as resources for the creative generation of new identities and lifestyles.

Poisonous consumption

There has long been a strand of thinking about culture that has been critical of the consumption practices of capitalist societies. For example, F.R. Leavis (Leavis and Thompson, 1933) held that the central task of cultural criticism was to define and defend the 'best' of culture against advertising, films and popular fiction with its 'addictions' and 'distractions'. Richard Hoggart's *The Uses of Literacy* (1957), widely considered to be one of the founding texts of cultural studies, explores the character of English working-class culture as it developed and changed from the 1930s through to the 1950s. Hoggart's sympathetic, humanist and detailed chronicle of the lived culture of the working class contrasts starkly with his acid account of the development of 'commercial culture' figured by the 'juke-box boy', the 'American slouch' and loud music. Indeed, to many who have been raised within commercial culture, Hoggart's view of working-class culture appears as nostalgia for the lost authenticity of a culture created from below.

The attitude of the quasi-Marxist Frankfurt School towards mass culture, at least as it was represented by Horkheimer and Adorno, is clearly stated in the title of their essay 'The Culture Industry as Mass Deception' (1979). They argue that cultural products are commodities produced by the culture industry that, while purporting to be democratic, individualistic and diversified, are in actuality authoritarian, conformist and highly standardized. Consumer culture impresses its uniform stamp on everything, and the apparent diversity of products is an illusion by which 'something is provided for all so none may escape' (Horkheimer and Adorno, 1979: 123). For Adorno, the consequence of standardized commodities is standardized reactions and the affirmation of life as it is.

Insofar as the work of the Frankfurt School has a contemporary heir, that nomination has fallen to Jürgen Habermas (1987, 1989), who documents the decline of the public sphere in the face of the development of capitalism towards monopoly. Habermas argues that the increased commodification of life by giant corporations transforms people from rational citizens to consumers of, amongst other things, the 'non-rational' products of the advertising and public relations industries. He is censorious of the instrumentality by which our day-to-day 'life-world' is colonized by 'system imperatives': that is, the subordination of social-existential questions to money and administrative power. In this context, it is worth reminding ourselves that advertising now sits at the heart of contemporary *public* life as national and local governments, political parties and campaign groups have become the largest purchasers of advertising services.

Brand power and commodity-signs

The early work on advertising and consumption within the emerging cultural studies of the 1970s was cast within the problematic of ideology and hegemony. Consequently, the textual and ideological analysis of advertising stressed the selling not just of commodities but also of ways of looking at the world. The job of advertising was to create an 'identity' for a product amid the bombardment of competing images by associating the brand with desirable human values. Acquiring a brand was not simply about purchasing a product; rather, it was also concerned with buying into lifestyles and values. Thus, for Williamson (1978), objects in advertisements are signifiers of meaning that we decode in the context of known cultural systems associating products in adverts with other cultural 'goods'. While an image of a particular product may denote only beans or a car, it is made to connote 'nature' or 'family'. In buying commodities, we emotionally invest in the associated image and so contribute to the construction of our identities through consumption.

In more contemporary vein, Baudrillard (1983) suggests that sign-value has replaced the use-value or exchange-value of commodities that is central to Williamson's analysis. In this view, consumerism is at the heart of a postmodern culture that is constituted through a continual flow of images that establishes no connotational hierarchy and thus no sense of value. Postmodern culture is argued to be literally and metaphorically 'superficial'. This is said to be a culture in which no objects have an 'essential' or 'deep' value; rather, value is determined through the exchange of symbolic meanings. That is, commodities have sign-value that confers prestige and signifies social value, status and power. A commodity is not an object with use-value but a commodity-sign. For Jameson (1984), who draws on the work of Baudrillard, this postmodern world represents the cultural style of late capitalism operating in a new global space.

Surveillance

Consumer culture appears to offer us diversity, choice and freedom. However, it is also implicated in forms of surveillance: for example, the development of electronic technologies that are intrinsic to contemporary life, such as CCTV cameras in urban malls and the use of shopping cards that record information for store management about consumer spending patterns and promotional activities. The computerized credit card, the home computer and the sophisticated television system that permits home banking, shopping, opinion polls, and so on, also allow corporations to collect massive amounts of information about users. Increasingly, the amount of money we have to spend, what we like to spend it on, our views on the environment, crime, taxation, our preference for political parties or laundry detergents, and so forth, are being used to draw detailed marketing profiles of individual households for targeting of potential buyers (Mosca, 1988).

Similarly, the new spaces of consumer culture, such as shopping malls and Disney World, are important because they consolidate the significance and power of culture as a form of commerce and social control. They arguably achieve this by imposing a form of meaning and managing social diversity through a combination of visual imagery and physical spatial control. This is a 'public' culture where civility and social interaction occur in the context of a tight security regime. Thus, Disney World aims for total control of space through the use of its own rules, vocabulary, norms, security force and even sanitation workers –most of whom are the relatively low-paid workforce of an ever-increasing service sector. Through its private management, spatial control and stimulating/simulated visual culture, Disney World is the new model for public space whose principles are echoed in numerous shopping malls (Zukin, 1996).

Consumption, resistance and lifestyle politics

Transgressive commodities

The arguments reviewed above have all implied that in various ways commodities are inherently 'unsound' for containing and transmitting world-views supportive of the capitalist status quo. In this context, resistance would be measured in terms of consumers' capacity to defy advertising and not to buy unnecessary commodities: that is, to generate alternative lifestyles and cultural forms that can offer challenges to consumerism. Given the limited evidence for such developments, this understanding of resistance would paint a bleak picture.

However, cultural critics have increasingly identified the propagation of creative, oppositional and resistant meanings in relation to the commodities produced by consumer culture. Thus, for Featherstone, 'the new heroes of consumer culture make a lifestyle a life project and display their individuality and sense of style in the particularity of the assemblage of goods, clothes, practices, experiences, appearance and bodily dispositions they design together into a lifestyle' (1991: 86).

Kaplan (1987) claims a transgressive and progressive role for postmodern music videos, which, she argues, offer no assured narrative position for the viewer, thereby undermining the status of representation as real or true. In particular, she explores the ambiguity of Madonna as a commodity-sign that deconstructs gender norms. For Kaplan, Madonna is able to 'alter gender relations and to destabilize gender altogether' (1992: 273). This is achieved, she suggests, because Madonna's videos are implicated in the continual shifting of subject positions involving stylized and mixed gender signs that question the boundaries of gender constructs.

On the one hand, as Kellner argues, any analysis of the place of Madonna in popular culture would need to take account of the fact that she has 'deployed some of the most proficient production and marketing teams in the history of popular music' (1997: 118). On the other hand, this argument does not in itself displace the analysis of Madonna as a sign (for, as Kellner suggests, the divide between cultural studies as textual studies and political economy is an unnecessary one).

Much depends, of course, on how one reads Madonna's performance, and in particular on how consumers construct, negotiate and perform a multiplicity of meanings. Though we can examine the ways in which texts work, we cannot simply 'read off' audiences' meaning production from textual analysis. Rather, audiences and consumers are active creators of meaning in relation to cultural signs. They bring previously acquired cultural competencies to bear on texts, so that differently constituted audiences will work with different meanings. At the very least, meaning is produced in the interplay between text and reader, so that the moment of consumption is also a moment of meaningful production. Thus, whether we read commodities as justifying capitalism or as the basis of resistance, we will still need to make a case with regard to the meanings created by concrete people in specific locations.

Creative consumption

Consumption-oriented cultural studies argues that while the production of popular music, film, television and fashion is in the hands of transnational capitalist corporations, meanings are produced, altered and managed at the level of consumption. For example, Fiske argues that popular culture is constituted by the meanings that people construct rather than those identifiable within texts. While he is clear that popular culture is very largely produced by capitalist corporations, he 'focuses rather upon the popular tactics by which these forces are coped with, are evaded or are resisted' (Fiske, 1989a: 8). Fiske argues that between 80 and 90 per cent of new products fail despite extensive advertising. Consequently, the culture industries have to work hard to get us to consume mass culture. Consumers are not passive dopes but discriminating active producers of meaning.

The work of McRobbie illustrates the transformation in thinking that has taken place within cultural studies. In her early work, McRobbie is suspicious of the consumer culture from which 'girl-culture' stems. For example, the magazine *Jackie* (McRobbie, 1991a) is held to operate through the codes of romance, domesticity, beauty and fashion, thereby defining the world of the personal sphere as the prime domain of girls. In her account of working-class girls, McRobbie (1991b) explores the way in which this culture of femininity is used by girls to create their own space while at the same time securing them for boyfriends, marriage, the family and children.

Later, McRobbie (1991c) critiques her own reliance on the analysis of documents. She suggests that girls are more active and creative in relation to girls' magazines and other forms of consumer culture than she had given them credit for. For example, she points to the productive, validating and inventive bricolage of fashion style that women originate as well as to the dynamic character of shopping as an enabling activity (McRobbie, 1989). McRobbie argues that the active and changing character of femininity is marked by the transformation of girls' magazines in response to the 'sophisticated and discerning young consumer' (1991c). This has involved a shift of attention from romance to pop music, fashion and a more self-confident sexuality.

Similarly, Willis (1990) argues that rather than being inherent in the commodity, meaning and value are constructed through actual usage. In general, as noted above (Chapter 4), it is argued that people range across a series of terrains and sites of meaning, actively producing sense within them, even though they are not of their own making. For Willis, contemporary culture is not meaningless or superficial but involves the active creation of meaning by all people as cultural producers. Thus, 'The symbolic creativity of the young is based in their everyday informal life and infuses with meaning the entirety of the world as they see it' (Willis, 1990: 98).

Young consumers assert their personal competencies through dancing and the customization of fashion and in doing so transform and recode the meanings of everyday objects. Willis argues that it is, ironically, capitalism and the expansion of consumerism that have provided the increased supply of symbolic resources for young people's creative work. Capitalism (in the world of work) may be that from which escape is sought, but it also provides the means and medium (in the domain of consumption) by which to do so. Thus, youth culture's consumption practices are able to offer resistance to the apparent passivity and conformity of consumer culture.

Resistance as style

For a number of writers within cultural studies, youth subcultures have been marked by the development of distinctive styles that are achieved through the transformation of the signs of commodities via the process of bricolage. These are said to act as a form of semiotic resistance to the dominant order. That is, objects that already carried sedimented symbolic meanings are resignified in relation to other artefacts in a new context. By way of example, Clarke (1976) points to the construction of the Teddy boy style, which was achieved through a combination of the otherwise unrelated Edwardian upper-class look, the boot-lace tie and large-soled 'brothel-creepers'.

For Hebdige (1979, 1988), 'style' is a signifying practice that, in the case of spectacular subcultures, is an obviously fabricated display of codes of meaning. Through the signification of difference, style constitutes a group identity. British punk was Hebdige's favoured exemplar. He argued that punk was not simply responding to the crisis of British decline manifested in joblessness, poverty and changing moral standards, but *dramatized* it. Punk appropriated the media language of crisis, recycling it in corporeal and visual terms. Punk style was an expression of anger and frustration cast in a language generally available but now resignified as symptomatic of a cluster of contemporary problems.

Bricolage in the hands of Clarke and Hebdige was conceived of as a process of dynamic and creative action contrasted to the apparently passive consumption of cultural industry commodities. Thus 'style' represented the 'real' and 'authentic' subculture in opposition to the media and the culture industries. However, Redhead (1990) challenges the whole notion of an authenticity of style that is located within youth culture. He suggests that any clear-cut distinction between the media, the culture industries and an oppositional and authentic youth subculture is problematic for the latter is 'heavily influenced and shaped by the global leisure industry of which pop is now structurally so much an integral part' (Redhead, 1990: 54). Hence the 'death of youth culture' is marked by the end of the relevance of the concept of an authentic subculture that played such a prominent part in cultural studies' understanding of youth. Style, it is now argued, involves bricolage without reference to the meanings of originals. Style has no underlying message or ironic transformation. It is the look and only the look.

Here, style is representative not of resistance but of classifications of power and markers of distinctions of taste (Thornton, 1995). Youth cultures are formed not outside and opposed to the media but within and through the media, so that the idea of a 'grass-roots, media-free, authentic subculture' cannot be sustained. Media, argues Thornton, are integral to the formation of subcultures and to young people's formulations of their own activities. For example, punk and house were marketed by subcultural entrepreneurs and record companies in and through moral panics and distinctions of 'hipness' that they helped to foster. Equally, in the perpetual search for significance, subcultures 'become politically relevant only when framed as such. Derogatory media coverage is not the verdict but the essence of their resistance' (Thornton, 1995: 137).

However, the birth of youth fashion and style in the media does not necessarily reduce style to meaninglessness. The end of authenticity is not the death of meaning as such, for postmodern bricolage can involve the creative recombination of existing items to forge new meanings. This creativity takes place 'inside the whale' of postmodern consumer capitalism, where the binary divisions of inside–outside and authentic–manufactured collapse. Nevertheless, while the generation of style is a form of creative consumption and one that marks a certain resistance to conformity, it does not offer a challenge to consumer culture *per se*. Indeed, as Thornton points out, operating successfully within club culture through generating subcultural capital requires a developed mastery of the distinctions between commodities.

Mass culture and popular culture

Western popular culture is primarily a commercially produced one and there is no reason to think that this is likely to change in the foreseeable future. Consequently, for cultural studies the very adoption of the term 'popular culture' rather than 'mass culture' signals a willingness to accept the creative role of ordinary people in the face of commodity culture. In taking popular culture seriously as that which is to be both valued and critically analysed, cultural studies works against the grain of the analyses of both the conservative Leavis and the Marxist Adorno. At the very least, the work of McRobbie, Willis and Fiske has the merit of displacing the idea of a monolithic and impenetrable culture industry that imposes its meanings on a passive set of consumers.

However, for its critics, this line of argument runs the risk of turning almost every piece of pop culture and youth style into resistance. Thus, McGuigan (1992) argues that the work of Fiske, Willis and others represents an uncritical embracing of the pleasures of consumer sovereignty in the marketplace. According to McGuigan, these writers have lost their conviction that there are grounds for criticizing the current order or for providing alternative visions. Equally, Morris (1996) finds a 'banality in cultural studies' by which an endless series of writers find resistance in popular culture at every turn. She parodies this as a formulation in which 'people in modern mediatized societies are complex and contradictory, mass cultural texts are complex and contradictory, therefore people using them produce complex and contradictory culture' (1996: 161). For Morris, what is missing is a balance sheet of gains and losses, of hope and despair. What is required, she suggests, is a critical edge that can articulate the notion that 'they always fuck us over' while constructing a space in which we can posit the utopian.

Audiences/consumers are *always* active, but this does not guarantee a challenge to the contemporary social order. In other words, activity as such should not be confused with resistance, for, by definition, consumption is an active process. The evidence that young consumers are active creators of meaning is overwhelming and irrefutable. Whether activity produces defiance or acquiescence, however, is ultimately a case-by-case empirical question.

Agency and activity do not have to imply resistance; they can also signify active appropriation of consumer values. Indeed, activity is required to take up world-views or 'ideology'. What matters is less the argument about whether consumers are active or not, – they are – but what kind of activity they are engaged in, and with what outcomes.

Put in this way, it is hard to imagine that we consumers are not implicated in consumer culture and the sense that happiness depends on having more of everything and the 'right' brands in particular. After all, we spend an unprecedented amount of time viewing adverts and buying commodities. Now, given my previous argument that consumer capitalism is here to stay, the question is: how do we both resist it and live with it?

Living in the wasteland: resistance and beyond

Resistance is not a fixed quality but is to be thought of relationally and conjuncturally. That is, resistance is not a singular and universal act that defines itself for all time; rather, it is constituted by repertoires of activity whose meanings are specific to particular times, places and social relationships. Resistance is not a quality of an act but a category of judgement about acts. It is a judgement that classifies the classifier.

For Bennett (1998), resistance is an essentially defensive relationship to cultural power experienced as external and 'other' by subordinate social forces. Here, resistance issues from relationships of power and subordination where a dominating culture is seeking to impose itself on subordinate cultures from without. Consequently, resources of resistance are to be located in some measure outside of the dominating culture. However, the bipolarity of Bennett's reading poses us a problem: namely that while capitalism is the stated target for resistance, in the era of consumerism all of us are immersed in, not separated from, consumer capitalism and the mass media. Where resistance is taking place it is commonly happening 'inside' consumer lifestyles, transforming commodities and using the mass media. There is no outside to consumer culture from which external resistance can be mounted.

Today, resistance may best be thought of 'as challenges to and negotiations of the dominant order which could not be assimilated to the traditional categories of revolutionary class struggle' (Hall, 1996e: 294). Thus, resistance is not best understood as a simple reversal of the order of high and low, of power and its absence. Contemporary cultural theory must give up on the idea of pure transcendence and accept that ambivalence and ambiguity occupy the space of resistance as exemplified by the transgressive character of the 'carnivalesque'.

The carnivalesque is a temporary reversal of the order of power through the rituals, games, mockeries and profanities by which the polite is overthrown by the vulgar and the king by the fool. However, the power of the 'carnivalesque', for Hall, lies not in a simple reversal of distinctions but in the invasion of the high by the low, creating 'grotesque' hybrid forms. The challenge is not simply to the high by the low, but to the very act of cultural classification by power.

Tactics and strategies

Similarly, de Certeau's account of resistance conceptualizes the resistive practices of everyday life as always already in the space of power. For de Certeau, as with Foucault (1980), there are no 'margins' outside of power from which to lay an assault on it or from within which to claim authenticity. De Certeau makes the distinction between the strategies of power and the tactics of resistance:

- A *strategy* is the means by which power marks out a space for itself distinct from its environs through which it can operate as a subject of will. Thus, the power of an enterprise involves the creation of its own space and the means by which to act separately from its competitors, adversaries, clients, and so forth.
- A *tactic* is a calculated action that must play on and within a terrain imposed on it. Tactics are the plays of the poacher, the ruses and deceptions of everyday life using the resources of 'the other' that seek to make space habitable. These include the devious productions of consumption, which 'does not manifest itself through its own products, but rather through its ways of using the products imposed by a dominant economic order' (de Certeau, 1984: xii–xiii).

Nevertheless, there is the clear limitation here that the aims of tactical resistance, if indeed they are articulated, are particular and do not represent a practical challenge to consumer culture as whole. In this sense, resistance, having only very localized targets, is frequently unsuccessful in bringing about change other than that of generating a new icon for consumer sales (e.g. the latest 'bad boys' of pop). On the other hand, resistance that is launched externally to consumer culture, if such is even possible, may mount a challenge of ideas and lifestyles but will by definition be marginalized discursively, symbolically and physically. Consequently, it is likely to have only very limited and largely symbolic achievements.

What is required is forms of resistance that mount a self-conscious assault on aspects of consumer capitalism from within the very culture that they oppose, remembering all the time that the best outcome we can expect is reform rather than revolution. This will take the form of creative consumption or conversely of consumer boycotts. Here consumer and ecological politics have much to offer. Greenpeace is one of the most successful of today's social and political organizations. Whatever the merits of the argument, the tactics deployed by Greenpeace against Shell during the Brent Spar campaign were exemplary in their use of a combination of media imagery, consumer campaigns and direct action.

Beyond resistance

A particularly insidious facet of consumer culture is the inherent claim that 'we' are not good enough as we are, but require to be enhanced in some way by commodities. We are perhaps not pretty enough, clever enough or rich enough to be happy. Alternatively, we are too fat, too slow or too dull ever to find a part-ner who might love us. Whatever the particularities of any given consumer item or advertising campaign, the collective outcome is a culture that is contin-ually telling us that we do not have enough nor are we good enough. This is especially problematic at a time when promotional communication is increas-ingly founded on visual images and the connotative values of signs with less and less appeal to even the semblance of rationality. We are not even asked to believe the argument that one washing powder cleans better than another; rather, we are enchanted by the feeling associated with key signs that happiness is at hand, if only . . .

For example, among the more powerful and influential representations of women that western culture promotes is the 'slender body' as a disciplinary cul-tural norm (Bordo, 1993). Slenderness and a concern with diet and self-monitoring are preoccupations of western media culture and its interest in a 'tighter, smoother, more constrained body profile'. Consequently, adverts target bulge, fat or flab and the desirability of flat stomachs and cellulite man-agement. Slenderness is a contemporary ideal for female attractiveness, so that girls and women are culturally more prone to eating disorders than are men. Having said that, it is perhaps no coincidence that we are witnessing a simulta-neous rise in the display of idealized male bodies in advertising and an increase in young men with eating disorders.

Paradoxically, advertising culture offers us images of desirable foods while proposing that we eat low-calorie items and buy exercise equipment. In the face of this contradiction, argues Bordo, the capacity for self-control and the con-tainment of fat is posed in moral as well as physical terms. The choice to diet and exercise is regarded as an aspect of self-fashioning requiring the production of a firm body as a symbol of gendered identity and the 'correct' attitude. The failure to exert the right degree of control, symbolically manifested in obesity and anorexia, is disciplined through, among other things, television talk-shows that feature portrayals of 'eating disorders' or the struggles of the obese to lose weight. *Oprah*, for example, has placed the presenter's struggle with weight gain at the centre of its strategy to humanize her.

Faced with the unsatisfying character of consumerism, we need to go 'beyond' resistance that is 'negative' in the simple sense of being against a clear enemy. Capitalism is not a reified object that is simply being manipulated by a conspiracy of the rich and powerful but is a set of all-embracing practices in which we are all implicated. Instead of vainly hankering after the revolution, we need to think about positive ways to live better within consumer capitalism. Thus, D. H. Lawrence once argued that the problem with industrial England was not just its inequality but its ugliness. In particular, a central problem with capitalism and consumerism in western post-scarcity cultures is its unsatisfying meaninglessness and continual suggestion that we are all inadequate.

This is a wasteland – a culture with a black hole of meaninglessness at its heart – that more and more of everything will not solve, for this particular monster feeds off precisely that desire.

What is required is a reappraisal of the qualitative aspects of cultural life through, for want of better words, emotional and spiritual intelligence (see Chapter 10). In the sense that I mean it, spirituality is cultural rather than metaphysical, practical more than textual, and open as opposed to doctrinaire. We also need to get beyond a zero-sum model of power with its sense that solutions to problems always involve 'taking over' or 'abolishing' something (though of course this notion remains relevant for particular cases) and develop instead new creative ways of living.

In particular, in the context of contemporary consumer culture, we need to say that identification with brand names and buying more commodities (along with the stress created by overwork in order to have the money to buy them) is not a route to happiness but a surefire recipe for eternal frustration. Not only can we never have all that we want, but also what we desire is all too often unable to deliver on its promise. Indeed, it fuels the desire for more of the unsatisfying pursuit of the same unsatisfying commodities, and so on.

Once we are beyond absolute material deprivation, as most people in the West are, then we can come to understand that happiness, or more precisely contentment, comes from within oneself. Of course, given the constitution of the subject in culture, then 'within' is also 'without'. Thus we need to be concerned with the overall *spiritual intelligence* (Zohar and Marshall, 2000) of any given culture. In any case, self-awareness, being in the present, self-autonomy, exercise, relaxation, common values and meanings, community, family, positive relationships, forgiveness and constructive and inspiring ethics aimed at reducing suffering are all more likely to bring contentment and self-worth than are consumer goods or excessive identification with work performance.

It is no accident that western culture is witnessing an unprecedented rise in anxiety and depression along with an associated fascination with self-help books. This is not attributable only to capitalism and consumer culture, for there are other factors in play (e.g. the loss of contact with issues of life, illness and death, the absence of positive family life, fragmentation and the decline of a common culture, etc.). However, consumer capitalism plays a significant part in the speed-up of work and consumption practices that underpins our culture of discontent.

Cultural studies needs to consider the ideas and practices that could help us move into a culture of contentment as much as it has thought about 'ideology' and class conflict.

Conclusions

I have argued that capitalism has continually transformed itself to the point that we no longer have a viable alternative to it. Indeed, capitalism is now victorious not only in the West but also on a global scale. In this context, the demise of a 'revolutionary politics' that could realize an alternative system seems to be marked by:

- the decline of socialism as an alternative systemic doctrine;
- the collapse of communism;
- the decline of the working class as a numerical and political force;
- the increasing disconnection between class and politics;
- the rise of social and cultural movements, including ecology politics and feminism, whose political claims are reformist (in the best sense of the word).

The transformations of post-war capitalism, and more particularly still of the last thirty years, have seen the power of class determinations and connections to culture and politics weakened. Nevertheless, class does still structure lives, as we can see clearly when we explore the inequalities of major western cities. Hence the concept of class needs to make a return into the vocabulary of cultural studies alongside the ubiquitous gender and race.

The consumer culture that now dominates the West is producing more discontent than happiness for its appeal to us works on the assumption that we are not good enough nor can we ever have enough. On the one hand, our response can only be resistance that is tactical and conjunctural rather than absolute and revolutionary. That is, resistance takes the form of the creative use of consumer goods, or, conversely, of campaigns aimed at consumer boycotts of particular products, including the use of direct action as media-oriented symbolism. On the other hand, we need to address seriously the sense of meaninglessness that lies at the centre of contemporary lives. This demands that we move away from simple confrontation with 'the enemy' and towards the development of ideas and practices that make life more rewarding for us. On occasion this may entail the 'winning of space' through 'alternative' lifestyles and communities that minimize contact with consumer capitalism, though they cannot of course ever escape from the totality of capitalist social relations.

9 Kaleidoscopic Cultural Studies:
Issues of Politics and Method

> **Central problem:**
> **Criticism vs policy: what are the politics of cultural studies?**

Injustices may not be perceived as injustices, even by those who suffer them, until somebody invents a previously unplayed role. Only if somebody has a dream, a voice, and a voice to describe the dream, does what looked like nature begin to look like culture, what looked like fate begin to look like a moral abomination. For until then only the language of the oppressor is available, and most oppressors have had the wit to teach the oppressed a language in which the oppressed will sound crazy – *even to themselves* – if they describe themselves as oppressed. (Rorty, 1995: 126)

Introduction

The multidisciplinary character of cultural studies has invariably made it difficult to pin down distinct boundaries that might mould the field into a coherent and unified academic discipline with clear-cut substantive topics, concepts and methods that would differentiate it from other disciplines. Thus, in order to distinguish itself as more than just 'anything goes', cultural studies has consistently identified the examination of culture, power and politics as unique to itself. Indeed, cultural studies can be understood as a body of theory generated by thinkers who regard the production of theoretical knowledge as a political practice.

For cultural studies, knowledge is never a neutral or detached phenomenon but rather a matter of positionality: of the place from which one speaks, to whom, and for what purposes. Hence, in addition to favouring the examination of representations that are both 'of' and 'for' subordinated social groups, cultural studies is partisan in its promotion of social and cultural change. Here, cultural politics has been conceived of as the power to name and to represent ourselves, where language is held to be constitutive of the world and a guide to action. This theoretical stance has implied an enabling connection to a series of collective cultural struggles organized around class, gender, race, sexuality and age that have sought to redescribe the social and cultural spheres in terms of specific values and hoped-for consequences.

In this chapter we shall be concerned with the interrelated issues of investigative methodology, cultural politics and cultural policy. We begin by exploring cultural politics in the context of the 'politics of difference'. This discussion will raise issues about the 'what' and the 'how' of cultural politics. We also inquire about potential agents of cultural change and the relationship between the politics of the signifier and the pursuit of cultural policy. These questions are implicitly tied up with the methodologies deployed within cultural studies. Overall, I argue that cultural studies is best advised to adopt a pragmatic stance that accepts a kaleidoscopic range of strategies encompassing the development of 'new languages', the symbolic politics of New Social Movements and the pursuit of cultural policy. Further, the character of politics in western 'democracies' is such that social and cultural change at an institutional level also requires engagement with the politics of social democracy.

The Politics of Culture and Power

The concept of culture directs our attention to questions of shared meanings and practices: that is, to the various ways we make sense of and act in the world. Of course, meanings are not simply floating 'out there'; rather, they are generated through signs, most notably those of language. Here, as a consequence of its engagement with semiotics, cultural studies has centred attention on questions of representation: that is, on how the world is socially constructed and represented to and by us. Given the constitutive place of language and the inability to locate an archimedean point from which to view the relationship between signs and an independent object world, representation is always 'someone's' point of view and never a mirror of reality capable of reflecting a universal truth. Thus, representation is always implicated in questions of power: who says what about whom, and with what consequences?

Though we commonly think of power as a force that individuals or groups deploy to achieve their aims or interests against the will of others, cultural studies has, after Foucault, stressed that power is also productive and enabling. Further, power is not thought to be organized in a bipolar way cohering into 'blocs'; rather, it is understood to circulate through all levels of society and all social relationships. That is, power is not simply the glue that holds the social together, or the coercive force which subordinates one set of people to another (though it certainly can be this), but is also a central part of the processes that generate and enable any form of action, relationship or social order.

In this sense, power, while certainly constraining, is also enabling. Having said that, cultural studies has shown a specific concern with subordinated groups, at first with class, and later with race, gender, age, and so forth. In this context, Bennett's (1998) 'element of a definition' of cultural studies holds it to be an interdisciplinary field in which perspectives from different disciplines can be selectively drawn on to examine the relations of culture and power.

In order to grasp the interplay of power and consent within culture, two related concepts were repeatedly deployed in cultural studies' early texts, namely ideology and hegemony. However, since I have already discussed what I take to be some of the limitations of these concepts (see Chapter 3), I will be directing my attention here to the more recent emergence of the politics of representation as manifested by 'the politics of difference'.

Power and the politics of difference

The theorization of the 'new' cultural politics of difference has come from a number of directions, though the work of Laclau and Mouffe (1985) and Hall (1988, 1990, 1992a, 1996a) has been of particular significance. Each retains the concept of hegemony but reworks it into a form of post-Marxism that draws on poststructuralist theory. Taking their lead from Derrida's concept of *différance* (difference and deferral), meaning is held by these writers to be inherently unstable. Consequently, culture is understood as a zone in which competing meanings and versions of the world contest each other for ascendancy and the pragmatic claim to truth. In particular, meaning and truth in the domain of culture are constituted within patterns of power that try to 'fix' their otherwise fluid character.

It is in this sense that the 'power to name', and to make particular meaningful descriptions stick, is a form of cultural politics. Issues of cultural representation are 'political' because the play of power that is intrinsic to questions of representation enables some kinds of knowledge and identities to exist while denying that to others. Representation matters since to describe women, for example, as full human beings and citizens with commensurate social rights and obligations is quite a different matter from regarding them as sub-human domestic workers with bodies designed for display. To use the language of citizenship to describe women is a different representation of common-sense and official world-views from one in which they are described as whores, tarts and servants. The language of citizenship legitimates the place of women in business and politics while the language of sexual and domestic servitude denies this place, seeking to confine women to the traditional spheres of domesticity and as objects of the male gaze.

The politics of representation, as currently understood within cultural studies, is concentrated on the 'politics of difference', which, according to West (1993), proceeds by way of:

- deconstruction;
- demythologization;
- demystification.

In general terms, *deconstruction* involves a reading of texts that challenges the tropes, metaphors and binaries of rhetorical textual operations. To deconstruct is to take apart, to undo, in order to seek out and display the assumptions of a text. In a more specifically Derridean sense, deconstruction involves the dismantling of hierarchical conceptual oppositions, such as man/woman, black/white, reality/appearance, nature/culture, reason/madness, and so on, that serve to guarantee truth claims by excluding and devaluing the 'inferior' part of the binary. In any case, the objective of deconstruction is to open to view the operations and assumptions of texts, including their world-views or 'ideologies'.

For West, the purpose of *demythologization* is to highlight the social construction of metaphors that regulate descriptions of the world and their possible consequences for classifying the social. That is, demythologization involves mapping the metaphors by which we live, along with their links to politics, values, purposes, interests and prejudices. Demythologization shows why we must speak not of History but of histories, not of Reason but of historically contingent forms of rationality. Thus, demythologization illustrates the social and cultural construction of our maps of the world and indicates to us the plasticity of identities.

Deconstruction and demythologization allow us to 'see through' the apparent solidity and habituation of cultural texts. However, in order for these insights to be translated into concrete cultural change, the development of critical positions and new theory must be linked to communities, groups, organizations and networks of people who are actively involved in social and cultural change. Thus, for West, *demystification* involves the describing and analysing of the complexity of institutional and other power structures in order to disclose options for transformative praxis. Such 'prophetic criticism' requires social analysis that is explicit and partisan in its moral and political aims.

Thus our attention is directed to the movement from textual analysis to overtly political action, or, rather, the necessary oscillation between textual analysis and practical politics.

However, the more common shift within cultural studies has been to take the language and methods of textual studies and to deploy them in the analysis of the social and cultural spheres. Hence, cultural studies has taken the practices of deconstruction and demythologization and, having first applied them to texts, now utilizes them in the broader analysis of culture, which is held to work 'like a language' or text (Chapter 2). In addition to the sidelining of economic reductionism, this approach has the advantages that West has already pointed us to, namely the de-naturalization of cultural texts and practices. However, the description and analysis of complex institutional power structures in order to disclose options for change is commonly absent. Worse still, the organic connections to communities, groups, organizations and networks of people who are actively involved in social and cultural change are largely non-existent. In this context, the question we need to ask is: who is able to act as the agent(s) for cultural change?

Cultural studies and the agents of cultural politics

Intellectuals and politics

In the context of the Gramscian cultural studies of the 1970s and 1980s, many writers within the field held the ambition of linking theorists with political movements in the model of the 'organic' intellectual. Here, cultural studies sought to play a 'demystifying' role by pointing to the constructed character of cultural texts. It aimed to highlight the myths and 'ideologies' embedded in texts in the hope of producing subject positions and real subjects, who are enabled to oppose subordination. Indeed, as a political theory, cultural studies has hoped to organize disparate oppositional groups into a politico-cultural alliance.

Within Gramscian thinking, traditional intellectuals are those persons who fill the scientific, literary, philosophical and religious positions in society, including in universities, schools, churches, the media, medical institutions, publishers and law firms. Though traditional intellectuals may be drawn from different class backgrounds, their status, position and functions lead them to view themselves as independent of any class allegiances or 'ideological' role. However, for Gramsci, they produce, maintain and circulate those ideologies constitutive of ruling-class cultural hegemony that become embedded and naturalized in common sense. For example, numerous analyses of contemporary media output have argued for the 'ideological' role of journalists, television producers and other media intellectuals (e.g. Hall et al., 1978).

By contrast, organic intellectuals are said to be a constitutive part of working-class (and later feminist, postcolonial, African-American, etc.) struggles. They are said to be the thinking and organizing elements of the counter-hegemonic class and its allies. As Gramsci put it, as a new class develops it creates 'organically . . . one or more strata of intellectuals which give it homogeneity and an awareness of its own function, not only economic but also in the social and political fields' (1971: 5). Given that Gramsci has an expansive notion of the organic intellectual, this role is to be played not only by those situated within the educational world but also by trade unionists, writers, campaigners, community organizers, teachers, and so forth.

However, there is little evidence to suggest that cultural studies writers have ever been 'organically' connected with political movements in any significant way. Rather, as Hall (1992a) has commented, cultural studies intellectuals acted 'as if' they were organic intellectuals or in the hope that one day they could be. Others, notably Bennett (1992), have been more sanguine in questioning whether cultural studies has ever been conceivable in terms of organic intellectuals. In particular, Bennett points out that the prime institutional sites for cultural studies are those of higher education. Consequently, though individuals and groups identified with cultural studies may try to forge connections outside of the academy with social and political movements, workers in cultural institutions, and cultural management, cultural studies shares its relative isolation from popular culture with most other academic disciplines.

As McGuigan has argued, the romantic and heroic conception of cultural studies as 'part of an intellectual guerrilla movement waging war on the borders of official academia' is 'now decidedly *passé*, not least because of the sheer success, in spite of obstructions to it, of cultural studies educationally and, indeed, in terms of research' (1997: 1). In the process of establishing a more secure institutional place in academic life, cultural studies has acquired a multitude of organizational bases, courses, textbooks and students. Indeed, it is difficult to see how the institutionalization and professionalization of cultural studies could have been avoided if it wanted to survive by carving out and maintaining a niche in the highly competitive and resource-poor higher education sector.

Class and new social movements

Cultural studies' early preoccupation with Marxism led many writers to be primarily concerned with the problems of economy, capitalism, class and culture, including the possibilities for revolutionary political transformation. Thus, it was with revolutionary class factions that organic intellectuals were intended to forge political links. However, the contemporary trajectory of cultural studies has been to de-centre class as a central and determining category. In theoretical terms this has been because culture is seen as having its own logic independently from class. In a more practical sense, the long-term recomposition of class relations and the decline of class as a predictor of politics, beliefs and cultural behaviour has led many thinkers to look elsewhere for the agents of social, political and cultural change (see Chapter 8).

The decline of the working class as a numerical and political force allied to the degeneration of socialism as an alternative systemic world-view marks the end of a revolutionary working-class politics in the West that could realize an alternative social order. I am not of course suggesting that class is no longer relevant to contemporary life or cultural politics. Indeed, in Chapter 8 I explicitly said otherwise. However, we can no longer look to class struggle as the primary vehicle of radical change, let alone the inevitable champion of universal liberation. Indeed, given that the emergence of cultural studies as an institutionally located enterprise did not coincide with an upsurge of class struggle, it has been the 'new' social and political movements of identity politics which have provided cultural studies with its alleged constituency.

New Social Movements are commonly seen as encompassing:

- civil rights struggles;
- feminism;
- ecology politics;
- peace movements;
- youth movements; and
- the politics of cultural identity.

According to Touraine (1981) and Melucci (1980, 1981, 1989), contemporary radical politics is becoming detached from class determinations and is increasingly organized through New Social Movements (NSMs). As characterized by these writers, NSMs are increasingly strident social and political collectivities based outside of the workplace, for orthodox class identifications and political strategies do not lie at their heart. Rather, the rise of NSMs appears to correlate with a reduction in trust in the major political parties and an interest in more direct forms of political action. Though it would be mistaken to see NSMs as entirely replacing class politics, conflict has been somewhat displaced from the opposition of manager and worker to a wider struggle for control over the direction of social, economic and cultural development. In particular, the axis of conflict has shifted to questions of identity, self-actualization and 'postmaterialist' values.

Thus, Giddens (1992) describes the axis of political activity in the West as having shifted from the 'emancipatory politics' of modernity, which were concerned with liberation from the exploitation and the constraints of tradition, to a concern with self-actualization, choice and lifestyle (see Chapter 10). That which Giddens calls 'life-politics' centres on questions of how to live a justifiable life in a global context. For Giddens, the more we 'make ourselves', the more the questions of 'what is a person?' and 'who do I want to be?' are raised in the context of global circumstances that no one can escape. For example, the recognition of the finite character of global resources and the limits of science and technology may lead to a sensible de-emphasis on economic accumulation and to the need to adopt new lifestyles. This reflexivity, involving the re-moralizing of social life, lies behind many contemporary social and political tendencies.

NSMs are more preoccupied with direct democracy and member participation than with representative democracy. Though the achievement of specific instrumental goals does form a part of their agenda, they are more concerned with their own autonomy and the value orientation of wider social developments. Indeed, Melucci (1989) casts them as having a 'spiritual' component (see Chapter 10), centred on the body and the 'natural' world, that acts as a source of moral authority.

NSMs are commonly marked out by their anti-authoritarian, anti-bureaucratic and even anti-industrial stance, alongside their loose, democratic and activist-oriented organizational modes. Consequently, the boundaries between particular movements are blurred in terms of value orientation, specific goals and overlapping flexible and shifting 'membership'. Though NSMs often engage in 'direct action', this is not usually aimed at the authority and personnel of orthodox representative politics (e.g. Members of Parliament or Congress) in the first instance. Rather, the initial symbolic protest commonly revolves around other actors or institutions in civil society, such as corporations, research establishments, military bases, oil rigs, road-building projects, and so forth.

The politics of NSMs challenge the cultural codes of institutionalized power relations through symbolic events and evocative language that lend them coherent form as an 'imagined community'. Hence the images generated by new social movements are core to their activities and act to blur the boundaries between their form and content. Indeed, many of the activities of NSMs are media events designed to give themselves popular appeal. Here, the symbolic languages of these movements are polysemic and thus broad enough to suit the imprecision of their aims while forming the basis of an alliance constituted by a range of otherwise disparate people. In this sense, more than traditional modern party politics, NSMs are expressly a form of cultural politics with which most cultural studies writers have felt an affinity.

Having said that, it remains difficult to see how the personnel and politics of cultural studies has engaged with NSMs any more than it did with class activists. Nevertheless, cultural studies practitioners can usefully go on writing deconstructive and demythologizing works for an audience some of whom will be drawn from NSMs and who may find intellectual clarification to be of benefit. That is,

---

Cultural studies can contribute to an intellectual 'clearing of the way' for political activists.

Texts, institutions and the politics of method

Of course, the success of the cultural studies enterprise will depend on the methods and modes of 'clarification' that the field adopts. The establishment of cultural studies as a department or programme within universities or as a subsection of another department – usually English literature – has coincided with an upsurge in the conceptualization of the field as a text-based discipline. Subsequently, cultural studies writers have commonly justified themselves with the argument that cultural criticism is a demythologizing aspect of cultural politics. Provided one drops the notion of 'exposing ideology' and settles for the perspective of redescription, this is an acceptable argument. Cultural criticism can act, albeit in a rather limited way for immediate practical purposes, as a tool for intervention in the social world. However, adoption of a certain deconstructive textualism along with the tone of methodological and ethical 'purity' has led some cultural studies writers into 'obscurity'.

This is not to say that the most 'obscure' and convoluted piece of writing possible is not valid in its own terms. Writing is obscure to the degree that it enacts a language used by a limited number of people. Though no language is entirely private, some are more restricted in their scope than others. Further, though the division of the public and private is culturally contingent (and the personal is political), nevertheless, there are some stories and some projects which have little or no public impact. We are entitled to write our own poems and construct our own private projects, and cultural theory has for many of us been a valuable part of this process. However, we should avoid over-inflating the public political value of our own private projects.

We should also try to avoid mistaking our ethical choices for the only viable ones while claiming them as 'radical public politics'. One of the dangers of amplifying the public impact of our ethical choices is that we expect culture and cultural identities to be more malleable than they turn out to be. That is, we mistake the 'world as we would like it to be' for 'the world as it is'. Or, to put that in a more epistemologically acceptable way, our stories do not prove to be very good predictors of political affairs. The revolutionary rhetoric of the cultural Left, which has provided emotional support for radical identities, has not turned out to be a particularly reliable guide to events or to effective action. However, the radical 'structure of feeling' that marks many cultural studies writers has prevented them from embracing the notion of gradualist reform.

Yet, under our current circumstances, the politics inherent to liberal democracies are the only politics in the West that are able to achieve structural change at the level of institutions and organizations. In this context, the radical rhetoric and stress on ethical style within cultural studies is of limited practical value. This does not mean that we have to accept liberal democracy as it stands. On the contrary, one of our aims must be to push for the extension of democratic practices within the liberal democratic framework. Further, though it sometimes leaves a bad taste in the mouth, this will commonly require engagement with social democratic political parties. The politics of NSMs, cultural policy and parliamentary politics are not mutually exclusive.

Cultural studies as writing

Although cultural studies engages in the rhetoric of populism, in practice most of the published work in the field reaches a very limited readership. In particular, an academic division of labour and the pressure to publish regularly and swiftly lead most of us to become rather opaque specialists. Not only do we work at limited aspects of whichever problem we are focused on, but we also tend to publish our work in forms that are not widely read. Ironically, specialization is one of the problems of a massive and expanding interdisciplinary field. It is just impossible to keep abreast of the sheer volume of literature available, let alone to take into account all the factors that are pertinent to our problem.

In addition, most cultural studies writers like to think of themselves as undertaking 'original' textual or theoretical work that pushes forward the boundaries of our thinking. This leads them to write in somewhat cryptic styles.

Of course such work is necessary in order to comprehend the world in new ways. However, its complex styles maintain the narrow specialist approach that in many ways runs counter to the populist ethos of cultural studies. The most ironic and senseless part of this approach is that only a small part of cultural studies work can be thought of as 'original' for most of it enacts the recycling of thinking demanded by universities and publishers. This is not in and of itself a problem, indeed it is entirely understandable when careers are at stake and students require to be taught. However, such work requires a simplicity and clarity of expression that is not always as evident as it should be.

Cultural studies needs to add to its repertoire a synthesizing approach that takes theoretical and empirical studies – including political economy, ethnography and textual analysis – and articulates them together. What is required, I am suggesting, is not one totalizing schema, but rather the generation of richer, more complex and multi-dimensional texts presented in more widely comprehensible styles. Thus it would be a welcome development if cultural studies were to develop more attempts to draw the various strands of the field together by juxtaposing and synthesizing the work of many writers around a specified topic. This is, in my view, the kind of thing Giddens has done well for the field of sociology and that we require within cultural studies as it reaches for what Willis (2000) has called a 'kind of maturity'.

Unfortunately, the stress in cultural studies on work that is embedded and historically and contextually specific, though to be encouraged on one level, militates against works of synthesis. Further, a cruelly ironic intellectual snobbery within cultural studies that identifies with academic-institutional demands for 'high'-level conceptualization operates against the production of popular works and quality textbooks wherein such a juggling act can take place.

The problem lies not with remote academic work per se *but with the clash between this approach and the pretensions of cultural studies to be politically relevant and engaged.*

Institutions and political economy

McGuigan (1992, 1996, 1997) and Kellner (1997), amongst others, have reacted to the recent stress on language, texts and identity in the field by asking cultural studies to engage more thoroughly with the institutions and political economy of culture. They argue that without such an analysis, criticism overlooks material inequalities and relations of power and thus becomes unable to apply the lever of change at the appropriate point (though this begs the question of how cultural studies is able to apply *any* kind of lever at any point). The claim is that where cultural studies fails to grasp the material circumstances and power relations that pertain between people, it lacks the means to bring about change.

Kellner (1997) rightly suggests that the divide between cultural studies (as textual studies) and political economy is a false one. He argues for a multiper-spectival approach that interrogates the relationships between political economy, representations, texts and audiences alongside an engagement with cultural policy. In this context, he recommends political economy to textual cultural studies as being able to show how cultural production takes place within specific historical, political and economic relations that structure textual meanings. In doing so, he calls attention to the fact that culture is produced within vectors of domination and subordination.

The arguments put by McGuigan and Kellner were timely reminders of the uses of political economy and the abuses of textualism. However, the argument for a multiperspectival approach has always been inherent within cultural stud-ies. Thus, the current stress on the 'circuit of culture' (du Gay et al., 1997) is a reworking of Hall's earlier (1981) encoding/decoding model. In this argument, each of the moments of the circuit – representation, regulation, consumption, production and identity – are articulated together and productive of meanings that are necessary for the continuation of the circuit but which are insufficient to determine the form and content of other instances. Thus the challenge is to grasp just how the moment of production inscribes itself in representation in each case without assuming that it can be 'read off' from economic relations. We would also be interested in the reverse case, namely how culture or representa-tion is implicated in the forms and modes of organization that production takes: that is, how the economic is cultural.

The ethnographic approach

Thus far, my focus has been on issues of method and substance as they relate to text and political economy. However, what remains absent is a discussion of living persons as readers of texts and as agents of change (see Chapter 2). The undervalued counter-weight to cultural studies' theoretical and textual focus has been an interest in the empirical investigation of 'readers' and consumers of texts from television to clothing.

Methodologically, rather than the textual approaches of semiotics, poststruc-turalism and deconstructionism, we have now entered the territory of reception studies and ethnography. The latter is an empirical and theoretical approach inherited from anthropology that seeks to generate detailed holistic description and analysis of cultures based on intensive fieldwork, the objective being the production of what Geertz (1973) famously described as 'thick descriptions' of 'the multiplicity of complex conceptual structures', including the unspoken and taken-for-granted assumptions that are made about cultural life.

Ethnographic cultural studies has been centred on the qualitative exploration of cultural values, meanings and life-worlds. However, in the context of media-oriented cultural studies, ethnography has also become a code-word for a range of qualitative methods, including participant observation, in-depth interviews and focus groups. Here, it is the 'spirit' of ethnography (i.e. qualitative under-standing of cultural activity in context) which has been invoked polemically against the tradition of quantitative communications research (see Morley, 1992).

In trying to 'represent the subjective meanings, feelings and cultures of others' (Willis, 1981: 91), ethnography has implicitly relied on a representationalist episte-mology and has thus opened itself up to considerable critique. In particular, not only is ethnography inevitably 'positional' knowledge, but also it is a genre of writing that deploys rhetorical devices, often obscured, to maintain its realist claims (Clifford and Marcus, 1986). This argument has led to the examination of ethno-graphic texts for their rhetorical devices, along with a more reflexive and dialogical approach to ethnography which demands that writers should elaborate on their own assumptions, views and positions. Further, consultation with the 'subjects' of research is required so that ethnography becomes less an expedition in search of 'the facts' and more a conversation between participants in a research process.

The critique of the representationalist epistemology that underpins ethno-graphic cultural studies is fundamentally correct for, as Wittgenstein, Rorty and Derrida, amongst others, have taught us, the 'real' is always already a repre-sentation. However, we need to be less concerned with questions of representational adequacy and more engaged in a politics of representation. That is, we need to be concerned with that which representations signify in an environment of social power, along with their potential consequences. In this context, the epistemological critique of ethnography does not leave it without worth or significance for its purposes do not lie in the production of a represen-tationally 'true' picture of the world. Indeed, ethnographies, writings in physical science and novels all involve socially agreed procedures that produce texts of more or less use to us in guiding our conduct.

The differences between these genres are not degrees of correspondence to reality but mat-ters of their purpose and style.

Thus, science has proved itself to be good at prediction and control of the nat-ural environment while ethnographies and novels have amongst their achievements the production of empathy and the widening of the circle of human solidarity (Rorty, 1989, 1991a). Ethnography has personal, poetic and political, rather than epistemological, justifications. However, this does not mean that we can abandon all methodical rigour, for the following reasons:

- Evidence and poetic style are pragmatically useful warrants for truth and action epistemologically equivalent to the procedural agreements of the physical sciences.
- The language of observation and evidence is among the reason-giving con-ventions that divide the genre of ethnography from the novel.
- The rejection of a universal objective truth is based on the impossibility of

word-world correspondence and therefore of accurate or adequate representation. This does not mean that we have to abandon word–word
translation. That is, we can achieve 'good enough' reporting of the speech or
action of others without making claims to universal truth. Thus, it is better to
use a tape recorder to document the utterances of research subjects than to
invent their speech because (a) we will be better able to translate and understand the words of others for practical purposes and (b) we will be better able
to predict the actions of others.

The problems of ethnography are problems of *translation* and *justification* not of
universal or objective truth. Since all languages are culture-bound and knowledge is positional, then languages, along with cultural and political discourses,
are in a sense incommensurable for there is no metalanguage of translation.
However, we can recognize others as language users. If we then consider languages to be constituted not by untranslatable and incompatible rules, but rather
by learnable skills, then the gap between languages and cultures is not for practical purposes unbridgeable after all.

In this view, ethnographic data can be seen as giving poetic expression to
voices from other cultures or from the 'margins' of our own cultures. However,
writing about such voices is to be regarded no longer as 'objective' scientific
work that reports on universal truth but as an exposition and reason-giving
narration that brings new voices into what Rorty (1980) calls the 'cosmopolitan
conversation of humankind'. Thus, ethnographic data can continue to be the
route by which our own culture is made strange to us through the generation of
new descriptions of the world. Further, through representing the previously
unrepresented, ethnographic work encourages dialogue and the expansion of
the 'we' of human solidarity.

Theoretically and politically, empirical reception and ethnographic research
stress persons as active agents. This view is in contrast to the widely held poststructuralist perspective by which subjects are interpellated by 'ideology' or fixed
into the subject positions of disciplinary discourses. Thus, in the necessary
oscillation between structure and agency, reception work has swung the pendulum
back towards the latter. Though this has sometimes gone too far in assuming
that readers can always resist the culture industries (see Chapters 7 and 8), it
does nevertheless put creative and active political subjects back on the agenda.
Further, ethnographic work has the potential to connect with individuals, organizations and networks of people who are, or could be, actively involved in the
politics of social and cultural change.

The politics that flow from a concern with the production of meaning within
human consciousness, which is shared by textual and ethnographic approaches,
have tended to operate on the level of signs, with a focus on changing the way
that people think. By contrast, Tony Bennett has been critical of cultural studies
for displacing its politics onto the level of signification and text at the expense of
a material politics of the institutions and organizations of culture.

The politics of policy

Bennett (1992, 1998) argues that the textual politics with which cultural studies has been engaged ignores the institutional dimensions of cultural power. He urges cultural studies to adopt a more pragmatic approach, to work with cultural producers and to 'put policy into cultural studies'. For Bennett, cultural politics should centre on policy formulation and enactment within the institutions that produce and administer the form and content of cultural products. His view is that cultural studies has been overly concerned with consciousness and the ideological struggle (as conceived through Gramsci) and not enough with the material technologies of power (as understood by Foucault).

According to Bennett, the Gramscian tradition has accorded little attention to the specificities of cultural institutions, technologies and apparatuses (concentrating instead on textual analysis and the personal rewards of a certain 'ethical style'). By contrast, Bennett's reading of Foucault suggests to him that a 'politics of detail' is required in relation to governmental technologies, cultural policy and cultural technologies. Here, culture is conceptualized as constituting 'a particular field of government' and social regulation. In Bennett's view, 'the relations of culture and power which most typically characterize modern societies are . . . now increasingly governmentally organized and constructed' (1998: 61). Thus, culture is caught up in, and functions as a part of, cultural technologies that organize and shape social life and human conduct.

In this context, the pertinent concept of *governmentality* stresses that processes of social regulation do not so much stand over and against the individual but are constitutive of self-reflective modes of conduct, ethical competencies and social movements. Governmentality designates the broad processes of regulation throughout the social order by which a population becomes subject to bureaucratic regimes and modes of discipline.

A cultural technology is part of the 'machinery' of institutional and organizational structures that produce particular configurations of power/knowledge. Thus, culture is a matter not simply of representations but also of institutional practices, administrative routines and spatial arrangement, that is, cultural technologies. In this context, cultural studies is urged to identify the different 'regions' of culture and their managerial operations: that is, to understand the divergent technologies of power and forms of politics associated with different domains of cultural practice and to work with other 'governmental' organizations of culture to develop policy and modes of strategic intervention.

It is unfortunate that the polemical tone of the so-called 'cultural policy debate' of the early 1990s led to a polarization of positions in terms of 'policy' vs 'cultural criticism'. Perhaps cultural studies' rather one-sided textual approach and lack of engagement with policy issues justified the stridency of the policy advocates. Nevertheless, it is clear that policy and criticism, the achievement of technical goals and changes in consciousness, are not opposites but complementary strategies. There is no necessary reason why cultural studies cannot attend to the important pragmatic calls of policy without relinquishing the role that 'critical cultural theory' has to play. Similarly, if it takes politics rather than posturing seriously, then cultural criticism does need to engage with policy questions.

If we are to achieve concrete cultural change in the context of modern organizational societies, then an engagement with institutional and policy matters is important. Nevertheless, given the rapidly changing socio-cultural contexts in which we live, it also remains necessary to reconsider continually the values and goals we hold dear and that make a policy orientation worthwhile. This is one of the reasons why cultural theory and criticism have continuing importance. Thus we require what Morris (1992) calls a 'critical outside', an unregulated site from which the actions of policy makers and organizational professionals can be scrutinized and criticized. Further, given the ascendancy of some damaging and dangerous ways of thinking within the West, the attempt to change people's minds must always be an option worth exploring.

A 'critical outside' could be constituted through a combination of cultural studies theory and the political actions of New Social Movements (though this formulation massively overrates cultural studies' contribution since NSMs do not need cultural studies as such). However, neither intellectuals nor NSMs are capable of bringing about radical change on their own. Intellectuals, at least the type cultural studies produces (as opposed to, say, some scientists or social policy makers), do not constitute a major lever of power in contemporary societies, while most NSMs (with the possible exception of the Greens) do not have radical *systemic* change as their goal.

In any case, 'revolution', in the sense of a complete overhaul of the social order through the seizure of a central point of power, is no longer an attractive or viable possibility.

The limits of human control and the politics of reform

There is little evidence of popular support for radical political change in the West, let alone 'cultural revolution'. Further, not only is power dispersed throughout the social order, making 'revolution' itself only a limited attack on power, but, as Giddens (1994) points out, we live in a runaway world that has not shown itself to be particularly amenable to tight human control. Indeed, the 'advance' of human knowledge and its consequent interventions has not led to greater certainty but is itself deeply implicated in unpredictability. That which Giddens calls 'manufactured uncertainty' is a *consequence* of human intervention. In particular, he points to globalization (action at a distance), the emergence of a post-traditional social order (where traditions must justify themselves) and the expansion of social reflexivity (which produces a dislocation between knowledge and control) as underlying the construction of doubtfulness.

Giddens displays an admirable willingness to accept that there are limitations to human perfectibility, while acknowledging the widespread influence of the unintended consequences of action. With this in mind, cultural policy needs to be specifically and carefully targeted with a clear sense of the intended outcomes along with the mechanisms and agents of transformation. Otherwise, as suggested by the literature on organizational change (Fullan with Stiegelbauer, 1991; Kanter, 1984; McCalman and Paton, 1992), we may well not get what we had hoped for. In particular, change takes place through a combination of push and pull, leadership and popular involvement, with the latter a crucial aspect of successful organizational change.

The culture and institutions of modernity have valued a so-called 'universal rationality' over tradition(s) because it has provided technical knowledge for the achievement of particular goals. Socialism and Marxism, as the underside of modernity, have also considered human social and cultural arrangements to be open to unlimited rational understanding, control and directed change. However, the universal rationality of modernity has manifested a tendency to override the local and particular, where knowledge is saturated by practice and provides a meaningful framework for action. We all work from within a tradition, and this is both necessary and inevitable. As Giddens (1994) suggests, ideals torn from a tradition (that are themselves constituted by continuity and change) are incapable of skilfully guiding human action. Here, many of the criticisms of modernity levelled by postmodernists regarding the 'dark side' of rationality and the danger of grand narratives resonate with some forms of 'philosophic conservatism'.

As Giddens argues, tradition offers both practical knowledge and, more significantly, wisdom or ritual truths that are enacted through repetition of practical formulae. However, what faces us now is the need not to defend tradition in the traditional way (i.e. because it is tradition), but to decide reflexively what aspects of traditions are *meaningful* to us in the present day. For example, the Green movement depends to some extent on a notion of 'conservation' – a conservative defence of the 'what is' or even 'what was' (including invented traditions). However, Green politics also require new and radical solutions in the form of, for example, resource-conserving energy provisions.

There is a similar balancing act to be achieved between conservation and change in relation to 'the family'. On the whole, 'the Left' has argued that the family is a place of oppression for women and children and a site for the generation of mental illness (Barrett and McIntosh, 1982; Hite, 1994; Laing, 1976). By contrast, 'the Right' has hailed the family as the bedrock of stable societies and the source of a primary human happiness. Consequently, changes in the family have been greeted with alarm by conservatives and blamed as the origins of many of our contemporary social woes. For example, there is currently much discussion about 'lost fathers' (Daniels, 1998), with some commentators arguing that the decline of fatherhood in America is the most extraordinary trend of our time and accounts for many of the social problems encountered there. Poverty, rising juvenile crime, eating disorders, suicide, depression, alcohol and drug abuse are all traced back to absent fathers.

Thus, it is maintained that children who grow up with one parent (usually the mother) are:

- two and a half times more likely to become teen mothers;
- twice as likely to drop out of school;
- one and a half times as likely to be out of school and out of work.

In America, 60 per cent of rapists, 72 per cent of adolescent murderers and 70 per cent of long-term prison inmates are said to come from fatherless homes (Popenoe, 1996). The argument that it is the absence of fathers *per se* that accounts for these figures is commonly countered by suggesting that the primary cause is the parental conflict and poverty that accompany single parenthood (McLanahan and Sandefur, 1994). It is argued that there is little evidence that children need a male parent so much as they need loving, nurturing, caring adults, a condition that can occur in a variety of family forms (Stacey, 1996). Indeed, some children are better off without the presence of their abusive father.

It is probably desirable for children to be actively parented by a man and a woman in a loving partnership. However, the anxiety about children living in one-parent families – which does have a basis in research evidence – is not best alleviated by a simple conservative 'return to family values'. Not only are women and children unlikely to accept a return to the traditional family, but we can now agree that there are many roads to happiness and a variety of workable kinship forms. These may include gay and lesbian parents, one-parent families embedded in a support network, shared parenthood with mobile children, and so forth. I am not myself bold or competent enough to say how the family 'should be', merely that we need to keep thinking about it and trying to come up with more satisfying solutions to living together and raising children. Indeed, contemporary changes in family life are part of an experiment in new ways of living.

Neither the call to family values nor the wilful ignoring of the consequences of the current crisis of the family for children and the social order is a plausible way to go forward. Rather, we need to develop and support new ways of living that sustain children and parents practically and emotionally. This requires creative and imaginative thinking developed through critique, dialogue and experiment, tempered with caution with regard to the best interests of children and driven by an emotional bravery. This path can be furthered through theoretical criticism and policy initiatives sponsored by the state and private-charitable organizations.

One of the reasons why many practitioners within cultural studies balk at policy strategies is that policy feels conservative in contrast to the more radical emotional 'structure of feeling' that constitutes most of the cultural Left.

However, a serious engagement with new forms of family living would constitute a radical – i.e. bold and daring – possibility for a critical policy orientation. By way of example, I want to argue that the development of policy related to 'emotional education' could form a necessary and practical aspect of the emergence of new family and gender relations.

Emotional education

In its early days British cultural studies had a strong interest in educational practices and policy, as evidenced in particular by Raymond Williams' engagement with the Workers' Educational Association and his concept of the 'long revolution'. Further, not only did Stuart Hall have a background as a schoolteacher (and co-author of a book on young people and the arts), but one of the early books produced at the Centre for Contemporary Cultural Studies concerned 'unpopular education' (Centre for Contemporary Cultural Studies, Education Group, 1981). However, since that time, questions of education have rarely been at the centre of the field. This is an oddity given that cultural studies is primarily located in educational institutions and that education policy and practice would seem to be the domains of cultural activity most open to the influence of cultural studies writers. I would suggest that facets of contemporary culture should encourage us to engage once more with this important zone of activity. In particular, the rise of psychological problems in the western world (e.g. anxiety, depression, eating disorders – see Chapter 10) suggests a need to explore the character and role of emotions within our lives through, amongst other things, the education system.

According to Goleman (1995), emotions can be classified into the following major categories:

- fear;
- joy;
- disgust;
- sadness;

- surprise;
- shame;
- love;
- anger.

During the mid-1990s Goleman popularized the notion of 'emotional intelligence' (EQ) based on his summary and discussion of the work of many neuroscientists and psychologists. Emotional intelligence is concerned with our own feelings and those of others. It is centred on self-awareness, motivation, compassion and empathy. As Goleman argued, emotional intelligence is a basic requirement for the effective use of intellectual intelligence (IQ). Clear, positive thinking and the successful deployment of intellectual skills need EQ. As Zohar and Marshall put it, 'If the brain areas with which we *feel* are damaged, we *think* less effectively' (2000: 3).

EQ, as Goleman defines it, allows us to judge what kind of situation we are in and to act appropriately. Stunted emotional intelligence leads us to be carried away with anger and fear and/or to become overly 'rational' with an inability to relate well to other people. This is significant in the context of a virtual epidemic of depression, addiction, attention deficit disorder and suicide across the western world. While these conditions are widely held to have genetic and biochemical roots, the 'predispositions' that genetics gives rise to are variously 'activated' or otherwise according to social and cultural circumstances. Further, as we noted above (Chapter 5), the increase in mental health problems that we are witnessing has been taking place over the last fifty years or so and is therefore too recent a phenomenon to be accounted for by genetic alteration in the human condition.

There is something about western culture that is promoting human unhappiness, and if that is not a question for cultural studies to take seriously, then it is hard to know what would be.

Blue days down under

In Australia, which ranks third in the world prescription rates for anti-depressants after Sweden and France (and closely followed by the USA, Canada, the UK, Germany and Italy), more than 8 million prescriptions were written in 1998. This represents a rise of 3 million prescriptions for anti-depressants since 1990. This has taken place in a country with a population of 18 million where depression has risen from the tenth most common problem seen by GPs to the fourth, with one in sixteen Australians meeting the criteria for depression (*The Sun Herald*, 5/11/00). A survey undertaken in the Illawarra area of the Australian state of New South Wales (Illawarra Public Health Unit, 1998) found the following:

- Some 75 per cent of the 1,939 year 6, 8 and 10 school students interviewed reported feeling unhappy, sad or depressed during the previous six months.
- For 21 per cent of these students (15 per cent of the total), this feeling had been *'almost more than I can take'*.
- At least 71 per cent of students reported that they had felt under strain, stress or pressure during the same period.
- For 16 per cent of these students (11 per cent of all students), this pressure had been *'almost more than I can take'*. That is, one in six students in the sample reported significant levels of stress and/or depression.

These levels of depression underpin a wide range of other problems: for example, 46 per cent of the students were unhappy with their body size, while 40 per cent of the participants reported drunkenness, with 25 per cent of students recounting drinking five or more drinks in the previous two weeks.

More alarming still, the overall suicide rate in Australia since the middle of the nineteenth century has increased about 24 per cent, with the number of suicides increasing sevenfold. In 1964 the rate was 10.4 per 100,000 population, and by 1990–2 it had increased to 12.9. Among young men (15–29) suicide rates increased from 5.8 per 100,000 in 1964 to 17.8 per 100,000 in 1990 (Hassan, 1997), later rising to 27.3 per 100, 000 (Lennane, 1997). In 1999, amongst men in the 25 to 39 age group, two out of five deaths were attributable to suicide and another 25 per cent to accidental poisoning, mainly though alcohol or drugs, and almost as many died from transport accidents, some of which will have been suicides (*Sun Herald*, 07/01/01).

Teaching emotional skills

According to Goleman (1995) and many educational psychologists, we can learn the skills necessary to combat some of these developments. Such skills would include the ability to motivate oneself, persist in the face of frustration, control impulsive behaviour, empathize with others, handle anger and become more self-aware about one's own emotional responses. Asked what is the thing they most want for their children, parents commonly say happiness. However, most schools pay scant attention to issues of emotional intelligence, stressing academic achievement and successful entry into the job market above all else.

As academic 'achievers', neither I nor most readers of this book are likely to want to deny the personal and social value of formal scholarly education. However, I would contend that most academic knowledge (content) is of direct use to only a minority of school students. Even the more durable learning skills that are acquired (outside of the three Rs), such as information retrieval, constructing and assessing arguments, gathering and evaluating evidence, and so forth, are underplayed in schools, while the more social and emotional skills like teamwork, co-operation, the ability to express oneself, independence, emotional self-awareness, and so forth, are commonly relegated to a gesture in the right direction.

Given the above, one must ask about what kind of culture it is that values success at work over happiness, academic knowledge over the mental health of young people, wealth creation and excessive consumption over social co-operation, military expansion over the reduction of violence, and so forth. Of course, none of these observations are new. Many psychologists have been saying this for a while now, and some educational administrations have taken the arguments on board. Certainly in the UK during the late 1980s and 1990s there was an expansion of curriculum areas entitled 'Personal and Social Education' (PSE) and 'Lifeskills' that attempted to address some of the important issues of emotional management.

Indeed, I spent some eight years in English schools working in just these areas. My experience was that even in situations where an education authority was supportive of these endeavours, individual schools would downplay them. Where a school management took the issues on board, many teachers would not, and where some teachers did, many students would not because the 'subject' was isolated in the curriculum provision and appeared to them to be of little worth compared to the traditional school work that our culture values. Indeed, one of the problems we face is the tendency not to regard PSE as a subject at all. Rather, it is thought better treated as a set of learnable skills that are addressed across the entire school curriculum. Having said that, the inability or unwillingness of the majority of teachers to engage systematically and seriously with 'emotional intelligence' has meant that even sympathetic schools have commonly been forced to segment PSE into a separated domain (or a ghetto) in order to undertake the work at all.

Needless to say, 'more education' is not the solution to all our problems, nor is the teaching and learning of emotional skills a panacea for the affective problems of young people, let alone the black hole of meaninglessness that sits at the heart of western culture (see Chapter 10). Nevertheless, emotional turmoil, personal meaninglessness, the repression of the moral questions of day-to-day life and the resources required to respond to them are vital issues for contemporary culture. We cannot simply declare the need for change and expect it to happen. We have to start the process of concrete change somewhere, and schools are an important site for us to work with.

Educational policy at all levels could address the crucial issues of teacher training, school curriculum content, skills acquisition and resource allocation in relation to emotional education. However, this is above all a question of *cultural* values that needs to be addressed through ongoing cultural critique, research and policy development that surely could and should be within the remit of cultural studies. Further, there is a considerable literature regarding 'organizational change' that puts the case for *cultural* change within schools (and other institutions) in order to enable policy initiatives to become workable in practice. In particular, educational policy has been continually thwarted by its 'hyperrational' mode of implementation. That is, policy is made on high and handed down to teachers to execute with little or no attention given to the cultures of schools as organizations and the conditions that underpin policy successes and failures.

In this context, classroom teachers have had little or no input and therefore neither much understanding nor proprietorship of the policies in question. Thus, with hardly a minute to spare in each busy day, policy is grudgingly brought into being, if at all. Given its delicate nature, and the need for new styles of teaching that stress skills, processes and participation within an environment of trust and confidentiality, emotional education cannot work properly under such conditions. The construction and implementation of policy regarding emotional education has to involve classroom teachers in more than a token way. Teachers must be one of the prime stakeholders in any such development.

Of course, teachers are not likely to take such a project seriously and enthusiastically unless educational authorities and school managements signal the sincerity with which they take emotional education by committing time and resources to it. Thus, organizational change requires leadership as well as ground-level participation. This argument has implications for cultural studies that extend beyond the particular policy instance under discussion. That is, if cultural studies is to take policy formation seriously, then it must also pay attention to the *processes* of organizational cultural change. To do otherwise is to commit the same sin as countless other organizational bureaucrats.

Conclusions

Cultural studies has always seen itself as a particularly politicized intellectual activity. Indeed, Stuart Hall once made the distinction between 'intellectual' (politically engaged) work and 'academic' work precisely to shore up the connections between cultural studies and cultural politics while differentiating it from other kinds of university-based activities. In this chapter, cultural politics was defined as the 'power to name', articulated with a series of collective social struggles. In particular, the politics of representation and difference have involved a move away from class as the central axis of politics towards questions of gender, race, age, ecology, and so forth, with various NSMs as the hoped-for agents of change.

I argued that the resistance of human culture to organized and directed revolutionary change, especially under the conditions of contemporary western democracies, has made reform the only possible and desirable way to move forward. However, in my view, cultural studies continues to overrate its own contribution to and connection with cultural and political change, with many practitioners more impressed with their own ethical stance than with the grubby politics of reform. I also suggested that cultural studies has tended to inflate the value of textual analysis and downplay both political economy and ethnography in ways that leave it isolated from the concerns of most people in western democracies. Ethnography in particular offers the possibility of direct contact with the everyday lives and cultural concerns of those extraordinary ordinary people in whose interests our politics are said to be forged.

I am convinced that cultural studies has made important intellectual contributions to our understanding of culture, power and politics. However, I have also been suggesting that the cultural politics of cultural studies have not been especially effective as forms of intervention. Consequently, cultural studies needs to adopt a more pragmatic approach to cultural politics and recognize the significance of cultural policy and the opportunities that it offers intellectuals for intervention. This must include not only policy formation but also the difficulties of implementation. In any case, no one investigative method or political strategy for cultural politics can be the 'correct' one. If I have stressed ethnography, reform and cultural policy, it is by way of contrast with the textual politics and revolutionary rhetoric that have predominated in cultural studies. In the end, the interdisciplinary character of cultural studies will continue to be reflected in a kaleidoscope of concepts, methods and political strategies, as indeed it should be.

10 Evolution and Emotion:

New Resources for Cultural Studies

Central problem:
Biology vs culture

> Genes don't care about suffering, because they don't care about anything. . . . The universe we observe has precisely the properties we should expect if there is, at bottom, no design, no purpose, no evil and no good, nothing but blind, pitiless indifference. . . . DNA neither cares nor knows. DNA just is. And we dance to its music. (Dawkins, 1995: 153–5)

> Darwin took [a] radical step toward uniting the mental and physical worlds, by showing how the mental world – whatever it might be comprised of – arguably owed its complex organization to the same process of natural selection that explained the physical organization of living things. Psychology became united with the biological and hence evolutionary sciences. (Tooby and Cosmides, 1992: 20)

Introduction

This chapter concerns the ongoing problem of the relationship between biology and culture, or, as it is commonly posed, nature vs nurture. This constitutes a 'problem' for cultural studies not so much because this issue has been widely discussed within the literature, but rather because it has been sidestepped.

As I see it, cultural studies has suffered by sealing itself off from the empirical rigours of science and the embodied nature of human beings. As such, I shall be putting the case that the languages of evolutionary biology/psychology, along with those of psychotherapy and a meaningful 'spirituality', would be valuable additions to the cultural studies vocabulary. On the face of it this would appear to be an odd, if not to say bizarre, combination of the pitilessly profane and the self-consciously sacred. However, in an indifferent universe it is in the nature of acculturated human beings to look for meaningful ways to live. In particular, I shall be suggesting that contemporary western culture is plagued by emotional discontents that form a link between biochemistry and the cultural need for a spirituality without God.

Evolutionary biology and cultural studies

If cultural studies adopted evolutionary biology/psychology (see Barkow et al., 1992; Buss, 1999a; 1999b; Dawkins, 1976, 1995; Dennett, 1995; Gribbin, 1998; Sterelny and Griffiths, 1999) as a backdrop to its work on culture, then we would be better able to draw a more naturalistic and holistic picture of human beings as animals that walk the earth adapting and changing themselves in the context of their environment. At this stage, I am presenting a philosophical and theoretical argument that will need its flesh and bones, its worked examples, to be developed more fully elsewhere.

An evolutionary view of culture suggests that it is formed as the legacy of our prior adaptations to our ancestral physical circumstances just as it now represents the human creation of a new 'synthetic' environment. It is often said that the complex character of human language and culture is what distinguishes us most obviously from other animals. However, we cannot presuppose human language, co-operation and culture; rather, they are built up from scratch over time within an evolutionary context. Human life is after all animal life. The development of language, the foundation stone of culture, probably depends on the evolutionary development of a 'language acquisition device', while the style and parameters of our thinking are shaped in part by the cognitive structures of the brain. Subsequently, we learn language as an integral part of learning how to do things within our environment and continue to develop language skills not so much through reasoning as through practice (see Chapter 2).

In any case, it is certainly a mistake to see language as either wholly cultural or biological in its operations since it is patently both. Indeed, as Buss (1999a, 1999b) argues, a whole series of binaries, such as nature vs nurture, culture vs biology, genes vs the environment, need to be jettisoned since that which makes human beings responsive to their immediate environment owes its existence to evolutionary processes.

To enable an alliance of evolutionary theory and cultural studies to work, and in order to avoid accusations of biological reductionism, we need to 'deconstruct' the opposition of nature and culture from both directions. On the one hand, culture is an outgrowth of human beings learning and adapting within their natural ancestral environment. On the other hand, not only is nature already a concept in language (and not a pure state of being beyond signs), but also the natural world has come under the sway of human knowledge and institutions. Thus we may speak of the 'socialization of nature'. Indeed, through the investigations of genetic science we are learning to intrude even further into the 'natural' human body.

Posed in Derridean terms, the character of the relations between biology and language is an undecidable question because inquiry is formed within an always already existent sign system. However, saying this is of limited usefulness to us in terms of coping with the world. For example, we need to make decisions about how to treat depression or carry out sex-changes. The languages of genetics, neuroscience and psychotherapy have proved more useful to us in dealing with these questions of biology, culture and language than has 'undecidability' or the Bible.

Evolutionary biology

According to Dennett,

> The fundamental core of contemporary Darwinism, the theory of DNA-based reproduction and evolution, is now beyond dispute among scientists. It demonstrates its power every day, contributing crucially to the explanation of planet-sized facts of geology and meteorology, through middle-sized facts of ecology and agronomy, down to the latest microscopic facts of genetic engineering. It unifies all of biology and the history of our planet into a single grand story. (1995: 20)

Evolutionary biology is a useful causal story that explains human organisms in terms of relationships and consequences in which history has no *telos*. It dispenses with the idea that either the human mind or the mind of God is the ultimate source of the universe, replacing them both with the mindless, purposeless and mechanical processes of natural selection. In doing so, evolutionary biology explores and explains the diversity of life on our planet, the processes of adaptation made by organisms in order to survive and the long-term development of species. Here, 'development' is the outcome of numerous acts of chance and environmental adaptation that make the 'direction' of human evolution contingent. Thus, 'progress' or 'purpose' can only be given meaning as a retrospectively told story.

As understood by Mayr (1982), the fundamentals of evolutionary theory can be grasped as a network of five components:

- The living world is not constant: evolutionary change has occurred.
- Evolutionary change has a branching pattern, indicating that contemporary species descended from remote ancestors.
- New species form when a population splits and the fragments diverge. That is, new species are accounted for by the isolation of sub-populations.
- Evolutionary change is gradual.
- The mechanism of adaptive change is natural selection.

Natural selection is held to be the inevitable outcome of the interaction of phenotypic (the actual physiology and conduct of an animal) variation, differential fitness and heritability. That is, organisms within a population will diverge in ways that leave some variants better suited than others to dealing with the problems that they face, notably those of resource limitations and population competition. These variants are likely to enable the creatures concerned to be able to survive and reproduce more successfully than can their contemporaries. If the characteristics that promote survival and reproduction are in part heritable, then subsequent populations will have a positive inclination towards heritable, advantageous traits. Hence, the characteristics of a given evolving species will be subject to change as the mechanisms that generate heritable variation add new traits to the evolving population. Thus does evolutionary theory demonstrate not only that modern species are the revised descendants of earlier species, but also that the mechanism for this process is natural selection (Darwin, 1985).

Evolution through natural selection is a 'mindless' and impersonal set of processes that unfold with guaranteed outcomes given initial conditions. That is, 'Life on Earth has been generated over billions of years in a single branching tree – the tree of life – by one algorithmic process or another' (Dennett, 1995: 51). An algorithm is a formal process that can be counted on logically to produce a specific outcome whenever it is run or instantiated. Long division and computer programs are algorithms. They do what they do and they do it every time. Further, no matter how impressive the results of algorithmic processes are to us, they are the outcome of individually mindless steps succeeding each other.

Evolution has no purpose; it is not for anything. Certainly it is not a set of processes designed to produce human beings; rather, it is a set of algorithmic processes that just happen to have created us through the generation of specific forms of DNA and genetic codes.

The place of genes

Dawkins is the prime architect of what has become known as the 'gene's-eye' view of evolution, constituted by a river of DNA that flows through time. This 'river out of Eden' is a river of information, a river of abstract instructions for assembling flesh and blood that passes through bodies but is not affected by them (genes do not blend but recombine independently). In Dawkins' terminology, genes are replicators that form lineages or chains, with each link being a copy of its predecessor in a way that organisms (and their traits) are not. That is, organisms are not copied, genes are. Of course, the successful reproduction of genes depends on their capacities for building robustly thriving bodies (vehicles or interactors) that survive their environment and reproduce. Thus organisms mediate the relationship of genes to the environment and further replication. In this context, evolutionary change is a consequence of cumulative selection over a very long period.

Genes are taken here to be variably sized chunks of DNA that have pheno-typic power, that is, they make a difference between one phenotypic trait and another. A phenotype is the manifested morphology, physiology and behaviour of an organism whereas a genotype or genome consists of the total collection of genes that an organism carries. DNA builds the brain and the body with minor differences accounting for the divergent character of human individuals' inher-ited temperaments. It is responsible for the chemically unique structure of individual brains as they develop within singular environments. We may under-stand genes as strings of digitally encoded information constructed from four symbols: A, T, G and C (Dawkins, 1995). This information can be encoded, recorded and decoded without degradation or change of meaning down millions of generations over aeons of geological time (variation in a genome comes through the multitude of gene combinations available to sexually repro-ducing organisms plus periodic errors in replication).

It is important to remember that genes exist in bodies and that physical forms inhabit environmental niches. In the long run, the genes that are good at sur-viving and reproducing are those that build bodies and traits that gather cumulative advantage in the environment. However, the specific phenotypic effects of genes are often variable depending on the environment (both the other genes in the body and the 'external' environment). Genes can then be seen as 'context-sensitive difference makers' (Sterelny and Griffiths, 1999: 99) that oper-ate within a whole 'developmental matrix', including the inheritance of non-genetic factors and modification of genetic consequences by developmental contexts. Nevertheless, from a 'gene's eye' view, DNA remains a privileged player in the game of life. But what is it that the language of genes allows us to understand?

The form of genetic explanation

As Sterelny and Griffiths (1999) argue, philosophy (and here I would include cultural studies) is important to biology because the latter's conclusions do not follow from the 'facts' alone but require interpretation. Equally, biology is impor-tant to philosophy because these conclusions do depend on the scientific evidence.

There is nothing in evolutionary biology that corresponds to the traditional notion of an essential and unbending human nature. There is no such thing as the 'genetic essence' of a species; rather, each population is a collection of indi-viduals with many genetic differences, and these differences are handed on to future generations in new combinations. Indeed, evolutionary theory relies on the possibility of the continual generation of genetic difference. One is human not because one possesses particular characteristics, but by dint of membership of a distinct population with a specific evolutionary history. Human beings form overlapping pools of genetic variation, not distinct races, each with its own genome. Indeed, information released by the Human Genome Project in February 2001 suggests that individuals are made up of some 30,000 genes, with each person sharing 99.9 per cent of his or her genetic material with other human beings.

One of the problems to plague evolutionary theory has been the charge of biological determinism or reductionism. This can be understood to mean that there are invariant features of human genetic endowment that are resistant to change and that provide explanations for features of human culture such as aggression no matter what other factors are present. A biological reductionist claim of this kind would involve saying that all men are more aggressive by nature, whatever the environment, than are women. There are no real biological determinists in this sense. No one imagines that a seed will grow in the same way no matter what kind of environment it is planted in. Rather, questions arise regarding the relationships between genes and the environment.

Here we may adopt a distinction put forward by Dennett (1995) between *greedy reductionism* and *good reductionism*. The former seeks to reduce all human behaviour to genes without recourse to intermediate causal steps. The latter seeks to explain phenomena through causal chains without resort to mysteries or miracles. Clearly 'greedy reductionism' is unacceptable, whereas the adoption of 'good reductionism' is merely to suggest that we can discover causal chains and explanations for human behaviour that include the role of genetic material.

Biologists agree that the body and behaviour of an organism are products of the interaction between genetic and environmental factors. A human genome is required if the 'environment' is to produce a human being, while no organsim can develop without suitable conditions. A stronger version of this argument would hold not only that genetics and environment are necessary, but also that a change in either one produces changes in the finished product. Thus, gene differences can contribute to widely varying phenotypes through environmental variation. Further, we cannot bracket off environment as a constant background, for a novel environment may produce a novel phenotype. That is, genes and other developmental factors interact with the environment in multifactorial, non-additive ways to produce variable outcomes (Sterelny and Griffiths, 1999).

Human culture and human biology have co-evolved and are indivisible in that culture forms an environment for the human body and feeds into evolutionary change. Hence environmental change, which includes the social and cultural aspects of human life, can change biological developmental outcomes. Of course the time-scales involved in human cultural change and evolutionary adaptations are radically different. The latter take place over aeons of time while the former is more obviously measured in decades. Thus, we currently operate with a human genome and brain structure that evolved a long time ago in quite different environmental (including cultural) circumstances from those in which we live today.

It is common to make a distinction between the notion of 'temperament', which is primarily genetic in origin but modified by environmental factors (such as parenting style), and 'personality' or 'identity', which is wholly cultural in its formation. It is argued that temperament is hard to change while personality is more plastic. Thus, the broad orientations that we have towards thrill seeking, anxiety, addiction, weight gain, sexuality (see Chapter 6), and so on, are held to be genetically formed (Hamer and Copeland, 1998) while the specificities of the way such orientations are worked out and manifested in any given person are cultural. What, then, do evolutionary biology and genetics have to contribute to cultural studies?

Biology in culture

The first valuable principle that evolutionary biology offers us is that all the people of the world are descended from the same ancestors and partake of the same fundamental genome. There may be vast tracts of cultural distance between us, but we remain members of the human species. Sometimes the cultural distance between us is apparently so vast that we see each other as different kinds of being because we think in such radically divergent ways. However, reassertion of the principle of shared biology – we are a species that shares overlapping gene pools – may help to bridge that gap and underpin the desirability of cultural moves such as a declaration of human rights. Further, the roots of emotional response are biochemical and, though emotions are culturally mediated, the sharing of broad emotional reactions is one of the features that binds us together as human beings. We all feel fear and we all have the potential to love.

Evolutionary biology also suggests the likelihood that there are cultural universals. For example, the evolutionary advantage that language gave to us means that all cultures use signs that have their roots in the biochemical capacities of the human brain. Subsequently, of course, we use different languages, that is, the forms of the universal are different. Further, although the specificities of various cultures are different, all human cultures include forms of sexuality, family relations, laughter, tears and rituals around birth, death and food. While cultural studies has been concerned with the particulars of culture and the local conjunctural character of culture, there is no reason why this cannot be set against the backdrop of cultural universals. Indeed, given its contemporary focus on living with difference, cultural studies might well benefit from exploring what human beings also have in common. It is at one and the same time the distinct and divergent ways that cultures construct meanings around sexuality, the family, death, and so forth, that are of interest to us even as we explore that which human beings also share.

One of the reasons why evolutionary biology and genetic science receive so little positive attention within the humanities is the suggestion they bring that there are limits to the plasticity of human capacities and behaviours (within the time-scale of existing human history). However, it is my view that acceptance of this 'fact' should come as something of a relief and saves us from the eternal frustration of seeking after the unattainable. Needless to say, there is the danger of making a mistake – of accepting the immutable character of that which is open to change – since adaptation in human beings has cultural as well as genetic explanations open to it. Hence, testing the waters of cultural change is usually worthwhile.

Nevertheless, we need to make judgements about when that experiment is no longer viable. Thus, feminism rightly challenged the claim that social inequality of the sexes was wholly grounded in biology and thus unalterable. However, as I argued in Chapter 6, it is now clear that there are limits to the plasticity of human gender-based behaviours. The human brain works the way it works and there is no point wishing that it functioned in some other way. However, this is not a recipe for a return to traditional gender roles, not least because fifty years of cultural change has demonstrated that transformation is possible in terms of many of our cultural arrangements.

From socio-biology to evolutionary psychology

In the context of the social sciences and humanities, much of the suspicion towards the conjunction of evolutionary biology and cultural analysis stems from the excesses of the socio-biology programme associated with E.O. Wilson (1975). In particular, this work tended to overlook the fact that culture enables the transmission from one generation to another of information and behavioural patterns in non-genetic form and that human adaptation can be cultural as well as biological. As Dennett (1995) argues, the ubiquity of territoriality within human cultures may be hard-wired but there is an equally plausible case for the territoriality being a culturally 'forced move'. There *may* be a genetic explanation to be had, but in the context of cross-cultural cross-fertilization it is unclear whether one can be found or whether we need one.

For some writers influenced by evolutionary biology, the linkage between genetic theory and culture is understood in terms of memes that are transferred from one mind to another (Dawkins, 1976; Dennett, 1995). A meme is understood to be the smallest cultural element that is able to replicate itself with reliability and fecundity. Examples would include the wheel, the alphabet, particular tunes or musical phrases, clothes fashions, books and ideas. The reproduction of a particular meme is not necessarily best for us; rather, memes are replicated simply because it is advantageous to themselves. However, the pressures of evolutionary adaptation and the role of our own esteem in relation to specific memes means that the general drift of meme replication is in line with our values (themselves a product of meme replication).

The broad implication of meme theory is that cultural evolution (understood as change not progress) takes place as a consequence of memes simply doing their own thing. Now, there is some dispute as to whether meme replication works exactly like genetic natural selection or whether this is simply an appealing analogy. Certainly the whole idea needs further work before it is likely to be of much operational use within cultural studies, though it may direct us to a greater consideration of the mechanisms of the transmission, reproduction and variation of culture.

Today, the more promising marriage of evolutionary theory and human cultural behaviour is to be found in the realm of evolutionary psychology. Here, there has been a turn away from the idea that different behaviours can be accounted for directly and only by genetically inspired adaptive selection. Instead, an interest has developed in the evolution of cognitive mechanisms that oversee our behaviour. It is important to be aware that 'evolutionary psychology advocates integration and consistency of different levels of analysis, not psychological or biological reductionism' (Buss, 1999b: 20). This is so because,

---

By themselves, psychological theories do not, and cannot, constitute theories of culture. They only provide the foundations for theories of culture. (Tooby and Cosmides, 1992: 88)

These foundations can be laid down by outlining the evolved psychological mechanisms that subsequently utilize and work over social and cultural inputs. It is the differential activation of these psychological mechanisms by divergent inputs in varied contexts that accounts for cultural diversity.

The fundamentals of evolutionary psychology

Evolutionary psychology suggests that human beings display the consequences of psychological mechanisms that arose as fitness-enhancing effects in our ancestral environments. Indeed, 'evolution by natural selection is the only known causal process capable of producing physiological and psychological mechanisms' (Buss, 1999b: 3). Subsequently, the concern of evolutionary psychology is to locate the cognitive mechanisms (and their functions) that underpin behaviour rather than trying to identify direct determination of behaviour by genes. Thus, evolutionary psychology is not a form of genetic determinism.

Human behaviour requires two particular ingredients: evolved adaptations and environmental input that triggers the development and activation of those adaptations (Buss, 1999a). For example, the class of possible human languages may depend on a single 'language acquisition device' within the brain, yet its different operations in divergent settings explain the range of human languages available to us. At the same time, all complex mechanisms require many hundreds or even thousands of genes for their development. Since the shuffling of genes at each reproductive moment makes it unlikely that the key combinations could be maintained if the gene coding for important mechanisms varied widely between individuals, our basic psychological mechanisms are almost certainly shared by all or most human beings (i.e. they are species-typical).

Evolutionary psychology does not suggest that human conduct is impervious to change. This is so because human beings can:

- change their own environments, including the variability of culture, and in doing so produce different behavioural outcomes;
- learn about their evolutionary predispositions in specific contexts and make self-conscious efforts to amend their actions in the light of new cultural circumstances.

For example, if men respond to certain triggers with violence more often than do women, or if men have lower thresholds of inferring sexual intent than do women, then both sexes may be able to learn to manage their responses more carefully. This may not always be easy but it is possible. It is also important to note that evolutionary psychology describes causal processes and outcomes; it does not impute motivations to human beings along the lines of seeking to maximize gene replication. Rather, evolution by natural selection fashions certain psychological mechanisms inclining people to particular behavioural decisions that have as their outcomes specific effects bestowing evolutionary advantages.

'Evolutionary psychologists', argue Sterelny and Griffiths (1999: 325), 'fiercely resist the division of labor between evolutionary and cultural theory.' This is not only because human cultural diversity is less profound than it may at first appear, but also because diversity itself has evolutionary explanations. Further, it is important to recognize that the human social group constituted at least one of the crucial selection environments for our ancestors. For example, the co-operative group may well have been the primary survival strategy for humans, and this would have selected for adaptations suited for co-operative living (Brewer and Caporael, 1990). Subsequently, because social adaptive problems were (and are) so crucial to human survival and reproduction, many of the most important evolved psychological mechanisms will be social in character (Buss, 1999b).

The evolved brain

The central argument of evolutionary psychology is that the human brain needs to be conceptualized as a series of evolved information-processing mechanisms or modules that are geared to performing specific tasks. That is, our brains have developed by way of solving certain problems posed by the environments in which we evolved.

When solutions were found to particular problems, they tended to be 'installed' in the brain for the foreseeable future, even though the scope of the resolution, and thus future capacities, was limited. Consequently, specific adaptations are not optimally designed for our ancestral environments, let alone for contemporary conditions. Rather, adaptations survive as long as they are 'good enough' and work in the environment of their genesis. Thus, evolutionary time-lag means that we are operating with brain mechanisms developed within and for an environment quite different from that of contemporary culture.

In this context, evolutionary psychology, as characterized by Cosmides and Tooby (1989, 1992), involves the search for domain-specific mental modules that are mandatory, opaque and informational-encapsulated mechanisms. That is, such modules are specific to food or sex or fear, and so forth, and do not deal with other functions. They are mandatory because a given person does not choose how to deal with a specific problem; rather, he or she is pre-structured to respond in particular ways. They are opaque because we cannot make these internal processes accessible to the conscious mind. And they are informational-encapsulated in the sense that they do not make use of information stored elsewhere in the cognitive system.

According to Buss (1999a: 47–9), an evolved psychological mechanism is a set of processes inside an organism with the following properties:

- An evolved psychological mechanism exists in the form that it does because it solved a specific problem of survival or reproduction recurrently over evolutionary history.
- An evolved psychological mechanism is designed to take in only a narrow slice of information.
- The input of an evolved psychological mechanism instructs an organism as to the particular adaptive problem it is facing.
- The input of an evolved psychological mechanism is transformed through decision rules into output.
- The output of an evolved psychological mechanism can be physiological activity, information to other psychological mechanisms, or manifest behaviour.
- The output of an evolved psychological mechanism is directed toward the solution to a specific adaptive problem.

In summary, an evolved psychological mechanism is a set of procedures within the organism that is designed to take in a particular slice of information and transform that information via decision rules into output that historically has helped with the solution to an adaptive problem. The psychological mechanism exists in current organisms because it led, on average, to the successful solution to a specific adaptive problem for that organism's ancestors. (Buss, 1999a: 49)

The fundamental argument is that domain-specific modules in the brain contribute to the shape of culture by providing the template for human thinking and the parameters of solutions to problems that we are likely to face. This would include the existence of specialized inference mechanisms that allow for the representations of culture to be transmitted from one mind to another through observation and/or interaction (Tooby and Cosmides, 1992). Of course, some aspects of culture, such as art, literature, film, music, and so forth, do not seem to have much to do with survival and reproduction. Nevertheless, it is argued by Pinker (1997) that people take pleasure from shapes, colours, sounds, stories, and so forth, whose mechanisms evolved in relation to other evolutionary tasks faced by our ancestors but which now enable us to appreciate and develop artistic endeavours.

It may be that evolutionary psychology remains over-simplified. It may also be the case that although functionally specific modules constitute the brain for the most part, there are other capacities that are of a more general character or encompass more than just one area of the brain. Nevertheless, evolutionary psychology and neuroscience offer us useful evidence and ways of thinking that are worthy of further exploration. By way of example, we shall examine aspects of the 'emotional brain' and its possible implications for the exploration of culture, bearing in mind my prior argument (in Chapter 5) that cultural studies has not paid adequate attention to the place of human emotions in its cultural analysis.

Evolution, culture and emotions

What is emotion?

Many of the major problems faced by western cultures involve psychological distress rather than material deprivation (which is not to say that the two do not often go hand in hand). These difficulties concern our relations with others (e.g. isolation, failed marriages, aggression and violence), our sense of meaninglessness, our addictions and our mental health. We work too hard and love too little (see Chapter 6 for this argument as it relates to men).

Such problems are partly biochemical, with emotions having evolutionary roots, and partly social, given that certain cultural conditions trigger fear, violence, depression, and so forth. These emotional responses are socially constructed to the degree that we interpret bodily responses in cultural ways. Consequently, what we require from cultural studies is an understanding of the way emotions are generated and comprehended by us. This would need to include the ability to recognize emotional responses and the thinking that is generated in tandem with them or indeed that triggers them off. It is in this sense that we need to develop more emotional and spiritual intelligence as resources within our culture that will enable us to deal better with ancestral emotions that are triggered by contemporary cultural circumstances.

Evolution tends to act on individual brain modules and their functions rather than on our gray matter as a whole. That is, to a large degree, specific brain adaptations underlie particular capacities. This argument would suggest that, rather than there being a single 'emotional system' in the brain, there are a series of different systems or modules that deal with particular emotions and which have evolved over long periods. Posed in evolutionary terms, emotions have emerged over the *longue durée* of our history and stayed with us because they have contributed to the survival of the species. That is, emotions deal with fundamental life tasks. Further, Darwin argued that signs of our feelings (e.g. facial expressions) communicate to others our emotional states, including anger, aggression and fear, so eliciting responses from them that lead to behaviour favourable to us.

On this basis, many contemporary evolutionary theorists (e.g. Plutchik, 1980) think that we have a set of 'hard-wired' basic emotions (sadness, surprise, disgust, anger, anticipation, joy, acceptance, fear) and a number of newer emotions that are a blend of the 'basic' emotional states (friendliness, alarm, guilt, sullenness, delight, anxiety, etc.). By contrast, writers committed to social constructionism (Gergen, 1994; Harré, 1986) tend to regard emotions as culturally formed, citing evidence for differing emotional responses within divergent cultures or social situations.

Ekman (1980) attempts to bridge these apparently conflicting explanations by suggesting that we have, on the one hand, universal bodily responses and facial expressions that are automatic and unlearned, and, on the other hand, learned cultural differences in emotional expression and display rules. That is, hardwired emotions are regulated by the conventions, norms and habits that people have developed to manage emotional expression. Display rules regulate who can show what emotion to whom and to what degree under given circumstances.

As a variation on this theme, Ortony and Turner (1990) argue that we have a number of bodily responses (e.g. a racing heart) that form the components of a variety of 'emotions' that are themselves organized and named by higher cognitive functions (appraisals). In this view, there are no basic emotions; rather, there are a series of primary responses that, in combination and under cognitive supervision, are held to be emotions. Thus, to a set of bodily responses we add a conscious 'feeling' from our working memory and words that not only label context-specific responses as 'fear', anger', 'love', and so forth, but which can themselves set off further emotional responses. That is, feelings result when we become consciously aware that an emotional system of the brain is active and we are able to name our perceptions and sensibilities (LeDoux, 1998).

We may operate with the broad notion that emotional behaviour is the outcome of a set of conditioned bodily responses and culturally modified cognitive appraisal mechanisms by which we learn about stimuli associated with natural triggers. Thus, we can understand emotion as brain biochemistry plus cognitive classificatory functions (with language as the most notable of these).

Indeed, discourses of emotion organize and regulate how we should understand bodily responses in given contexts. Nevertheless, the speed at which the body responds to a given set of circumstances to produce, let us say, fear-inspired flight is much faster than any cognitive and linguistic 'understanding' can be. Thus we often react in an emotionally driven manner before we are able to think in a more self-conscious way. As Parrott and Harré argue, we need to pursue two lines of investigation:

> On the functional side we are looking at emotion displays and feelings that have a role in social control, for example embarrassment, shame and guilt. On the somatic side we are taking up the great insight of Luria (1996), that learning new practices reshapes the human brain and nervous system. Taking the two lines of investigation together, we are looking at the way patterns of social control enhance the natural human responses and develop specific cultural action patterns, thereby creating the neural basis on which those very responses and patterns depend. We are attempting to bridge the gap between the approaches of the neuroscientist and the cultural psychologist. (1996: 2)

As such, we will be interested in:

- the biologically embodied dimension of emotions;
- the role of emotions in social settings (including the constitutive place of language and the generation of display rules);
- the degree of cultural variation that surrounds emotions.

Needless to say, we must be interested in the interaction between these three orders of emotion.

From an evolutionary perspective (Tooby and Cosmides, 1992), emotions invoke circumstances that have repeatedly occurred throughout our developmental history and that cause us to appraise current events in the light of our ancestral past. Thus, the structure of the past overlays an interpretive net on the present. This is particularly noticeable in the case of the pervasive fear and its related emotions (anxiety, obsession, panic, etc.) that underpin human existence and whose consequences show up with regularity in the courts and the consulting rooms of psychotherapists. This is in part because some people have more sensitive fear systems than others (i.e. biology shapes both a general fear response and differences between people based on genetic coding) and in part because we enact responses that are no longer appropriate to contemporary cultural conditions.

Thus, a particular cultural circumstance, let us say a disagreement at work or a rebuffed romantic advance, sets off a conditioned response (which is interpreted by our consciousness and working memory as fear and anger) that is no longer useful to anyone in that social situation. Or, more dramatically, childhood trauma lays down 'emotional memories' in the form of neural pathways that condition future associative responses. Hence the need to acquire an awareness of our bodily responses and to use our cultural competences to observe, redescribe and amend our behaviour where necessary, as in a number of psychotherapeutic interventions. Psychotherapy, it can be argued, enables the cortex, associated with 'thinking', to exert controls over the more emotional aspects of the brain (e.g. the amygdala, which is connected with fear responses). This may work either through conscious verbal control or by way of rewiring the brain in ways that eradicate certain forms of brain pathway (known as extinction).

Emotions and psychotherapy

In 1994, about 51 million Americans aged 18 and older were diagnosed with some form of mental illness. About 11 million of those involved substance abuse. Of the remaining 40 million, more than half were accounted for by the category of 'anxiety disorders' and somewhat less than half by 'mood disorders' (especially depression), with schizophrenia and assorted other conditions accounting for the rest (LeDoux, 1998). As I argued in Chapters 5 and 9, there is now considerable evidence of an epidemic of depression, suicide and drug abuse in western cultures. I argued that explanations for depression and its associated social difficulties lie in a combination of biological, psychological and cultural analysis. In particular, the time-scale of the current explosion of anxiety, and so forth, suggests social and cultural causes that are related to feelings of anger, low self-esteem and powerlessness which are rooted in family trauma and a loss of connection with others.

Psychotherapy is in part concerned with the way in which childhood experiences are re-enacted in adult relationships. In particular, though such experiences range from the clearly traumatic to apparently minor incidents, it is the child's *interpretation* of events that is more significant than what 'actually happened'. A common strategy of psychotherapeutic intervention involves the learning of more appropriate and unthreatening language with which to recognize and manage emotional (i.e. bodily) responses. Indeed, the growth of identity as an autonomous adult self-narrative necessitates the breaking free from parent–child relationships as the determinant of present emotions and behaviour. Here, cognitive language processes located in the cerebral cortex can, up to a point, be used to contain and regulate the brain's emotional fear circuits (located in and around the amygdala and hippocampal systems of the brain), which operate outside of conscious direction (LeDoux, 1998).

As noted above (Chapter 5), there is a growing consensus amongst psychologists and psychiatrists that the best results in the treatment of depression are currently achieved through a combination of anti-depressant drugs and psychotherapy. The roots of depression are planted in genetic and biochemical dispositions intertwined with family trauma. Indeed, one of the most fascinating aspects of current research is the evidence that personal experience, including the way we think, can alter the biochemistry of the brain. Thus, family trauma changes biochemistry just as changing our patterns of thinking alters brain biochemistry (LeDoux, 1998; Luria, 1996). Indeed the evidence that Seligman (1990) cites to suggest that pessimism depletes the immune system while optimistic thinking boosts it suggests the ability of thought to amend the body (indeed it collapses the mind–body distinction).

Emotion works at the permeable interface between language and the body, with causal flows taking place in either direction. That is, thinking generates and can change biochemical emotional responses while these chemical actions can set off a stream of thoughts. Current thinking in neuroscience suggests that all thoughts have an affective dimension, so that a concept of 'emotion-thought' is a useful one. Here, the rewriting of the self with which psychotherapy is implicated involves not just words but new conduct and not just new conduct but alterations in biochemistry. Further, the emotional identifications described by psychoanalysis, which for Hall (1996a) and Butler (1993) suture discourse to the psyche, or the language which constitutes or 'does' emotion for Gergen (1994), can be put 'under the description' of biochemistry. Language digs deep down into the body so that questions of biochemistry and neurology are pertinent to human emotions and the quest for meaning.

The problem of meaning

In Chapter 9, we noted that emotional intelligence (EQ) is concerned with feelings – our own and those of others. It is centred on self-awareness, motivation, compassion and empathy and is a basic requirement for the effective use of intellectual intelligence (IQ). Underdeveloped emotional intelligence opens us up to being overpowered by anger and fear and/or to become overly 'rational' with an inability to relate well to other people.

Emotional intelligence enables us to evaluate our situation and to act appropriately within it. By contrast, Zohar and Marshall (2000) argue that spiritual intelligence (SQ) challenges and reconstructs the parameters and purposes of our lives and asks about the very boundaries of our life's circumstances. That is, it is our meaning-giving, contextualizing and transformative intelligence that constitutes SQ. However, the line between emotional and spiritual intelligence is somewhat arbitrary, and certainly thin, since a spiritual experience is commonly also an affective one. Here I would reiterate a point I made in Chapter 1, namely that I am talking of a sceptical, reflexive and ironic spirituality that has its place in our lives as the way to arrive at meaningful understandings of our existential and emotional questions. This does not require metaphysical foundations or the abdication of rationality.

Spiritual intelligence

Spiritual intelligence can be understood as the forging of a mental happiness and contentment that is based not on gaining material possessions, status or social position, but on developing meaning, self-awareness, love and compassion. Thus, spirituality addresses such human questions as 'Why was I born?' 'Who am I?' 'What is the meaning of my life?'

According to the psychologists Zohar and Marshall,

> We are driven, indeed we are defined, by a specifically human longing to find mean-
> ing and value in what we do and experience. We have a longing to see our lives in
> some larger, meaning giving context, whether this is the family, the community, a
> football club, our life's work, our religious framework or the universe itself. We have
> a longing for something that gives us and our actions a sense of worth. (2000: 4)

Zohar and Marshall argue that the quest for meaning has both an evolutionary
and a neurological basis. For example, the quest for meaning is thought to have
first brought human beings out of the trees some two million years ago and
given rise to the symbolic imagination, the evolution of language and the
extraordinary growth of the human brain. While IQ and EQ both enable us to
learn a language, we invent new languages and new situations and behaviours
with our third kind of intelligence (i.e. SQ). Indeed, human beings' use of SQ,
which includes the meaning-generating capacities of language and symbolic
representation, has enhanced the growth of the brain.

Zohar and Marshall present two kinds of neurological evidence for spiritual
intelligence:

- the so-called 'God spot', which is located among the neural connections in
  the temporal lobes of the brain;
- 40-Hz neural oscillations that 'bind together' and contextualize cognitive
  experiences.

When investigated using brain-scan techniques, key neural connections in the
temporal lobes light up with activity whenever subjects are exposed to discussion of spiritual or religious topics, suggesting that the brain has evolved to
engage with spiritual questions of life and death. That is, the capacity to raise
spiritual questions is 'hard-wired' into our brains. In addition, connections
between the temporal lobes and the limbic system give such occurrences a special emotional quality – an affective experience as opposed to an intellectual
belief. This includes intensity of emotions such as love, peacefulness, serenity
and the feeling that one is in harmony with one's surroundings.

However, according to Zohar and Marshall, the neurological basis of spiritual
experience does not guarantee that we can use it creatively, that is, develop a
spiritual intelligence that brings context, meaning, purpose and direction to our
lives. This, they argue, belongs more readily to the second kind of evidence that
they discuss, namely the detection of 40-Hz oscillations across the whole of the
brain by new magneto-encephalographic technology.

Research shows that bundles of neurones situated all over the brain oscillate
simultaneously at about 40 Hz when exposed to the same object. These neural
oscillations enable the brain to communicate with itself and give our consciousness a unity without which the world would consist of meaningless
fragments. That is, neural oscillations help to 'bind together' specific perceptual

or cognitive experiences, placing the activity of specific local neurones or groups of neurones within a larger (meaningful) context.

By analogy, Zohar and Marshall describe specific perceptions, thoughts and emotions as waves, or excitations of energy, on the ocean or background of 'inert' energy. They hypothesize that the 'many voices' of separate neural oscillations are pulled together into the 'one voice of the choir' and that this process takes the form of quantum holism. That is, many individual parts are so fully integrated as to function as a single unified whole. In any case, the disclosure that 40-Hz oscillations occur across the whole brain suggests that consciousness is an intrinsic property of the brain. Consciousness just *is* and does not depend on external stimulation.

The neurological function of SQ is to integrate all our intelligences, thereby making us the intellectual, emotional and spiritual creatures that we are. Indeed, SQ can be characterized as 'unitive thinking', understanding that is holistic and grasps the overall context that links component parts. We use SQ to be creative, flexible and visionary. In doing so, SQ draws our attention to the existential problems of loss, pain, illness and grief in addition to the central 'meaning' issues of good and evil, life and death. According to Zohar and Marshall, to experience the spiritual is to be in touch with the 'something more' that confers added meaning and value to our lives. That search for meaning is the primary motivation of our lives, and it is when this deep-seated need is unmet that we feel shallow or empty. The search for meaning takes a variety of forms; it may, but equally may not, be religious in an orthodox sense. Thus,

> That spiritual 'something more' may be a deeper social reality or social web of meaning. It may be an awareness of or attunement to the mythological, archetypal or religious dimensions of our situation. It may be a sense of some more profound level of truth or beauty. And/or it may be an attunement to some deeper, cosmic sense of wholeness, a sense that our actions are parts of some greater universal process. Whatever our specific sense of the spiritual, without it our vision is clouded, our lives feel flat and our purposes dreadfully finite. (Zohar and Marshall, 2000: 18)

Modernity, meaninglessness and self-identity

The people of most pre-modern societies had living traditions of family, community, morality and gods into which they were embedded. The traditions of the community encapsulated spiritual insights and values so that any given person could relate to questions of meaning through his or her culture. Traditional societies were less self-consciously reflexive than those located within modernity and were more obviously underpinned by 'associative (emotional) thinking'.

Today, modern western-style societies have few meaningful collective traditions or communities, the conventional family is in disarray and our God(s) has been declared well and truly dead (and with no sign of imminent resurrection).

In this sense, ours is a spiritually poor culture whose answers to our existential questions revolve around 'more of everything': that is, quantity over quality. Further, we have overdeveloped some characteristics of human capacities (e.g. rationality) in relation to others (love, empathy, care and artistic creativity) and so become unbalanced. This is evidenced by the rise in addictions, mania, depression, low self-esteem and self-indulgent, self-centred behaviour. These phenomena are described by Jobst et al. (1999) as 'diseases of meaning'.

Perhaps readers find the language of 'spiritual intelligence' rather esoteric and consider it inappropriate for a book about cultural studies. However, the central theme of meaninglessness that I am pursing is already embedded in the work of some leading contemporary thinkers. For example, Lasch (1980, 1985) characterizes the western world as a 'culture of narcissism', and later as a 'culture of survivalism'. Here, self-centred individuals, encouraged by a consumer culture that offers them the good life but delivers only a hollow echo of meaningfulness, become increasingly apathetic. This trend is further advanced by the rise of bureaucratic organizations that wield apparently arbitrary powers over us, and by the decline of the traditional family and its underpinning of meaningful human relations.

According to Giddens, 'Personal meaninglessness – the feeling that life has nothing worthwhile to offer – becomes a fundamental psychic problem in circumstances of late modernity' (1991: 9). He argues that we should understand this phenomenon in terms of a repression of the moral questions that day-to-day life poses, but which are denied answers. That is, we are separated from the moral resources necessary to live a full and satisfying existence. Giddens explores the generation of meaninglessness as an aspect of what he calls 'the sequestration of experience'.

This process involves the separation of day-to-day life from contact with experiences of sickness, madness, criminality, sexuality and death that raise potentially disturbing existential questions. That is, the development of hospitals, asylums, the 'privatization of passion' and an apparent disconnection from nature rob most people of direct contact with events and situations that link the individual life-span to broad issues of morality and death. Here, basic aspects of life-experience and morality are removed from the regularities of everyday life as a consequence of the security won through the routinization of day-to-day activities.

The establishment of relative security in key domains of human life through the acceptance of routines lacks moral meaning and can be experienced as 'empty' practices. This takes place in the context of high modernity where self-identity becomes internally referential and individuals live primarily no longer by extrinsic moral precepts but by means of the reflexive organization of the self. However, this reflexive project of the self has to be carried out 'in a technically competent but morally arid social environment' where 'mastery . . . substitutes for morality' (Giddens, 1991: 201–2).

The sequestration of experience serves to 'contain' many forms of anxiety that might otherwise threaten our sense of security. Yet the conditions of late modernity generate their own forms of anxiety. For example, we have by necessity to construct ourselves reflexively in a world with few certainties or maps of meaning to guide us and in the context of a 'risk society'. Here, the very processes of risk calculation generate anxieties. Further, in a context that lacks external referents and in which our lives are understood in terms of individual projects and plans, 'fateful moments' confront the individual with disturbing implications that he or she may lack the moral resources to cope with. Most notable amongst these would be a confrontation with death or madness without the aid of moral frameworks and rituals that connect the individual to wider cultural and cosmic forces.

However, whereas Lasch paints a pessimistic picture of the overpowered individual, Giddens' argument offers some hope, for in his view the very reflexive character of contemporary culture is generating new possibilities as well as dangers. For Giddens, the more we 'make ourselves', the more significant moral and political questions about 'what a person is' and 'who I want to be' are raised. This involves the re-moralizing of social life. For example, developments in biological science lead us to ask questions about what life consists of, the rights of the unborn, claims on the body and the ethics of genetic research. These concerns lie behind many contemporary New Social Movements (Chapter 9).

Thus 'life-politics' concerns self-actualization, choice and lifestyle centred on the reflexive ethics of 'How shall we live?' It revolves around the creation of justifiable forms of life that will promote self-actualization in a global context.

A path with heart

There are many ways to develop emotional and spiritual intelligence: through public service, for example, or the loving and nurturing of families and communities, or by way of intellectual investigation and/or artistic creation. In any case, whatever course we take needs to be a path of commitment – a path with heart. This requires self-awareness, including a sound understanding of one's own emotional and cognitive patterns. To some extent this comes through a capacity to use personal difficulties to learn about, and to take responsibility for, our own lives. Commonly, given the nature of contemporary western culture, this also demands of us the ability to be 'field-independent'. For Zohar and Marshall (2000), such self-awareness can be developed through meditation, poetry, walking in nature, listening to music, paying attention to life, and keeping and reviewing a daily diary.

For Jack Kornfield (1994) a path with heart entails, amongst other things, examining the values we live by and asking such questions as 'Where do we put our time, our strength, our creativity, our love?' And 'Does what we are choosing reflect what we most deeply value?' Above all, we are urged to consider our life in the context of our inevitable death. 'What would it be like to live with the knowledge that this may be our last year, our last week, our last day?' For, as Kornfield suggests, when people come to the end of their lives they do not look back and ask about how much money they have or how many books they wrote but 'Did I live fully?' And above all, 'Did I love well?'

Kornfield argues that a 'mature spirituality' enables us to let go of rigid and idealistic ways of being and discover flexibility and joy in our life that brings ease, kindness and compassion. More specifically, he describes the qualities of spiritual maturity as being non-idealistic in the sense that it does not seek to perfect our world or ourselves but is founded on self-acceptance and our capacity to love in the context of human relationships. Or, as Salman puts it, wisdom (understood psychologically) involves 'the capacity to see, under-stand, and live-out what has been given, the ability to reach for what is not given and transcend the boundaries of fate, and the mysterious process of creating meaning and new experience where there had been none before' (2000: 82). Thus spiritual maturity demands that we are continually questioning and investigating our lives so that we may find a wise and compassionate relationship to all things. Further, while we may have little direct control over much of what happens to us in our lives, we can 'choose' how we relate to our experiences.

As Kornfield suggests, contemporary western culture encourages us to pursue a fantasy life. Ours is a society of denial that conditions us to protect our-selves from any difficulty or discomfort, including pain, insecurity, loss and death. To insulate ourselves from the natural world, we have air conditioning, insurance polices and a whole array of ways by which we seek to colonize and control the future. Thus, as discussed above, we shut away the elderly, sick and mentally ill within institutions where the existential truth of these states is hidden from us. In addition, the widespread existence of addictions to alcohol, heroin, sex, and so forth, marks the compulsively repetitive attachments we use to deny the difficulties of our lives.

One of the most telling of our addictions, Kornfield argues, is to S P E E D > > >

- fast work,
  - fast leisure,
    - fast cars,
      - fast food.

This habitual obsession makes it impossible to stay connected to ourselves, let alone to others, with the consequence that people are isolated and lonely. They are at war with themselves and with the external world. Spiritual practice, argues Kornfield, is about stopping the 'war within' by staying in the present moment rather than drifting off into the fantasies of our thought patterns that are driven by desire/attraction and fear/aversion. Further, recognizing and accepting that there are pain and sorrow as well as joy and happiness in our own lives lead us to the realization that there are pain, sorrow, joy and happiness in all people's lives.

It may be objected that spiritual practice and psychotherapy are isolated self-centred activities that will encourage rather than subvert the western preoccupation with self. However, psychotherapy and spiritual training require open and honest forms of communication so that the development of self-awareness in context of developing relationships, rather than in isolation, is at the heart of best practice in each domain. For example, both spiritual practice and psychotherapy address the wild swinging between grandiosity and low self-esteem that accompanies the attempt to shore up unrealistic self-images. This is an acute phenomenon in western cultures, which value competition, achievement, material wealth and being a 'winner'.

No doubt many readers are still wondering what 'spiritual intelligence' and psychotherapy have to do with cultural studies. Let me elaborate on their relevance to each other:

- It is open to us to investigate spiritual practices and psychotherapy as cultural activities. Indeed, the whole range of cultural practices that come under the banner of religion, spirituality and the 'New Age' have received scant attention from cultural studies yet they remain, on a global scale, important aspects of human life. Indeed, the levels of popular interest in self-help books, therapy, Buddhism and New Age practices should tell us something important about the unmet needs of human beings within western culture.
- I have argued that a good deal of the problems encountered within western culture are emotional and spiritual in form. In particular, we need to recognize the emotional dimension to cultural and political life. Too often the political and cultural Left is disappointed with other people because it fails to understand that what it takes to be 'rational' analysis is insufficient to comprehend human beings' motivations and actions. In this sense, cultural studies would be well advised to explore different kinds of knowing – a project that feminism has already made a start on.
- Notions of emotional and spiritual intelligence offer levers for cultural studies to further explore the mutual constitution of the personal and the political. As Giddens (1984) has demonstrated, the macro formations of human societies are 'virtual structures' that are recursive in character, being constructed in and through the everyday activities and accounts of actors. Thus, a concentration on the micro-practices of emotional life and psychotherapy is not a distraction from the 'important' work of macro-analysis and social change any more than is an attention to micro-linguistics as the building blocks of culture. Rather, they are a necessary complement to, and underpinning of, cultural change.

Most of the problems faced by contemporary humanity are created by humans themselves, and it is not some kind of wishy-washy liberal sentimentality to argue that war, starvation, poverty, exploitation and psychological suffering are the products of our minds and that we need to change them. Cultural studies needs to explore the workings of such minds even as it investigates the constitution of subjectivity and identity by language and culture. That is, we require a form of cultural psychology that is rooted in evolutionary processes.

Conclusions

In this chapter I have argued that western culture is the site of an epidemic of psychological suffering that cultural studies should find worthy of investigation. The picture that I painted was one of emotional dislocation and meaninglessness that has its roots in biochemistry and culture. In particular, many of the problems of emotion and meaning are rooted in psychological mechanisms developed throughout our evolutionary history that are now inappropriate for contemporary cultural conditions. Overall, I argued that evolutionary theory, notably evolutionary psychology, could provide cultural studies with the background required by which to integrate biological and cultural investigation.

Genetics and evolutionary psychology can offer us useful ways of looking at the world that can assist us to keep our feet on the ground of the embodied self. However, the issues of anxiety, depression, substance abuse, and so forth, that I discussed cannot be understood only as biochemical questions for their growth has occurred within a time-scale that only cultural change can explain. Consequently, I suggested that cultural studies might explore questions of emotionally charged meaning both as a contemporary cultural occurrence and as a mode of intervention.

Whereas evolution involves causal chains that operate within an indifferent universe, human culture consists of practices and meanings that allow us not only to survive in the physical world but also to thrive (or not) in an emotionally satisfying and meaningful way. Here, evolutionary psychology can assist us in understanding the way in which the brain works and the causal chains that have given rise to our particular type of mind and its patterns of thinking. At the same time, cultural studies can help us to comprehend the way that this specific human mind operates in the context of the self-created environments of culture. However, to undertake this project more adequately than it has done to date, cultural studies needs to engage more fully with the emotional aspects of human life. To do so we will need to break down the unnecessary and illusory distinction between biology and culture.

Keywords in Cultural Studies

Acculturation This refers to those social processes by which we learn the knowledge and practices that enable us to be members of a culture. The ability to 'go on' in a culture requires the learning and acquisition of language, values and norms through imitation, practice and experimentation. Key sites and agents of acculturation would include the family, peer groups, schools, work organizations and the media. The processes of acculturation represent the nurture side of the so-called 'nature vs nurture' debate. Consequently they are looked to by theorists of social constructionism as providing the basis by which actors acquire those concepts and maps of meaning that constitute a way of life and a way of seeing. The argument that subjectivity and identity are the products of acculturation is strong within cultural studies. This suggests that what it means to be a person is changeable and related to definite social and cultural conjunctures.

Active audience The concept of the active audience stresses the capability of readers and viewers to be dynamic creators and producers of meaning rather than being passive receptors of the meanings generated by texts. This paradigm emerged in the early 1980s in reaction to the 'hypodermic model' of audiences, whereby the meanings of texts appear to be injected directly into the minds of audiences without modification. Overall, the active audience paradigm represented a shift of interest from numbers to meanings, from textual meaning to textual meanings in the plural and from the general audience to particular audiences. Within this framework, audiences are understood to be active creators of meaning in relation to texts and do so on the basis of previously acquired cultural competencies forged in the context of language and social relationships.

Anti-essentialism This concept alludes to the idea that words are not held to have referents with essential or universal qualities. Rather, being discursive constructions, categories change their meanings according to time, place and usage. For example, since words do not refer to essences, identity is not a fixed universal 'thing' but a description in language. In this sense, identities are plastic and malleable, so that what it means to be a woman or an American is not stable but subject to constant modifications and mutations. In particular, for post-structuralism there can be no truths, subjects or identities outside of language, a language which has no stable referents and therefore no fixed truths or identities. Consequently, the objects of language are not fixed or universal things but meaningful descriptions that through social convention come to be 'what counts as truth' (i.e. the temporary stabilization of meaning).

Articulation   The concept of articulation suggests a temporary unity of discursive elements that do not have to 'go together'. An articulation is the form of the connection that *can* make a unity of two different elements under certain conditions. Articulation suggests expressing/representing and a joining together so that, for example, questions of gender may connect with race but in context-specific and contingent ways. Thus, intersections between race, ethnicity, nation, class, age and gender can be understood in terms of the articulation of these criss-crossing discourses. Hence, the concept of articulation enables that unity thought of as 'society' to be considered as the unique historically specific temporary stabilization of the relations and meanings of different levels of a social formation. The idea of articulation is also deployed to discuss the relationship between culture and political economy. Thus, culture is said to be 'articulated' with moments of production but not determined in any 'necessary' way by that moment, and vice versa.

Culture   The concept of culture does not represent an entity in an independent object world but is best thought of as a mobile signifier that enables distinct ways of talking about human activity that stress divergent uses and purposes. The concept of culture is thus political and contingent. Indeed, insofar as contemporary cultural studies has a distinguishing take on the concept of culture, it is a political one that stresses the intersection of power and meaning with a view to promoting social change and improving the human condition as 'we' would define it. In a general sense, cultural studies emphasizes that culture is:

- ordinary in that it concerns everyday life and not simply the arts;
- constituted by shared social *meanings*, that is, the various ways we make sense of the world;
- the product of the creative capacity of common people to construct meaningful practices;
- concerned with tradition and social reproduction but also creativity and change;
- constructed through processes of meaning production designated as signifying practices;
- to be understood as produced symbolically in language as a 'signifying system'.

Today, culture is less a matter of locations with roots than of hybrid and creolized cultural routes in global space. Cultures as syncretic and hybridized products of interactions across space are thought of as carving routes rather than possessing roots. They are constellations of temporary coherence or knots in the field of social space that are the product of relations and interconnections from the very local to the intercontinental.

Cultural materialism   The concept of cultural materialism draws our attention to the idea that the meanings and representations that we designate as 'culture' are generated through material processes under particular physical and social circumstances. Thus, cultural materialism is concerned to explore the questions of how and why meanings are inscribed at the moment of production. That is, cultural materialism explores signifying practices in the context of the means and conditions of their construction. Traditionally, this has focused on the connections between cultural practices and political economy, though, strictly speaking, this is a rather narrow definition of cultural materialism. Thus, Williams understands cultural materialism to involve 'the analysis of all forms of signification . . . within the actual means and conditions of their production' (1981: 64–5).

Cultural Policy   In its simplest form, cultural policy is concerned with the administration of those institutions that produce and administer the form and content of cultural products. This would include museums, government departments of education/arts/culture/media /sport, and so forth, schools, institutions of higher education, theatre administration, television organizations (public and commercial), record companies and advertising agencies. However, within the context of cultural studies, questions of policy formation and enactment are connected to wider issues of cultural politics. That is, cultural policy is not only a technical problem of administration, but also one of cultural values and social power set in the overall context of the production and circulation of symbolic meanings. In any case, cultural policy is concerned with the regulation and management of culture.

Cultural politics   In broad terms we may consider cultural politics to be the 'power to name' or to write 'new languages' (and to make them stick). One of the central arguments of cultural studies is that its object of study, culture, is a zone of contestation in which competing meanings and versions of the world have fought for ascendancy and the pragmatic claim to truth. In particular, meaning and truth in the domain of culture are constituted within patterns of power. Thus, cultural politics can be understood in terms of the power to name and represent the world, where language is constitutive of the world and a guide to action. In contemporary terms, cultural politics has been conceived of as a series of collective social struggles organized around class, gender, race, sexuality, age, and so forth, which seek to redescribe the social in terms of specific values and hoped-for consequences. In its engagement with cultural politics, cultural studies has sought to play a 'demystifying role' by pointing to the constructed character of cultural texts.

Deconstruction   This concept is associated with Derrida's 'undoing' of the binaries of western philosophy and its extension into the fields of literature (e.g. de Man) and postcolonial theory (e.g. Spivak). To deconstruct is to take apart, to undo, in order to seek out and display the assumptions of a text. In particular, deconstruction involves the dismantling of hierarchical conceptual oppositions, such as man/woman, black/white, reality/appearance, nature/culture, reason/madness, and so forth, that serve to guarantee truth by excluding and devaluing the 'inferior' part of the binary. Thus, speech is privileged over writing, reality over appearance, men over women. The purpose of deconstruction is not simply to reverse the order of binaries but also to show that they are implicated in each other. Deconstruction seeks to expose the blind spots of texts, the unacknowledged assumptions upon which they operate. This includes the places where a text's rhetorical strategies work against the logic of its arguments: that is, the tension between what a text means to say and what it is constrained to mean.

Discourse   For Foucault, from whom cultural studies derives its usage of this term, discourse 'unites' both language and practice and refers to the production of knowledge through language which gives meaning to material objects and social practices. Though material objects and social practices 'exist' outside of language, they are given meaning or 'brought into view' by language and are thus discursively formed. Discourse constructs, defines and produces the objects of knowledge in an intelligible way while excluding other forms of reasoning as unintelligible. Repeated motifs or clusters of ideas, practices and forms of knowledge across a range of sites of activity constitute a discursive formation. This is a pattern of discursive events which refer to, or bring into being, a common object across a number of sites.

Globalization   This refers to the increasing multi-directional economic, social, cultural and political global connections across the world and our awareness of them. It is widely held that since the early 1970s we have witnessed a phase of *accelerated* globalization marked by a new dimension of time-space compression and propelled by transnational companies' search for new sources of profit, involving the speed-up of production and consumption turnover assisted by the use of information and communication technology. Patterns of population movement and settlement established during colonialism and its aftermath, combined with the more recent acceleration of globalization, particularly of electronic communications, have enabled increased cultural juxtaposing, meeting and mixing on a global scale. This suggests the need to escape from a model of culture as a locally bounded 'whole way of life'. Consequently globalization and global cultural flows cannot be understood through neat sets of linear determinations but are better comprehended as a series of overlapping, over-determined, complex and chaotic conditions which, at best, cluster around key 'nodal points'.

Hegemony Culture is constructed in terms of a multiplicity of streams of meaning and encompasses a range of ideologies and cultural forms. However, it is argued that there is a strand of meanings which can be called authoritative or ascendant. The process of making, maintaining and reproducing these governing sets of meanings and practices has been called hegemony. This involves a temporary closure of meaning supportive of the powerful. Hegemony thus involves the process of making, maintaining and reproducing the governing sets of meanings of a given culture. A hegemonic bloc never consists of a single socio-economic category but is formed through a series of alliances in which one group takes on a position of leadership. For Gramsci, hegemony implies a situation where an 'historical bloc' of ruling-class factions exercises social authority and leadership over the subordinate classes through a combination of force and, more importantly, consent. (See Chapter 3 for a wider discussion of the concept of hegemony.)

Identity The concept of identity pertains to cultural descriptions of persons with which we emotionally identify. Identity is cultural since the resources that form the material for identity formation – language and cultural practices – are social in character. The anti-essentialist position commonly adopted within cultural studies stresses that identity is a process of *becoming* built from points of similarity and difference. There is no essence of identity to be discovered; rather, cultural identity is continually being produced within the vectors of resemblance and distinction. Of course, identity is a matter not only of self-description but also of social ascription.

The concept of identity is further deployed in order to link the emotional 'inside' of persons with the discursive 'outside'. That is, identity represents the processes by which discursively constructed subject positions are taken up (or otherwise) by concrete persons' fantasy identifications and emotional 'investments'. The de-centred or postmodern self involves the subject in shifting, fragmented and multiple identities. Here, persons are composed not of one but of several, sometimes contradictory, identities. If we feel that we have a unified identity from birth to death, it is only because we construct a comforting story or 'narrative of the self' about ourselves.

Ideology Within Gramscian cultural studies, ideology has been understood in terms of ideas, meanings and practices which, while they purport to be universal truths, are better understood as maps of cultural significance. Above all, ideology is not separate from the practical activities of life but is a material phenomenon rooted in day-to-day conditions. Ideologies provide people with rules of practical conduct and moral behaviour. The whole concept of ideology has come under scrutiny for it involves at least two central problems: (1) the problem of *scope*, that is: 'Do all groups have ideologies, or only the powerful?' and (2) the problem of *truth*, that is: 'Can we understand ideology as being counterposed to truth? Consequently, the concept of ideology can be understood in the following ways:

- world-views of dominant groups which justify and maintain their power and which are counterpoised to truth;
- world-views of any social groups which justify their actions and which are counterpoised to truth;
- world-views of dominant groups which justify and maintain their power but which cannot be counterpoised to truth; however, they can be subject to redescription and thus do not have to be accepted;
- world-views of any social groups which justify their actions but which cannot be counterpoised to truth; however, they can be subject to redescription and thus do not have to be accepted.

I have argued (see Chapter 3) that it is untenable to counterpoise the concept of ideology to truth and that all social groups have ideologies. As such, ideology cannot be seen as a simple tool of domination but should be regarded as discourses which have specific *consequences* for relations of power at all levels of social relationships.

Power   Power is commonly thought of in terms of a force by which individuals or groups are able to achieve their aims or interests against the will of others. Power here is constraining (power over) in the context of a zero-sum model (you have it or you do not) and organized into binary power blocs. However, cultural studies has, after Foucault, stressed that power is also productive and enabling (power to), that it circulates through all levels of society and all social relationships. Foucault regards knowledge as implicated with power, hence his concept of *power/knowledge*. By power/knowledge is meant a mutually constituting relationship between power and knowledge so that knowledge is indissociable from regimes of power. Knowledge is formed within the context of the relationships and practices of power and subsequently contributes to the development, refinement and proliferation of new techniques of power. However, no simple uncontaminated 'truth' can be counterpoised to power/knowledge for there is no truth outside of it.

Representation   This is the process whereby signifying practices appear to stand for or depict another object or practice in the 'real' world. It is better described as a 'representational effect' since signs do not stand for or reflect objects in a direct 'mirroring' mode. That is, representation is not a neutral depiction of values, meanings and knowledges which exist beyond its boundaries; rather, it is *constitutive* of those very values, meanings and knowledges. That is, representation gives meaning to material objects and social practices which are brought into view and made intelligible to us in terms which representation delimits.

To understand culture is to explore how meaning is produced symbolically through the signifying practices of representation. Signs, and language in particular, are a central concern of cultural studies for they are the means and medium for the generation of significance or meaning. Thus, to investigate culture is to explore how meaning is produced symbolically as representations through the actions of signifying practices. Here, meaning is generated through difference, the relation of one signifier to another, rather than by reference to fixed entities in an independent object world.

Resistance   Resistance could be understood in terms of one force meeting another where both are forces and resistances: that is, it could be a simple descriptive of the balance of forces. We may have no interest in the outcome of resistive forces. However, in the context of cultural studies, to describe an act as resistance is a matter not of truth or falsity but of utility and value. Given cultural studies' commitment to a cultural politics of insubordination and the politics of difference, resistance is *a normative* concept with success measured strategically against normative criteria. Hence, resistance is not a quality of an act but a category of judgement about acts. Resistance is a distinction of value which classifies the classifier. It is a judgement that reveals the values of the cultural studies critic. Resistance issues from relationships of power and subordination in the form of challenges to and negotiations of the ascendant order. Resistance is relational and conjunctural.

Subjectivity   This refers to the condition and processes of being a person or self. For cultural studies, subjectivity is often regarded as an 'effect' of discourse because it is constituted by the subject positions which discourse obliges us to take up. This includes the characteristics of agency and identity which discursive subject positions enable for a speaking subject. A subject position can be understood in terms of empty spaces or functions in discourse from which the world makes sense. Here, discourse constitutes the 'I' through the processes of signification, and the speaking subject is dependent on the prior existence of discursive positions. For Foucault, bodies are 'subject to' the regulatory power of discourse by which they become 'subjects for' themselves and others.

Theory   Theory can be understood as narratives which seek to distinguish and account for the general features that describe, define and explain persistently perceived occurrences. It can also be grasped as a tool, instrument or logic for intervening in the world through the mechanisms of description, definition, prediction and control. Theory construction is a self-reflexive discursive endeavour which seeks to interpret and intervene in the world. It involves the thinking through of concepts and arguments, often redefining and critiquing prior work, with the objective of offering new tools with which to think about our world. This has maintained a high-profile position within cultural studies. Theoretical work can be thought of as a crafting of the cultural signposts and maps by which we are guided. Cultural studies has rejected the empiricist claim that knowledge is simply a matter of collecting facts from which theory can be deduced or against which it can be tested. That is, 'facts' are not neutral and, without theory, no amount of stacking up of 'facts' produces a story about our lives.

References

Abercrombie, N., Hill, S. and Turner, B. (1980) *The Dominant Ideology Thesis*. London: Allen & Unwin.

Aglietta, M. (1979) *A Theory of Capitalist Regulation: The US Experience*. London: Verso.

Althusser, L. (1969) *For Marx*. London: Allen Lane.

Althusser, L. (1971) *Lenin and Philosophy and Other Essays*. London: New Left Books.

Ang, I. (1985) *Watching Dallas: Soap Opera and the Melodramatic Imagination*. London: Methuen.

Ang, I. (1996) *Living Room Wars*. London and New York: Routledge.

Appadurai, A. (1993) 'Disjuncture and Difference in the Global Cultural Economy' in P. Williams and L. Chrisman (eds) *Colonial Discourse and Post-Colonial Theory*. Hemel Hempstead: Harvester Wheatsheaf.

Arnold, M. (1960) *Culture and Anarchy*. Cambridge: Cambridge University Press (orig. 1869).

Austin, J. (1999) *Zen and the Brain*. Cambridge, MA: MIT Press.

Austin, J.L. (1962). *How To Do Things With Words*. Oxford: Oxford University Press.

Barker, C. (1997) *Global Television: An Introduction*. Oxford: Blackwell.

Barker, C. (1999) *Television, Globalization and Cultural Identities*. Milton Keynes: Open University Press.

Barker, C. (2000) *Cultural Studies: Theory and Practice*. London and Thousand Oaks, CA: Sage.

Barker, C. and Galasinski, D. (2001) *Cultural Studies and Discourse Analysis: A Dialogue on Language and Identity*. London and Thousand Oaks, CA: Sage.

Barkow, J., Cosmides, L. and Tooby, J. (eds) (1992) *The Adapted Mind: Evolutionary Psychology and the Generation of Culture*. Oxford: Oxford University Press.

Barrett, M. and McIntosh, M. (1982) *The Anti-Social Family*. London: Verso.

Barthes, R. (1967) *The Elements of Semiology*. London: Cape.

Barthes, R. (1972) *Mythologies*. London: Cape.

Baudrillard, J. (1983) *Simulations*. New York: Semiotext(e).

Bauman, Z. (1991) *Modernity and Ambivalence*. Cambridge: Polity.

Beck, C. (1997) *Everyday Zen*. London: Thorsons.

Bell, D. (1973) *The Coming of the Post-Industrial Society*. New York: Basic Books.

Bennett, T. (1992) 'Putting Policy into Cultural Studies' in L. Grossberg, C. Nelson and P. Treichler (eds) *Cultural Studies*. London and New York: Routledge.

Bennett, T. (1998) *Culture: A Reformer's Science*. St Leonards: Allen & Unwin.

Bennett, T., Martin, G., Mercer, C. and Woollacott, J. (eds) (1981) *Popular Television and Film*. London: British Film Institute.

Bennett, T., Mercer, C. and Woollacott, J. (eds) (1986) *Popular Culture and Social Relations*. Milton Keynes: Open University Press.

Berman, M. (1982) *All That Is Solid Melts Into Air*. New York: Simon & Schuster.

Best, B. (1997) 'Over-the-Counter-Culture: Retheorizing Resistance in Popular Culture' in S. Redhead with D. Wynne and J. O'Connor (eds) *The Clubcultures Reader: Readings in Popular Cultural Studies*. Oxford: Blackwell.

Bhabha, H. (1994) *The Location of Culture*. London and New York: Routledge.

Biddulph, S. (1994) *Manhood*. Sydney: Finch.

Billig, M. (1997) 'From Texts to Utterances' in M. Ferguson and P. Golding (eds) *Cultural Studies in Question*. London and Newbury Park, CA: Sage.

Bly, R. (1991) *Iron John: A Book About Men*. London: Element.

Bordo, S. (1993) *Unbearable Weight: Feminism, Western Culture and the Body*. Berkeley: University of California Press.

Brah, A. (1996) *Cartographies of Diaspora*. London: Routledge.

Brewer, M. and Caporael, L. (1990) 'Selfish Genes versus Selfish People: Sociobiology as Origin Myth' *Motivation and Emotion*, 14: 237–43.

Buckingham, D. (1987) *Public Secrets: EastEnders and its Audience*. London: British Film Institute.

Buss, D. (1999a) *Evolutionary Psychology: The New Science of the Mind*. Needham Heights, MA: Allyn & Bacon.

Buss, D. (1999b) 'Evolutionary Psychology: A New Paradigm for Psychological Science' in D. Rosen and M. Luebbert (eds) *Evolution of the Psyche*. Westport, CT: Praeger.

Butler, J. (1990) *Gender Trouble*. London and New York: Routledge.

Butler, J. (1991) 'Imitation and Gender Subordination' in D. Fuss (ed.) *Inside/Out: Lesbian Theories, Gay Theories*. London: Routledge.

Butler, J. (1993) *Bodies That Matter*. London and New York: Routledge.

Centre for Contemporary Cultural Studies, Education Group (1981) *Unpopular Education: Schooling and Social Democracy in England since 1944*. London: Hutchinson.

Chambers, I. (1986) *Popular Culture: The Metropolitan Experience*. London: Methuen.

Chambers, I. (1990) 'Popular Music and Mass Culture' in J. Downing, A. Mohammadi and A. Sreberny-Mohammadi (eds) *Questioning the Media*. London: Sage.

Chodorow, N. (1978) *The Reproduction of Motherhood*. Berkeley: University of California Press.

Chodorow, N. (1989) *Feminism and Psychoanalytic Theory*. Cambridge: Polity.

Christen, Y. (1991) *Sex Differences: Modern Biology and the Unisex Fallacy*. New Brunswick, NJ: Transaction Publishers.

Clarke, J. (1976) 'Style' in S. Hall and T. Jefferson (eds) *Resistance Through Rituals: Youth Subcultures in Post-War Britain*. London: Hutchinson.

Clifford, J. (1992) 'Traveling Cultures' in L. Grossberg, C. Nelson and P. Treichler (eds) *Cultural Studies*. London and New York: Routledge.

Clifford, J. and Marcus, G. (eds) (1986) *Writing Culture*. Berkeley: University of California Press.

Cohen, S. (1980) 'Symbols of Trouble: An Introduction to the New Edition', in *Folk Devils and Moral Panics: The Creation of the Mods and Rockers*. London: Martin Robertson.

Collard, A. with Contrucci, J. (1988) *Rape of the Wild*. London: Women's Press.

Collins, J. (1989) *Uncommon Cultures*. London and New York: Routledge.

Connell, R.W. (1995) *Masculinities*. Cambridge: Polity.

Cosmides, L. and Tooby, J. (1989) 'Evolutionary Theory and the Generation of Culture', *Ethology and Sociobiology*, 10: 51–97.

Cosmides, L. and Tooby, J. (1992) 'Cognitive Adaptations for Social Exchange' in J. Barkow, L. Cosmides and L. Tooby (eds) *The Adapted Mind*. Oxford: Oxford University Press.

Crofts, S. (1995) 'Global *Neighbours*?' in R. Allen (ed.) *To Be Continued . . . Soap Opera Around the World*. London and New York: Routledge.

Crook, J. and Fontana, D. (eds.) (1990) *Space in Mind*. Shaftesbury: Element Books.

Crook, S., Pakulski, J. and Waters, M. (1992) *Postmodernization*. London and Thousand Oaks, CA: Sage.

Dahlgren, P. (1995) *Television and the Public Sphere*. London and Newbury Park, CA: Sage.

Daniels, C. (ed.) (1998) *Lost Fathers*. London: Macmillan.

Darwin, C. (1985) *On the Origin of Species*. New York: Penguin (orig. 1859).

Davidson, D. (1984) *Inquiries into Truth and Interpretation*. Oxford: Clarendon Press.

Davis, M. (1990) *City of Quartz: Excavating the Future of Los Angeles*. London. Verso.

Dawkins, R. (1976) *The Selfish Gene*. Oxford: Oxford University Press.

Dawkins, R. (1995). *River Out of Eden: A Darwinian View of Life*. New York: Basic Books.

de Certeau, M. (1984) *The Practice of Everyday Life*. Berkeley: University of California Press.

Dennett, D. (1995) *Darwin's Dangerous Idea: Evolution and the Meanings of Life*. London: Penguin.

Derrida, J. (1976) *Of Grammatology*. Baltimore: Johns Hopkins University Press.

du Gay, P., Hall, S., Janes, L., Mackay, H. and Negus, K. (1997) *Doing Cultural Studies*. London and Thousand Oaks, CA: Sage

Edwards, D. and Potter, J. (1992) *Discursive Psychology*. London: Sage.

Ekman, P. (1980) 'Biological and Cultural Contributions to Body and Facial Movement in the Expression of Emotions' in A.O. Rorty (ed.) *Explaining Emotions*. Berkeley: University of California Press.

Elias, N. (1978) *The History of Manners: The Civilizing Process, Vol. 1*. Oxford: Blackwell.

Elias, N. (1982) *State Formation and Civilization: The Civilizing Process, Vol. 2*. Oxford: Blackwell.

Fairclough, N. (1992). *Discourse and Social Change*. Cambridge: Polity.

Faludi, S. (1991) *Backlash: The Undeclared War Against American Women*. London: Vintage.

Faludi, S. (1999) *Stiffed: The Betrayal of the Modern Man*. London: Chatto and Windus.

Farrell, W. (1993) *The Myth of Male Power*. Sydney: Random House.

Featherstone, M. (1991) *Consumer Culture and Postmodernism*. London and Newbury Park, CA: Sage.

Featherstone, M. (1995) *Undoing Culture: Globalization, Postmodernism and Identity*. London and Newbury Park, CA: Sage.

Fiske, J. (1987) *Television Culture*. London: Methuen.

Fiske, J. (1989a) *Understanding Popular Culture*. London: Unwin Hyman.

Fiske, J. (1989b) *Reading the Popular*. London: Unwin Hyman.

Forward, S. (1990) *Toxic Parents: Overcoming Their Hurtful Legacy and Reclaiming Your Life*. New York: Bantam Books.

Foucault, M. (1972) *The Archaeology of Knowledge*. New York: Pantheon.

Foucault, M. (1973) *The Birth of the Clinic*. London: Tavistock.

Foucault, M. (1977) *Discipline and Punish* London: Allen Lane.

Foucault, M. (1979) *The History of Sexuality, Vol. 1: The Will to Truth*. London: Penguin/Allen Lane.

Foucault, M. (1980) *Power/Knowledge*. New York: Pantheon.

Foucault, M. (1984a) 'What is the Enlightenment?' in P. Rabinow (ed.) *The Foucault Reader*. New York: Pantheon.

Foucault, M. (1984b) 'Nietzsche, Genealogy, History' in P. Rabinow (ed.) *The Foucault Reader*. New York: Pantheon.

Foucault, M. (1985) *The Uses of Pleasure. The History of Sexuality, Vol. 2*. Harmondsworth: Penguin.

Foucault, M. (1986) *The Care of the Self: The History of Sexuality, Vol. 3*. Harmondsworth: Penguin.

Freud, S. (1977) *Three Essays on Sexuality. The Pelican Freud Library, Vol. 7*. Harmondsworth: Penguin (orig. 1905).

Fukuyama, F. (1989) 'The End of History?' *The National Interest*, No. 16.

Fukuyama, F. (1992) *The End of History and the Last Man*. Harmondsworth: Penguin.

Fullan, M. with Stiegelbauer, S. (1991) *The New Meaning of Educational Change*. London: Cassell.

Gazzaniga, M. (1980) 'The Role of Language for Conscious Experience: Observations from Split-Brain Man' in H. Kornhuber and L. Deecke (eds) *Progress in Brain Research*. Amsterdam: Elsevier.

Geertz, C. (1973) *The Interpretation of Culture*. New York: Basic Books.

Genova, J. (1995) *Wittgenstein: A Way of Seeing*. New York: Routledge.

Gergen, K. (1994) *Realities and Relationships*. Cambridge, MA and London: Harvard University Press.

Giddens, A. (1979) *Central Problems in Social Theory*. London: Macmillan.

Giddens, A. (1984) *The Constitution of Society*. Cambridge: Polity.

Giddens, A. (1989) *Sociology*. Cambridge: Polity.

Giddens, A. (1990) *The Consequences of Modernity*. Cambridge: Polity.

Giddens, A. (1991) *Modernity and Self-Identity*. Cambridge: Polity.

Giddens, A. (1992) *The Transformation of Intimacy*. Cambridge: Polity.

Giddens, A. (1994) *Beyond Left and Right*. Cambridge: Polity.

Gillespie, M. (1995) *Television, Ethnicity and Cultural Change*. London and New York: Routledge.

Gilligan, C. (1982) *In a Different Voice*. Cambridge, MA: Harvard University Press.

Gilroy, P. (1987) *There Ain't No Black in the Union Jack*. London: Unwin Hyman.

Gilroy, P. (1993) *The Black Atlantic*. London: Verso.

Gilroy, P. (1997) 'Diaspora and the Detours of Identity' in K. Woodward (ed.) *Identity and Difference*. London and Thousand Oaks, CA: Sage.

Goldthorpe, J. (1982) 'On the Service Class, its Formation and Future' in A. Giddens and G. Mackenzie (eds) *Social Class and the Division of Labour*. Cambridge: Cambridge University Press.

Goldthorpe, J. and Lockwood, D. (1968) *The Affluent Worker*. Cambridge: Cambridge University Press.

Goleman, D. (1995) *Emotional Intelligence*. New York: Bantam Books.

Gorz, A. (1982) *Farewell to the Working Class*. London: Pluto Press.

Gramsci, A. (1971) *Selections from the Prison Notebooks*, eds Q. Hoare and G. Nowell-Smith. London: Lawrence and Wishart.

Gribbin, J. (1998) *Almost Everyone's Guide to Science*. London: Phoenix.

Grossberg, L., Nelson, C. and Treichler, P. (1992) 'Cultural Studies: An Introduction' in L. Grossberg, C. Nelson and P. Treichler (eds) *Cultural Studies*. London and New York: Routledge.

Gurevitch, M., Levy, M. and Roeh, I. (1991) 'The Global Newsroom: Convergence and Diversities in the Globalisation of Television News' in P. Dahlgren and C. Sparks (eds) *Communication and Citizenship*. London and New York: Routledge.

Gutting, G. (1999) *Pragmatic Liberalism and the Critique of Modernity*. Cambridge: Cambridge University Press.

Habermas, J. (1987) *The Philosophical Discourse of Modernity*. Cambridge: Polity.

Habermas, J. (1989) *The Structural Transformation of the Public Sphere*. Cambridge, MA: MIT Press.

Hall, S. (1972) *On Ideology: Cultural Studies 10*. Birmingham: Centre for Contemporary Cultural Studies.

Hall, S. (1977) 'Culture, the Media and the Ideological Effect', in J. Curran, M. Gurevitch and J. Woolacott (eds) *Mass Communications and Society*. London: Edward Arnold.

Hall, S. (1981) 'Encoding/Decoding' in S. Hall, D. Hobson, A. Lowe and P. Willis (eds) *Culture, Media, Language*. London: Hutchinson.

Hall, S. (1988) *The Hard Road to Renewal*. London: Verso.

Hall, S. (1990) 'Cultural Identity and Diaspora' in J. Rutherford (ed.) *Identity: Community, Culture, Difference*. London: Lawrence & Wishart.

Hall, S. (1992a) 'Cultural Studies and its Theoretical Legacies' in L. Grossberg, C. Nelson and P. Treichler (eds) *Cultural Studies*. London and New York: Routledge.

Hall, S. (1992b) 'The Question of Cultural Identity' in S. Hall, D. Held and T. McGrew (eds) *Modernity and its Futures*. Cambridge: Polity.

Hall, S. (1996a) 'Who Needs Identity? in S. Hall and P. du Gay (eds) *Questions of Cultural Identity* London: Sage.

Hall, S. (1996b) 'On Postmodernism and Articulation: An Interview with Stuart Hall', ed. L. Grossberg, in D. Morley and D.-K. Chen (eds) *Stuart Hall*. London: Routledge.

Hall, S. (1996c) 'Gramsci's Relevance for the Study of Race and Ethnicity' in D. Morley and D.-K. Chen (eds) *Stuart Hall*. London: Routledge.

Hall, S. (1996d) 'New Ethnicities' in D. Morley and D.-K. Chen (eds) *Stuart Hall*. London: Routledge.

Hall, S. (1996e) 'For Allon White: Metaphors of Transformation' in D. Morley and D.-K. Chen (eds) *Stuart Hall*. London: Routledge.

Hall, S. (1997) 'The Work of Representation' in S. Hall (ed.) *Representation*. London and Thousand Oaks, CA: Sage.

Hall, S. and Jacques, M. (eds) (1989) *New Times: The Changing Face of Politics in the 1990s*. London: Lawrence & Wishart.

Hall, S., Critcher, C., Jefferson, T., Clarke, J. and Roberts, B. (1978) *Policing the Crisis: Mugging, the State and Law and Order*. London: Macmillan.

Halpern, D. (1992) *Sex Differences in Cognitive Abilities*. London: Lawrence Erlbaum Associates.

Hamer, D. and Copeland, P. (1998) *Living with Our Genes*. New York: Doubleday.

Harding, J. (1998) *Sex Acts*. London and Thousand Oaks, CA: Sage.

Harré, R. (ed.) (1986) *The Social Construction of Emotion*. Oxford: Blackwell.

Harvey, D. (1989) *The Condition of Postmodernity*. Oxford: Blackwell.

Hassan, R. (1997) 'Suicide Trends in Australia' in K. Healey (ed.) *Suicide, Vol. 84*. Sydney: Spinney Press.

Hebdige, D. (1979) *Subculture: The Meaning of Style*. London and New York: Routledge.

Hebdige, D. (1988) *Hiding in the Light*. London: Comedia.

Held, D. (1992) 'Liberalism, Marxism and Democracy' in S. Hall, D. Held and T. McGrew. (eds) *Modernity and its Futures*. Cambridge: Polity.

Herman, J. (1992) *Trauma and Recovery*. New York: Basic Books.

Hite, S. (1994) *The Hite Report on the Family*. London: Bloomsbury.

Hobson, D. (1982) *Crossroads: Drama of a Soap Opera*. London: Methuen.

Hoggart, R. (1957) *The Uses of Literacy*. Harmondsworth: Penguin.

Horkheimer, M. and Adorno, T.W. (1979) 'The Culture Industry as Mass Deception', in *The Dialectic of Enlightenment*. London: Verso (orig. 1946).

Hoskins, C., McFadyen, S., Finn, A. and Jackel, A. (1995) 'Film and Television Co-productions: Evidence from Canadian–European Experience', *European Journal of Communication*, 10 (2).

Illawarra Public Health Unit (1998) *Illawarra Youth Health Survey*. Wollongong: Area Health Authority.

Irigaray, L. (1993) *Sex and Genealogies*. New York: Colombia University Press.

Irigaray, L. (1985a) *The Speculum of the Other Woman*. Ithaca, NY: Cornell University Press.

Irigaray, L. (1985b) *This Sex Which Is Not One*. Ithaca, NY: Cornell University Press.

James, W. (1890) *Principles of Psychology*. New York: Holt.

Jameson, F. (1984) 'Postmodernsim or the Cultural Logic of Late Capitalism', *New Left Review*, 46.

Jobst, K., Shostak, D. and Whitehouse, P. (1999) 'Diseases of Meaning: Manifestations of Health, and Metaphor', *Journal of Alternative and Complementary Medicine*, 6 (5).

Johnson, S. and Meinhof, U. (eds) (1997) *Language and Masculinity*. Oxford: Blackwell.

Jordan, G. and Weedon, C. (1995) *Cultural Politics: Class, Gender, Race and the Postmodern World*. Oxford: Blackwell.

Kabat-Zinn, J. (1990) *Full Catastrophe Living: Using the Wisdom of Your Body and Mind to Face Stress, Pain, and Illness*. New York: Delta.

Kanter, R. (1984) *The Change Masters: Corporate Entrepreneurs at Work*. London: Allen & Unwin.

Kaplan, E. (1987) *Rocking Around the Clock: Music, Television, Postmodernism and Consumer Culture*. Boulder, CO: Westview Press.

Kaplan, E. (1992) 'Feminist Criticism and Television' in R. Allen (ed.) *Channels of Discourse, Reassembled*. London and New York: Routledge.

Kellner, D. (1992) 'Popular Culture and the Construction of Postmodern Identities' in S. Lash and J. Friedman (eds) *Modernity and Identity*. Oxford: Blackwell.

Kellner, D. (1997) 'Overcoming the Divide: Cultural Studies and Political Economy' in M. Ferguson and P. Golding (eds) *Cultural Studies in Question*. London and Newbury Park, CA: Sage.

Kelly, G.A. (1955) *The Psychology of Personal Constructs*. New York: Norton.

Kerr, C., Dunlop, K., Harbison, F. and Mayers, C. (1973) *Industrialism and Industrial Man*. Harmondsworth: Penguin.

Kimura, D. (1996) 'Sex, Sexual Orientation and Sex Hormones Influence Human Cognitive Function', *Current Opinion in Neurobiology*, 259.

Kornfield, J. (1994) *A Path with Heart*. London: Rider.

Kornfield, J. (2000) *After the Ecstasy, the Laundry*. London: Rider.

Kristeva, J. (1986a) 'Women's Time' in T. Moi (ed.) *The Kristeva Reader*. Oxford: Blackwell.

Kristeva, J. (1986b) 'Revolution in Poetic Language' in T. Moi (ed.) *The Kristeva Reader*. Oxford: Blackwell.

Kuhn, T.S. (1962) *The Structure of Scientific Revolutions*. Chicago and London: University of Chicago Press.

Lacan, J. (1977) *Écrits: A Selection*. London: Tavistock.

Laclau, E. and Mouffe, C. (1985) *Hegemony and Socialist Strategy: Toward a Radical Democratic Politics*. London: Verso.

Laing, R.D. (1976) *The Politics of the Family*. Harmondsworth: Penguin.

Lasch, C. (1980) *The Culture of Narcissism*. London: Edward Arnold.

Lasch, C. (1985) *The Minimal Self*. London: Picador.

Lash, S. and Urry, J. (1987) *Disorganized Capitalism*. Cambridge: Polity.

Leavis, F. R. and Thompson, D. (1933) *Culture and the Environment*. London: Chatto & Windus.

LeDoux, J. (1998) *The Emotional Brain*. London: Phoenix.

Lee, J. (1991) *At My Father's Wedding*. New York: Bantam Books.

Lennane, J. (1997) 'Youth Suicide: Why Us?' in K. Healey (ed.) *Suicide, Vol. 84*. Sydney: Spinney Press.

Liebes, T. and Katz, E. (1991) *The Export of Meaning*. Oxford: Oxford University Press.

Lull, J. (1991) *China Turned On: Television, Reform and Resistance*. London: Routledge.

Lull, J. (1997) 'China Turned On (Revisited): Television, Reform and Resistance' in A. Sreberny-Mohammadi, D. Winseck., J. McKenna and O. Boyd-Barrett (eds) *Media in a Global Context*. London: Edward Arnold.

Luria, A.R (1996) *Human Brain and Psychological Processes*. New York: Harper & Row.

Lyotard, J.-F. (1984) *The Postmodern Condition*. Minneapolis: University of Minnesota Press.

McCalman, J. and Paton, R. (1992*) Change Management: A Guide to Effective Implementation*. London: Paul Chapman.

McGuigan, J. (1992) *Cultural Populism*. London: Routledge.

McGuigan, J. (1997) 'Introduction' in J. McGuigan (ed.) *Cultural Methodologies*. London: Sage

McGuigan, J. (1996) 'Cultural Populism Revisited' in M. Ferguson and P. Golding (eds) *Cultural Studies in Question*. London and Newbury Park, CA: Sage.

Mackinnon, C. (1987) *Feminism Unmodified*. Cambridge, MA and London: Harvard University Press.

Mackinnon, C. (1991) 'Difference and Domination' in K. Bartlett and R. Kennedy (eds) *Feminist Legal Theory*. Boulder, CO and London: Westview Press.

McLanahan, S. and Sandefur, G. (1994) *Growing Up with a Single Parent*. Cambridge, MA: Harvard University Press.

McLean, C., Carey, M. and White, C. (eds) (1996) *Men's Ways of Being*. Boulder, CO: Westview Press.

McQuail, D., De Mateo, R. and Tapper, H. (1992) 'A Framework for Analysis of Media Change in Europe in the 1990s' in K. Siune and W. Truetzschler (eds) *Dynamics of Media Politics: Broadcasting and Electronic Media in Western Europe*. London and Newbury Park, CA: Sage.

McRobbie, A. (1989) *Zoot Suits and Second-Hand Dresses*. London: Macmillan.

McRobbie, A. (1991a) '*Jackie*: Romantic Individualism and the Teenage Girl' in A. McRobbie *Feminism and Youth Culture*. London: Macmillan.

McRobbie, A. (1991b) 'Working-Class Girls and the Culture of Femininity' in A. McRobbie *Feminism and Youth Culture*. London: Macmillan.

McRobbie, A. (1991c) '*Jackie* and *Just Seventeen* in the 1980s' in A. McRobbie *Feminism and Youth Culture*. London: Macmillan.

Marx, K. (1961) 'The Preface to a Contribution to the Critique of Political Economy' in T. Bottomore and M. Rubel (eds) *Karl Marx: Selected Writings in Sociology and Social Philosophy*. London: Pelican.

Marx, K. and Engels, F. (1970) *The German Ideology*. London: Lawrence & Wishart (orig. 1845–6).

Massey, D. (1998) 'The Spatial Construction of Youth Cultures' in T. Skelton and G. Valentine (eds) *Cool Places: Geographies of Youth Cultures*. London and New York: Routledge.

Mayr, E. (1982) *The Growth of Biological Thought: Diversity, Evolution and Inheritance*. Cambridge: Cambridge University Press.

Mellody, P. (1987) *Facing Co-Dependence*. San Francisco: HarperCollins.

Melucci, A. (1980) 'The New Social Movements: A Theoretical Approach', *Social Science Information*, 19 (2).

Melucci, A. (1981) 'Ten Hypotheses for the analysis of New Movements' in D. Pinto (ed.) *Contemporary Italian Sociology*. Cambridge: Cambridge University Press.

Melucci, A. (1989) *Nomads of the Present*. London: Hutchinson Radius.

Mercer, K. (1994) *Welcome to the Jungle: New Positions in Black Cultural Studies*. London and New York: Routledge.

Miller, D. (1995) 'The Consumption of Soap Opera: *The Young and the Restless* and Mass Consumption in Trinidad' in R. Allen (ed.) *To Be Continued . . . Soap Opera Around the World*. London and New York: Routledge.

Mitchell, J. (1974) *Psychoanalysis and Feminism*. London: Allen Lane.

Moir, A. and Jessel, D. (1991) *BrainSex: The Real Differences Between Men and Women*. London: Mandarin.

Moir, A. and Moir, B. (1998) *Why Men Don't Iron: The Real Science of Gender Studies*. London: HarperCollins.

Morley, D. (1980) *The Nationwide Audience*. London: British Film Institute.

Morley, D. (1992) *Television, Audiences and Cultural Studies*. London and New York: Routledge.

Morris, M. (1992) 'A Gadfly Bites back', *Meanjin*, 51 (3).

Morris, M. (1996) 'Banality in Cultural Studies' in J. Storey (ed.) *What is Cultural Studies? A Reader*. London and New York: Edward Arnold.

Mosca, V. (1988) 'Introduction: Information in the Pay Society' in V. Mosca and J. Wasko (eds) *The Political Economy of Information*. Madison: University of Wisconsin Press.

National Drug Strategy (1995) *Household Survey*. Canberra: Australian Government.

Newcombe, H. (1988). 'One Night of PrimeTime' in J. Carey (ed.) *Media, Myth, Narrative*. London and Newbury Park, CA: Sage.

Nicholson, L. (ed.) (1990) *Feminism/Postmodernism*. London and New York: Routledge.

Nicholson, L. (1995) 'Interpreting Gender' in L. Nicholson and S. Seidman (eds) *Social Postmodernism*. Cambridge: Cambridge University Press.

Nielsen Media Research (1999)
 http://www.nielsenmedia.com/reports_available/reports.html

Nietzsche, F. (1967) *The Will to Power*. New York: Random House (orig. 1901).

Nixon, S. (1997) 'Exhibiting Masculinity' in S. Hall (ed.) *Representation*. London and Thousand Oaks, CA: Sage.

O'Hagen, A. (1999) *Our Fathers*. London: Faber & Faber.

Ortony, A. and Turner, T.J. (1990) 'What's Basic about Basic Emotions? *Psychological Review* 97: 315–31.

Parrott, G. and Harré, R. (1996) 'Introduction', in G. Parrott and R. Harré (eds) *The Emotions: Social, Cultural and Biological Dimensions*. London and Newbury Park, CA: Sage.

Pears, D. (1971) *Wittgenstein*. London: Fontana.

Pfeil, F. (1995*) White Guys*. London: Verso.

Pieterse, J. (1995) 'Globalization as Hybridization', in M. Featherstone, S. Lash and R. Robertson (eds) *Global Modernities*. London and Newbury Park, CA: Sage.

Pinker, S. (1994) *The Language Instinct: How the Mind Creates Language*. New York: Morrow.

Pinker, S. (1997) *How the Mind Works*. New York: Norton.

Plutchik, R. (1980) 'Emotion: A General Psychoevolutionary Theory' in R. Plutchik and H. Kellerman (eds) *Emotion: Theory, Research and Experience*. New York: Academic Press.

Popenoe, D. (1996) *Life without Father*. New York: Free Press.

Popper, K. (1959) *The Logic of Scientific Discovery*. London: Hutchinson (orig. 1934).

Potter, J. and Wetherell, M. (1987) *Discourse and Social Psychology: Beyond Attitudes and Behaviour*. London and Thousand Oaks, CA: Sage.

Real, T. (1998) *I Don't Want to Talk About It: Men and Depression*. Dublin: Newleaf.

Redhead, S. (1990) *The End-of the-Century Party: Youth and Pop Towards 2000*. Manchester: Manchester University Press.

Rich, A. (1986) *Of Women Born*. London: Virago Press.

Robertson, R. (1992) *Globalization*. London and Newbury Park, CA: Sage.

Robins, K. (1991) 'Tradition and Translation: National Culture in its Global Context' in J. Corner and S. Harvey (eds) *Enterprise and Heritage: Crosscurrents of National Culture*. London: Routledge.

Rorty, R. (1980) *Philosophy and the Mirror of Nature*. Cambridge: Cambridge University Press.

Rorty, R. (1989) *Contingency, Irony and Solidarity*. Cambridge: Cambridge University Press.

Rorty, R. (1991a) *Objectivity, Relativism, and Truth: Philosophical Papers, Vol. 1*. Cambridge: Cambridge University Press.

Rorty, R. (1991b) *Essays on Heidegger and Others: Philosophical Papers, Vol. 2*. Cambridge: Cambridge University Press.

Rorty, R. (1995) 'Feminism and Pragmatism' in R.S. Goodman (ed.) *Pragmatism*. New York: Routledge.

Rorty, R. (1998a) *Achieving Our Country*. Cambridge, MA: Harvard University Press.

Rorty, R. (1998b) *Truth and Progress: Philosophical Papers, Vol. 3*. Cambridge: Cambridge University Press.

Rose, J. (1997) *Sexuality in the Field of Vision*. London: Verso.

Rose, N. (1996) 'Identity, Genealogy, History' in S. Hall and P. du Gay (eds) *Questions of Cultural Identity*. London and Newbury Park, CA: Sage.

Rowe, D. (1996) *Depression*. London and New York: Routledge.

Salman, S. (2000) 'The Wisdom of Psychological Creativity and *Amor Fati*' in P. Young-Eisendrath and M. Miller (eds) *The Psychology of Mature Spirituality*. London: Routledge.

Salmans, S. (1997) *Depression*. London: HarperCollins.

Sartre, J.-P. (1967) *Words*. London: Penguin.

Sassen, S. (1996) 'Rebuilding the Global City: Economy, Ethnicity and Space' in A.D. King (ed.) *Re-presenting the City*. London: Macmillan.

Saussure, F. de (1960) *Course in General Linguistics*. London: Peter Owen (orig. 1916).

Schiller, H. (1969) *Mass Communications and the American Empire*. New York: Augustus M. Kelly.

Schiller, H. (1985) 'Electronic Information Flows: New Basis for Global Domination?', in P. Drummond and R. Patterson (eds) *Television in Transition*. London: British Film Institute.

Seidler, V. (1989) *Rediscovering Masculinity: Reason, Language and Sexuality*. London: Routledge.

Seligman, M. (1990) *Learned Optimism*. Sydney: Random House.

Sepstrup, P. (1989) 'Research into International Television Flows: A Methodological Contribution', *European Journal of Communication*, 4.

Shotter, J. (1993) *Conversational Realities*. London and Newbury Park, CA: Sage.

Shweder, R. (1995) 'Cultural Psychology: What is It?' in N. Rule Goldberger and J. Bennet Veroff (eds) *The Culture and Psychology Reader*. New York and London: New York University Press.

Silverstone, R. (1994) *Television and Everyday Life*. London and New York: Routledge.

Smith A.D. (1990) 'Towards a Global Culture?' in M. Featherstone (ed.) *Global Culture*. London and Newbury Park, CA: Sage.

Soja, E. (1989) *Postmodern Geographies*. London: Verso.

Stacey, J. (1996) *In the Name of the Family: Rethinking Family Values in a Postmodern World*. Boston: Beacon Press.

Staten, H. (1984) *Wittgenstein and Derrida*. Lincoln: University of Nebraska Press.

Sterelny, K. and Griffiths, P. (1999) *Sex and Death: An Introduction to Philosophy of Biology*. Chicago and London: University of Chicago Press.

Straubhaar, J. (1992) 'What Makes News? Western, Socialist, and Third World Television Newscasts Compared in Eight Countries' in F. Korzenny and S. Ting Toomey (eds) *Mass Media Effects Across Cultures*. London and Newbury Park, CA: Sage.

Straubhaar, J. (1997) 'Distinguishing the Global, Regional and National Levels of World Television' in A. Sreberny-Mohammadi, D. Winseck, J. McKenna and O. Boyd-Barrett (eds) *Media in a Global Context*. London: Edward Arnold.

Thompson, E.P. (1963) *The Making of the English Working Class*. New York: Vintage.

Thornton, S. (1995) *Club Cultures: Music, Media and Subcultural Capital*. Cambridge: Polity.

Thussu, D. K. (2000) *International Communication: Continuity and Change*. London: Edward Arnold.

Tooby, J. and Cosmides, L. (1992) 'The Psychological Foundations of Culture' in J. Barkow, L. Cosmides and L. Tooby (eds) *The Adapted Mind*. Oxford: Oxford University Press.

Touraine, A. (1981) *The Voice and the Eye: An Analysis of Social Movements*. Cambridge: Cambridge University Press.

Turner, G. (1990) *British Cultural Studies: An Introduction*. London: Unwin Hyman.

van Dijk, T.A. (1997) 'The Study of Discourse' in T.A. van Dijk (ed.) *Discourse as Structure and Process*. London: Sage.

Varis, T. (1974) 'Global Traffic in Television', *Journal of Communication*, 24.

Varis, T. (1984) 'International Flow of Television Programmes', *Journal of Communication*, 34 (1).

Viney, L. (1996) *Personal Construct Therapy: A Handbook*. Norwood, NJ: Ablex.

Watts, A.(1957) *The Way of Zen*. London: Thames & Hudson.

Watts, A. (1968) *Psychotherapy East and West*. New York: Ballatine Books.

Weedon, C. (1997) *Feminist Practice and Poststructuralist Theory*. Oxford: Blackwell.

Wernick, A. (1991) *Promo Culture*. London and Newbury Park, CA: Sage.

West, C. (1993) *Keeping Faith*. London and New York: Routledge.

Widdicombe, S. and Wooffitt, R. (1995) *The Language of Youth Subcultures*. Hemel Hempstead: Harvester Wheatsheaf.

Williams, R. (1965) *The Long Revolution*. London: Penguin.

Williams, R. (1981) *Culture*. London: Fontana.

Williams, R. (1983) *Keywords*. London: Fontana.

Williams, R. (1989) *Resources of Hope*. London: Verso

Williamson, J. (1978) *Decoding Advertisements*. London: Marion Boyars.

Willis, P. (1977) *Learning to Labour*. Farnborough: Saxon House.

Willis, P. (1978) *Profane Culture*. London: Routledge & Kegan Paul.

Willis, P. (1981) 'Notes on Method' in S. Hall, D. Hobson, A. Lowe and P. Willis (eds) *Culture, Media, Language*. London: Hutchinson.

Willis, P. (1990) *Common Culture*. Milton Keynes: Open University Press.

Willis, P. (2000) 'Foreword' to C. Barker, *Cultural Studies: Theory and Practice*. London and Thousand Oaks, CA: Sage.

Wilson, E.O. (1975) *Sociobiology: The New Synthesis*. , MA: Harvard University Press.

Wittgenstein, L. (1957) *Philosophical Investigations*. Oxford: Blackwell.

Wittgenstein, L. (1969) *On Certainty*. New York: Harper Torch Books.

Wittgenstein, L. (1980). *Culture and Value*. Oxford: Blackwell.

Woodward, K. (1997) 'Motherhood: Identities, Meanings and Myths' in K. Woodward (ed.) *Identity and Difference*. London and Thousand Oaks, CA: Sage.

Young-Eisendrath, P. and Miller, M. (2000) 'Beyond Enlightened Self-Interest: The Psychology of Mature Spirituality in the Twenty-First Century' in P. Young-Eisendrath and M. Miller (eds) *The Psychology of Mature Spirituality*. London: Routledge.

Zohar, D. and Marshall, I. (2000) *SQ: Spiritual Intelligence: The Ultimate Intelligence*. London: Bloomsbury.

Zukin, S. (1996) *The Culture of Cities*. Oxford: Blackwell.

Index